Linguistics
and
New Testament
Greek

Linguistics and New Testament Greek

Key Issues in the Current Debate

David Alan Black
and
Benjamin L. Merkle, eds.

Baker Academic

a division of Baker Publishing Group
Grand Rapids, Michigan

Published by Baker Academic
a division of Baker Publishing Group
PO Box 6287, Grand Rapids, MI 49516-6287
www.bakeracademic.com

Printed in the United States of America

Library of Congress Cataloging-in-Publication Data
Names: Black, David Alan, 1952– editor. | Merkle, Benjamin L., 1971– editor.
Title: Linguistics and New Testament Greek : key issues in the current debate / David Alan Black and Benjamin L. Merkle, eds.
Description: Grand Rapids, Michigan : Baker Academic, [2020] | Includes bibliographical references and indexes.
Identifiers: LCCN 2020007330 | ISBN 9781540961068 (paperback) | ISBN 9781540963444 (casebound)
Subjects: LCSH: Greek language, Biblical. | Bible. New Testament—Language, style.
Classification: LCC PA695 .L56 2020 | DDC 487/.4—dc23
LC record available at https://lccn.loc.gov/2020007330

Unless otherwise indicated, Greek text is from UBS[5].

Unless otherwise indicated, Scripture translations are the author's own.

In keeping with biblical principles of creation stewardship, Baker Publishing Group advocates the responsible use of our natural resources. As a member of the Green Press Initiative, our company uses recycled paper when possible. The text paper of this book is composed in part of post-consumer waste.

20   21   22   23   24   25   26   7   6   5   4   3   2

To the students at
SOUTHEASTERN BAPTIST THEOLOGICAL SEMINARY

Contents

   Randall Buth

9. Electronic Tools and New Testament Greek   195
   Thomas W. Hudgins

10. An Ideal Beginning Greek Grammar?   213
    Robert L. Plummer

11. Biblical Exegesis and Linguistics: *A Prodigal History*   227
    Nicholas J. Ellis

    Postscript: Where Do We Go from Here?   247
    Benjamin L. Merkle

    Glossary   261
    Contributors   265
    Scripture and Ancient Writings Index   269
    Author Index   271
    Subject Index   275

Abbreviations

General

//	parallel	LXX	Septuagint (Greek version of the Jewish Scriptures)
acc.	accusative		
adj.	adjective	n	note
ca.	*circa*, about	nom.	nominative
cf.	*confer*, compare	NIF	Natural Information Flow
chap(s).	chapter(s)	no(s).	number(s)
d.	dative	NT	New Testament
ed(s).	editor(s), edited by, edition	OT	Old Testament
e.g.	*exempli gratia*, for example	pl.	plural
ESOL	English to Speakers of Other Languages	p(p).	page(s)
		repr.	reprinted
f.	feminine	SBL	Society of Biblical Literature
fig.	figure	SFL	Systemic Functional Linguistics
gen.	genitive	SIL	Summer Institute of Linguistics
ind.	indicative	subj.	subjunctive
IPA	International Phonetic Alphabet	v(v).	verse(s)

Scripture Editions and Translations

ASV	American Standard Version	NA²⁸	*Novum Testamentum Graece*, Nestle-Aland, 28th ed.
AT	author's translation		
CSB	Christian Standard Bible	NASB	New American Standard Bible
ESV	English Standard Version	NEB	New English Bible
KJV	King James Version	NIV	New International Version (2011)

NKJV	New King James Version	TEV	Today's English Version (=
NRSV	New Revised Standard Version		Good News Bible)
	(1989)	UBS⁵	*The Greek New Testament*,
RSV	Revised Standard Version		United Bible Societies, 5th ed.
SBLGNT	Michael W. Holmes, ed., *The Greek New Testament: SBL Edition*		

Old Testament Apocrypha and Pseudepigrapha

Jdt.   Judith   1–2 Macc.   1–2 Maccabees

Apostolic Fathers

Barn.	Epistle of Barnabas
FPap 3.14	Papias, *Fragments* 3.14, in "Papias and Quadratus," Loeb Classical Library 25, *The Apostolic Fathers*, vol. 2, ed. and trans. Bart D. Ehrman (Cambridge, MA: Harvard University Press, 2003)
Herm. Mand.	Shepherd of Hermas, Mandates
Herm. Sim.	Shepherd of Hermas, Similitudes
Ign. *Rom.*	Ignatius, *To the Romans*

Secondary Sources and Collections

BDAG	W. Bauer, F. W. Danker, W. F. Arndt, and F. W. Gingrich, *A Greek-English Lexicon of the New Testament and Other Early Christian Literature*, 3rd ed. (Chicago: University of Chicago Press, 2000)
BDF	Friedrich Blass, Albert Debrunner, and Robert W. Funk, *A Greek Grammar of the New Testament and Other Early Christian Literature* (Chicago: University of Chicago Press, 1961)
CILT	Current Issues in Linguistic Theory
ICC	International Critical Commentary
INTF	Institut für neutestamentliche Textforschung
JETS	*Journal of the Evangelical Theological Society*
JSNTSup	Journal for the Study of the New Testament Supplement Series
Louw-Nida	Johannes P. Louw and Eugene A. Nida, eds., *Greek-English Lexicon of the New Testament: Based on Semantic Domains*, 2nd ed. (New York: United Bible Societies, 1989)
MJTM	*McMaster Journal of Theology and Ministry*
NCBC	New Century Bible Commentary

NICNT   New International Commentary on the New Testament
NIGTC   New International Greek Testament Commentary
NMLB   Newson's Modern Language Books
OAL   Oxford Applied Linguistics
OPTAT   *Occasional Papers in Translation and Textlinguistics*
SDR   Strumenti per la didattica e la ricerca
TSL   Typological Studies in Language
WBC   Word Biblical Commentary

Preface

Where Did We Come From?

DAVID ALAN BLACK

Recently I ordered a book edited by Stanley Porter and Don Carson called *Discourse Analysis and Other Topics in Biblical Greek*.[1] Though reprinted by Bloomsbury in 2015, it was first published by Sheffield Academic Press way back when the ark landed on Ararat (1995). Most of my students weren't even alive back then. I originally read this book when it first came out, but I have a big reading problem: I can never read a good book only once. This disorder started when I was in seminary and reading books by F. F. Bruce and Bruce Manning Metzger. I've long been a fan of books about linguistics, so when I ordered this one, I knew I was in for some pleasant surprises. I will give you one example. The irrepressible Moisés Silva, in his chapter titled "Discourse Analysis and Philippians," writes the following (keep in mind that Silva is discussing his growing confusion about the character of Greek discourse analysis):

> Every researcher seems to be following his or her own agenda—usually quite an expansive agenda. Certain that the problem was not the early onset of senility, I picked up the recent and fine collection of papers edited by David Black,

1. Stanley E. Porter and D. A. Carson, eds., *Discourse Analysis and Other Topics in Biblical Greek* (London: Bloomsbury, 2015).

with the hopes of clarifying matters once and for all. My anxiety, however, was only aggravated to realize in a fresh way that discourse analysis is about . . . *everything*! It is grammar and syntax, pragmatics and lexicology, exegesis and literary criticism. In short, fertile ground for undisciplined minds.[2]

Silva's was a tough chapter to get through because it is so blatantly honest and on target. As he puts it, "The more I read the more lost I feel."[3] There's no need to fool ourselves into thinking that our discipline (New Testament Greek) has gotten any less confusing since Silva wrote that chapter twenty-four years ago. What to do? Hold a conference, of course!

Two years ago, having previously organized three major New Testament conferences on our campus, I asked my colleague Benjamin Merkle if he would be interested in helping me organize yet another one, this time a summit dealing with the intersection of linguistics and New Testament Greek.[4] To this request he graciously agreed, and the book you now hold in your hands is the result of our joint effort to try to help our Greek students become more familiar with the significant contributions that linguistics can make to their study of New Testament Greek. In this preface I will endeavor to briefly explain the reasons we felt such a conference was necessary. In the postscript, my co-editor, who is currently writing (with Robert Plummer) a new beginning grammar of New Testament Greek, will summarize his impressions of the conference and make some suggestions as to where he thinks the discipline of New Testament Greek studies is likely to go in the future.

One of the most notable features of New Testament Greek scholarship during the past ten to twenty years has been the recovery of our temporarily mislaid interest in the science of linguistics. In the mid- to late twentieth

2. Moisés Silva, "Discourse Analysis and Philippians," in Porter and Carson, *Discourse Analysis*, 102. The "collection of papers" to which Silva is referring is David Alan Black, with Katharine Barnwell and Stephen Levinsohn, eds., *Linguistics and New Testament Interpretation: Essays on Discourse Analysis* (Nashville: B&H Academic, 1993).

3. Silva, "Discourse Analysis and Philippians," 102.

4. Those three conferences were Symposium on New Testament Studies: A Time for Reappraisal, April 6–7, 2000; The Last Twelve Verses of Mark: Original or Not, April 13–14, 2007; and Pericope of the Adulteress Conference, April 25–26, 2014. I had the privilege of editing the papers from these conferences. The fruit of the first conference was published in the form of two books, the first edited with my colleague David R. Beck and titled *Rethinking the Synoptic Problem* (Grand Rapids: Baker Academic, 2001) and the second titled *Rethinking New Testament Textual Criticism* (Grand Rapids: Baker Academic, 2002). The papers from the second conference were published under the title *Perspectives on the Ending of Mark* (Nashville: B&H Academic, 2008). The third conference resulted in the collection of essays I edited with Jacob Cerone for the Library of New Testament Studies Series titled *The Pericope of the Adulteress in Contemporary Research* (London: T&T Clark, 2016).

century, teachers of New Testament Greek were generally preoccupied with more or less traditional approaches to Greek grammar that often involved little more than lists of paradigms and principal parts. But now many of us who teach Greek are convinced that God has given us insights from the science of linguistics that can and should inform our traditional approaches to exegesis. At the same time we realize that our discipline is far behind in this area, and we have a long way to go to catch up. This book is one attempt to bring New Testament Greek studies up to speed. It contains eleven papers delivered at a conference called Linguistics and New Testament Greek: Key Issues in the Current Debate, held on the campus of Southeastern Baptist Theological Seminary on April 26–27, 2019. The editors confess that they are not specialists in the science of linguistics and have no particular expertise in most of the subjects treated in this volume. (You will notice that neither of us read papers at the conference.) Moreover, each topic is uniquely complex and has attracted a very extensive literature, only some of which we have been able to explore. Yet we venture to offer to the reading public (mostly those who have had at least one year of Greek instruction) a book that will hopefully help ordinary students of Greek think more linguistically about the language they are studying.

Proverbs 27:17 might well have been a suitable motto for our conference: "As iron sharpens iron, so one person sharpens another" (NIV). In its original context, this proverb is about individuals. But could it not also apply to Greek and linguistics? Each subject is a challenge to the other, for better or for worse. In fact, many if not most evangelicals today would argue that there is a strong correlation between the Bible and science, between Greek and linguistics. God is the God of nature as well as Scripture, of reason as well as revelation. During the so-called Enlightenment, of course, many abandoned the Bible for science altogether. To them, the Bible seemed incompatible with their Western culture and with its scientific approach to all things in the universe. Conversely, some Christians withdrew from the world of science, asking themselves, "Can anything good come out of Athens?"[5] In recent years, however, the Bible and science have moved closer together. It has become apparent to many New Testament scholars that Greek is, in fact, a *language* just like any other human language, even though God used it to inscripturate his divine truth. And if it is true that Koine Greek is a language,

---

5. An insightful documentation of these developments can be found in Mark A. Noll, *Between Faith and Criticism: Evangelicals, Scholarship, and the Bible in America* (Grand Rapids: Baker, 1991). To read about details specific to the NT not only in America but also in Europe, see the standard treatment in Stephen Neill and N. T. Wright, *The Interpretation of the New Testament, 1861–1986*, 2nd ed. (Oxford: Oxford University Press, 1988).

then the science of linguistics has much to commend it.[6] It seems clear that the main alternative—viewing the Greek of the New Testament as sui generis, as a kind of Holy Ghost language—has little evidence for it compared with a linguistic understanding of how languages work.[7]

In the past century, the study of New Testament Greek has gradually moved from viewing Greek as a special field of study to viewing it as a part of the broader science of linguistics. The shift began well before I published my book *Linguistics for Students of New Testament Greek* in 1988. This new forward impetus was based on the groundbreaking work of nineteenth-century and early twentieth-century New Testament Greek scholars, including Winer, Blass, Moulton, and A. T. Robertson.[8] Since then,

6. One excellent defense of this idea is Moisés Silva, *God, Language and Scripture: Reading the Bible in the Light of General Linguistics* (Grand Rapids: Zondervan, 1990). For an attempt to locate the phenomena of language in a theological framework, see Vern S. Poythress, *In the Beginning Was the Word: Language—a God-Centered Approach* (Wheaton: Crossway, 2009). Recent interest in the application of modern linguistics to the study of the biblical languages is evidenced by a series of works intended to introduce biblical language students to linguistic concepts. In addition to my *Linguistics for Students of New Testament Greek: A Survey of Basic Concepts and Applications*, 2nd ed. (Grand Rapids: Baker, 1995), there is also Peter Cotterell and Max Turner, *Linguistics and Biblical Interpretation* (London: SPCK, 1989); Peter James Silzer and Thomas John Finley, *How Biblical Languages Work: A Student's Guide to Learning Hebrew and Greek* (Grand Rapids: Kregel, 2004); Constantine R. Campbell, *Advances in the Study of Greek: New Insights for Reading the New Testament* (Grand Rapids: Zondervan, 2015); and Douglas Mangum and Josh Westbury, eds., *Linguistics and Biblical Exegesis* (Bellingham, WA: Lexham, 2017).

7. For the crucial role of the papyri in deconstructing the idea of "Holy Ghost Greek," see James Hope Moulton, *Prolegomena*, vol. 1 of *A Grammar of New Testament Greek*, 3rd ed. (Edinburgh: T&T Clark, 1908), 2–5. Somewhat different is Nigel Turner's evaluation of the "inner homogeneity of Biblical Greek." See Nigel Turner, *Style*, vol. 4 of *A Grammar of New Testament Greek* (Edinburgh: T&T Clark, 1976), 2. See also his comments in Nigel Turner, *Syntax*, vol. 3 of *A Grammar of New Testament Greek* (Edinburgh: T&T Clark, 1963), 9:

> I do not wish to prove too much by these examples, but the strongly Semitic character of Bibl. Greek, and therefore its remarkable unity within itself, do seem to me to have contemporary significance at a time when many are finding their way back to the Bible as a living book and perhaps are pondering afresh the old question of a "Holy Ghost language." The lapse of half a century was needed to assess the discoveries of Deissmann and Moulton and put them in right perspective. We now have to concede that not only is the subject-matter of the Scriptures unique but so also is the language in which they came to be written or translated. This much is plain for all who can see, but the further question arises, whether such a Biblical language was the creature of an hour and the *ad hoc* instrument for a particular purpose, or whether it was a spoken language as well, something more than an over-literal rendering of Semitic idioms, a permanent influence and a significant development in the language. Students of Greek await the answer with interest.

8. Georg Benedikt Winer, *Grammatik des neutestamentlichen Sprachidioms* (Leipzig: Vogel, 1822); English translation: *A Treatise on the Grammar of New Testament Greek*, trans. W. F. Moulton, 3rd ed. (Edinburgh: T&T Clark, 1882); Friedrich Blass, *Grammatik des*

New Testament scholars have been split over whether or not exegesis allows for the full integration of linguistics into biblical studies. Some scholars have even felt threatened by this new approach to the study of the Greek of the New Testament.[9] However, since evangelicals believe that God is the unifier of the cosmos, the editors are convinced that no one should feel intimidated by the various models of linguistic research that have become available over the past century.

Among the branches of linguistics, comparative-historical linguistics proved to be the most interesting to New Testament scholars of the past century. Robertson's *Grammar of the Greek New Testament in the Light of Historical Research*—affectionately known to students as his "Big Grammar"—moved biblical studies in this direction like no other work that preceded it. Then discoveries in the field of semantics began to inform our discipline, resulting in groundbreaking works like Johannes Louw's *Semantics of New Testament Greek* and Moisés Silva's *Biblical Words and Their Meaning*.[10] Currently it looks like the field of New Testament Greek linguistics has begun to burgeon far beyond anyone's wildest imaginations, owing in large part to the tireless efforts of scholars like Stanley Porter, Stephen Levinsohn, and Steven Runge, all three of whom contributed papers to this volume.[11] If, for example, we take lexical semantics as a trustworthy approach, books like *Biblical Words and Their Meaning* become indispensable. Clearly our

---

neutestamentlichen Griechisch (Göttingen: Vandenhoeck & Ruprecht, 1896), the tenth edition of which (better known as Blass-Debrunner-Funk [BDF]) was translated and updated as Friedrich Blass, Albert Debrunner, and Robert W. Funk, *A Greek Grammar of the New Testament and Other Early Christian Literature* (Chicago: University of Chicago Press, 1961); James Hope Moulton, Wilbert Francis Howard, and Nigel Turner, *A Grammar of New Testament Greek*, 4 vols. (Edinburgh: T&T Clark, 1908–76); and A. T. Robertson, *A Grammar of the Greek New Testament in the Light of Historical Research* (New York: Hodder & Stoughton, 1914).

9. One of the most prominent in this regard is the late Robert L. Thomas. See Robert L. Thomas, "Modern Linguistics versus Traditional Hermeneutics," *Masters Seminary Journal* 14, no. 1 (Spring 2003): 23–45.

10. J. P. Louw, *Semantics of New Testament Greek* (Atlanta: Scholars Press, 1982); Moisés Silva, *Biblical Words and Their Meaning: An Introduction to Lexical Semantics*, rev. ed. (Grand Rapids: Zondervan, 1994).

11. Stanley Porter has been one of the most prolific proponents of linguistic exegesis of the Greek NT. He has authored or coauthored 28 books and edited or co-edited 124 books and journal volumes. His most important works include *Verbal Aspect in the Greek of the New Testament, with Reference to Tense and Mood* (New York: Peter Lang, 1989) and *Idioms of the Greek New Testament*, 2nd ed. (Sheffield: Sheffield Academic, 1994). Stephen H. Levinsohn's most important work is *Discourse Features of New Testament Greek: A Coursebook on the Information Structure of New Testament Greek*, 2nd ed. (Dallas: SIL International, 2000). Steven E. Runge's *Discourse Grammar of the Greek New Testament: A Practical Introduction for Teaching and Exegesis* (Peabody, MA: Hendrickson, 2010) is an essential work in the field.

discipline could do without such exegetical fallacies as illegitimate totality transfer, etymologizing, and anachronistic interpretation.[12] With the rise of the field of biblical linguistics, evidence that the Greek of the New Testament is in fact not sui generis has risen dramatically, putting even more pressure on the claim that the New Testament is composed of "Holy Ghost Greek."

In my chapter "The Study of New Testament Greek in the Light of Ancient and Modern Linguistics," published in 1991 and revised in 2001, I noted several potentially fruitful areas of research for Greek scholars.[13] Allow me to quote them here and then make a few brief comments about the progress made since I originally wrote these words:

1. The problem of the reticence to break the traditional mold and strike out for newer and more productive territory. No longer can students of Greek be considered knowledgeable if they still believe *the* grammar they were taught; it is now painfully obvious that there are *many* grammars—traditional, structural, transformational, etc.—and that each of these comes in a wide variety of sizes and shapes. And it seems a reasonable assumption that more will follow.

2. The problem of the atomization of methods currently employed in New Testament philology. To take just one example, in the United States, Chomskyan linguistics once held the day, but today several other methods are being employed, such as Kenneth Pike's Tagmemics, Charles Fillmore's case grammar, and Sydney Lamb's stratificational grammar. This diversity, including significant terminological confusion, remains a problem, and this situation is only exacerbated by the recent influx of methods currently in vogue in Europe.

3. The present crisis over the nature of "New Testament Greek." What is to be done about the strongly Semitic character of New Testament Greek, and can one speak of New Testament Greek as a linguistic subsystem when a comprehensive grammar of Hellenistic Greek has yet to be written?

12. As pointed out in Silva, *Biblical Words and Their Meaning*, 137–69. See also D. A. Carson, *Exegetical Fallacies*, 2nd ed. (Grand Rapids: Baker, 1996).

13. David Alan Black, "The Study of New Testament Greek in the Light of Ancient and Modern Linguistics," in *New Testament Criticism and Interpretation*, ed. David Alan Black and David S. Dockery (Grand Rapids: Zondervan, 1991), 379–406. The items listed are from pp. 404–5. This book was revised and renamed in 2001, and numbers 8 and 9 were added to the list. See David Alan Black, "The Study of New Testament Greek in the Light of Ancient and Modern Linguistics," in *Interpreting the New Testament: Essays on Methods and Issues*, ed. David Alan Black and David S. Dockery (Nashville: Broadman & Holman, 2001), 230–52.

4. The problem of defining the relationship between linguistics proper and New Testament "philology," which itself can refer both to *Literaturwissenschaft* (the study of the New Testament as a part of ancient Greek literature) and *Sprachwissenschaft* (the study of the Greek of the New Testament). This duel between diachronic and synchronic approaches must, it seems to me, be resolved if New Testament scholarship is to arrive at a synthesis capable of using the best of both approaches to language.

5. The riddle of the Greek verbal system: Can the tense structure of New Testament Greek continue to be described in terms of a rigid time structure when the latest research indicates that verbal aspect is the predominant category of tense (see especially the recent works by Buist Fanning and Stanley Porter)?

6. The challenge posed by "rhetorical criticism" in taking us beyond hermeneutics and structuralism. The recent revival of interest in rhetoric in New Testament studies bodes well for the future of our discipline, but neither James Muilenburg nor his school has produced a workable model of rhetorical criticism (though F. Siegert's 1984 dissertation is a positive step in the right direction).

7. The mention of structuralism raises the onerous hermeneutical question concerning surface and deeper linguistic meaning in the interpretation of New Testament texts, a question posed most radically by Erhardt Güttgemanns (1978) but certainly not by him alone.

8. The value of linguistics for New Testament Greek pedagogy. There are signs that a linguistic approach is becoming more acceptable to a new generation of Greek teachers. Phonology is seen as useful in that it helps students see that many seeming irregularities about Greek are perfectly normal and operate according to certain phonological "rules" in the language, while morphology is especially helpful in acquiring and retaining vocabulary and in understanding the Greek verb system. The "slot and filler" approach to grammar used by the present writer in his *Learn to Read New Testament Greek* (expanded edition, 1994) helps students *understand* what they are learning (instead of just requiring them to memorize a phalanx of linguistic minutiae). Semantics reminds us that meaning is the ultimate goal of all linguistic analysis and that both syntagmatic and paradigmatic relations deserve careful study.

9. Finally, the place of discourse analysis (textlinguistics) requires further discussion. Traditional studies of New Testament Greek have tended to ignore the macrostructure of a given text (the "forest"), emphasizing

instead the trees and the tiny saplings. It is everywhere apparent that New Testament exegesis remains somewhat "word-bound," though more and more seminarians are being exposed to the dangers of a "wall motto" or "bumper sticker" mentality in doing exegesis. Discourse analysis is especially helpful in doing exegesis above the sentence level and promises to become a standard instrument in the pastor's toolbox.

Fortunately, there is evidence that, in all of these areas, significant progress has been made since 2001: (1) More and more New Testament Greek scholars are eager to engage in linguistically oriented research when it comes to the language of the New Testament. (2) Although the problem of atomization remains, conferences like the one in Great Britain on the Greek verb have made serious strides forward.[14] (3) Today one can speak of a consensus among New Testament scholars that the Greek of the New Testament, although it is often characterized by Septuagintalisms, is related to Koine Greek as a whole. (4) Most agree that exegesis requires both a diachronic approach and a synchronic one. (5) Even those who argue that time is grammaticalized in the indicative mood in Greek would affirm that Koine Greek is largely aspectual in nature. (6) Rhetorical criticism is duly recognized as an indispensable step in exegesis in many of our current handbooks. (7) The issue of deep versus surface structures has become a fairly common theme in our hermeneutical primers. (8) Our most recent evangelical introductory grammars of New Testament Greek have consciously adopted linguistically aware methodologies.[15] (9) The practice of discourse analysis among New Testament scholars is perhaps as common today as it was uncommon three or four decades ago.

With this brief summary, we can see that the field of New Testament Greek linguistics has made a number of discoveries that challenge evangelicals' traditional approach to exegesis. It has also made other discoveries that challenge the methodological certainty of our exegetical methods. Unfortunately, evangelicals have not found as much common ground as we would like for a unified response to modern linguistic science. All can (and do) agree that the Bible is God's inspired Word and that it is crucial for people to recognize this. However, there is as of yet no agreement on the detailed model (or models) of

14. These conference papers were published as Steven E. Runge and Christopher J. Fresch, eds., *The Greek Verb Revisited: A Fresh Approach for Biblical Exegesis* (Bellingham, WA: Lexham, 2016).

15. Here I am thinking especially of Stanley E. Porter, Jeffrey T. Reed, and Matthew Brook O'Donnell, *Fundamentals of New Testament Greek* (Grand Rapids: Eerdmans, 2010); Rodney J. Decker, *Reading Koine Greek: An Introduction and Integrated Workbook* (Grand Rapids: Baker Academic, 2014).

linguistics that should prevail in our schools and seminaries. Other questions arise as well: How should Koine Greek be pronounced? How many aspects are there in the Greek verb system, and what should we call them? Should the term "deponency" be used anymore? What is the unmarked word order in Koine Greek? What is the proper place of discourse analysis in exegesis? What are the semantics of the perfect tense-form? How should linguistics affect our classroom pedagogy? These are basic and central matters that should not be overlooked amid our intramural disputes.

To be sure, the speakers at our conference did not agree among themselves on many of these topics. We should not be surprised to find such disagreement. After all, evangelical New Testament scholars are not united in many other areas of interpretation, including the mode of baptism, the biblical form of church government, eschatology, and whether miraculous gifts are valid today. Despite our disagreements, however, we should not throw up our hands in despair but should continue to seek solutions in all these areas. We hope that the papers included here will give all of us helpful suggestions for making progress in relating the New Testament to the science of linguistics. For an evangelical, both nature and Scripture are sources of information about God. But because both have fallible human interpreters, we often fail to see what is there. Ideally, scientists (whether secular or evangelical) should favor the data over their pet theories.

I draw this preface to a close with some final thoughts. For two thousand years, Christian theologians have taught that God is a rational God and that humankind is made in God's image and likeness. Moreover, God has given us in nature and in Scripture a double revelation of himself. All scientific research is based on the conviction that the universe is intelligible and that there is a fundamental correspondence between the mind of the scientist and the data that he or she is investigating. And what connects the objective universe with the human mind is precisely what we call rationality.

It is no accident that many if not most of the pioneers of the scientific enterprise were Christian men and women.[16] They believed that a rational God had stamped his rationality both upon the world and upon themselves as they attempted to investigate the natural world. Thus every scientist, whether consciously or not, in the words of the seventeenth-century astronomer Johannes Kepler, is "thinking God's thoughts after Him."[17] And if the scientist

16. See especially James Hannam, *The Genesis of Science: How the Christian Middle Ages Launched the Scientific Revolution* (Washington, DC: Regnery, 2011).
17. My attempts to track down the exact source of this quotation have proven fruitless. Yet I know of no scientist other than Kepler to whom it is attributed. All seem to agree that the sentiments, if not the exact words, are an accurate reflection of his thinking on the subject.

is doing that, so is the student of the Bible, for in Scripture we have an even fuller revelation of God than what we find in the natural order. If, therefore, God has created us as rational beings, are we going to neglect his revelation, both in nature and in Scripture? A thousand times no, for the Christian doctrine of revelation, far from being an unreasonable thing, is an eminently reasonable doctrine.

Many pastors and even New Testament professors in our schools do not think they are exegeting God's revelation in nature when they study Greek grammar. But that doesn't mean they aren't. All study of language is linguistic by its very nature, whether or not we are aware of it. This is not to say that New Testament Greek linguists have completed the task of relating the biblical and scientific data to each other. Further investigation and reflection, long after the publication of this book, will still be needed in this area. Our desire in organizing our linguistics conference was that, far from treating science as an enemy, we should all realize that science is simply the process of studying general revelation. Our hope is that God will continue to reveal himself to us as long as we do not rule out divine inspiration in the process.

Linguistics is, of course, a large subject. No one can ever hope to master its entire scope. Nevertheless, it is obvious that students of New Testament Greek can and should have a working knowledge of linguistics. Although the editors have not solved all the problems involved with integrating New Testament Greek with linguistics, least of all by providing another book on the subject, certain things are clear. We who study and teach New Testament Greek cannot be satisfied with superficial answers. We must carefully scrutinize the pages of general revelation and consider how they may influence our current approach to Greek exegesis. If we need to be cautious in our handling of the scientific data, we also need to be hopeful and optimistic. Further, we must welcome the new approach and not remain locked into traditional methods of Greek instruction. Even the simplest application of linguistics can benefit our beginning students enormously. Finally, we must all be willing to subordinate our own pet theories and preferences to what will best serve the believing communities in which we worship and serve. Love and mutual respect are to be the hallmarks of all we do as New Testament scholars (John 13:35).

These prefatory words are meant to be nothing more than an entrée into the papers read at our linguistics conference. The editors sincerely hope that the chapters will help to identify what is essential and inessential in an era of renewed curiosity about the language of the New Testament.

1

Linguistic Schools

STANLEY E. PORTER

This chapter is concerned with linguistic schools and their impact upon the study of the Greek language of the New Testament. As I shall explain, the study of New Testament Greek has not been clear in its methodologies. The result is a widely accepted positivist view of language in which the Greek language is seen as a "thing" predescriptive in nature—that is, there is an essentialist nature of the Greek language that we, as Greek grammarians and linguists, have progressively discovered over the years and now know. At this stage, we are no longer engaging in new descriptions of Greek but are fine-tuning our previous, agreed-upon understandings. The major problem with this viewpoint is that it is not only out of keeping with virtually every other field of study but also clearly wrong for Greek.

A case in point is the discussion of verbal aspect over the last thirty years. The Greek verbal system was previously described as temporal, even if this was not entirely satisfactory, and we must recognize that Greek, on at least some occasions, is concerned not just with *when* an action took place as signified by a verb but with *how* it took place. Many will be familiar with this discussion over the semantics of the Greek tense-forms and their relationship to *Aktionsart*, or "kind of action." Thirty or more years ago, however, the notion of verbal aspect was introduced as a better description of the Greek verbal edifice. According to aspect theory, the Greek verbal system was aspect prominent, not tense prominent, so that the Greek tense-forms were used to represent the subjective conception of processes by the language user, not the time at which the event occurred. The result was a debate over the semantics of the Greek verbal system and whether aspect or tense was prominent, both of which had implications for understanding the entire Greek language. I have an opinion of which view is correct, but that is not important here. What is important is that the traditional view of Greek sounds much more like a description of German, a heavily tensed language, or perhaps even more importantly of English, a tensed language that also has categories for kinds of action. I suspect that the understandings of German and English were, for many of those in the discussion, far more important in their examinations of Greek than attempting to offer a description of Greek without drawing upon these well-established categories, especially as they represented the first language of the analyst.

The resistance to an aspectual view of Greek is probably not based upon actual examination of the language—something I attempted to do.[1] By at least one accounting, there are as many tenseless as tensed languages among the world's languages.[2] Rather, such resistance is often based upon prior belief that the semantics of the Greek verbal system had already been resolved—if not by the ancient Greeks themselves, then by the Latin grammarians or surely by the nineteenth-century comparative philologians. This simply is not true. Much of what is labeled as linguistic description is projection of one's prior understanding of language, often one's first language, upon another language. That is why linguistic models are so important. Linguistic models—and the linguistic schools of thought that grow up around them—are attempts to find conceptual structures by which to examine language without accepting what we have been told or what we assumed without further reflection and without imposing our own language upon another. These attempts instead provide a linguistic framework that acknowledges its presuppositions and helps us to think about language in new ways, using the resources of the linguistic model.

In this chapter, I wish to examine the major linguistic schools that are currently productively functioning within New Testament Greek studies. In this regard, biblical studies is a problematic discipline since it often demands that a scholar be an expert in a variety of methods, such as linguistics. Most biblical scholars are at least competent in the historical-critical method, as

---

1. Stanley E. Porter, *Verbal Aspect in the Greek of the New Testament, with Reference to Tense and Mood* (New York: Peter Lang, 1989).

2. See Jo-Wang Lin, "Tenselessness," in *The Oxford Handbook of Tense and Aspect*, ed. Robert I. Binnick (Oxford: Oxford University Press, 2012), 668–95, esp. 669; cf. criteria for determining tensed and tenseless languages (670–71).

well as knowledgeable about other post-historical-critical methods, such as social-scientific criticism, literary criticism, and the like. Linguistics, however, is not like that. The methodological boundaries are much more strongly and exclusively drawn, to the point that some may be aware of "linguistic wars" among those who have called into question others' methods. In that sense, being a master of several different methods is not just unpracticed but is often frowned upon, because it implies an inappropriate crossing of boundaries. Therefore, I cannot claim to be an expert in all of the approaches or schools that I will be discussing, but I will attempt to do the best that I can in presenting each one, offering some representative examples of scholars within these schools of thought, and then making some evaluative comments.

■ What Are Linguistic Schools?

Before I divide the linguistic world into its various schools, I must ask what constitutes a linguistic school and how I decide what constitutes a linguistic school within New Testament Greek studies. In 1980, Geoffrey Sampson published his *Schools of Linguistics*, an excellent introduction up to the time of publication. He defines a linguistic school thus: "Often one individual or a small group of original minds has founded a tradition which has continued to mould approaches to language in the university or the nation in which that tradition began; between adherents of different traditions there has usually been relatively limited contact."[3] I will use this definition to define schools of linguistics, with the minimum publication requirement of at least two major monographs or the equivalent in the field of linguistics or linguistic theory and at least two major monographs in the field of New Testament Greek studies, and with some sign of continuing work using the approach. I realize that by imposing this requirement I run the risk of excluding approaches to linguistics that some might follow and find useful. However, the notion of a school, as Sampson indicates, implies a tradition that continues to shape scholarship, rather than simply an individual who develops a particular idea (although I will make a significant exception to this rule). I can offer only a rough outline of the schools of thought as reflected by those who follow a tradition, recognizing that individual scholars will have their own variations upon its major concepts. I am sure that I will overlook some schools of thought in other countries, as I concentrate upon English-language scholarship. I also concentrate upon what Sampson calls "core" linguistic fields, not

3. Geoffrey Sampson, *Schools of Linguistics* (Stanford, CA: Stanford University Press, 1980), 9.

what he terms "peripheral branches," so I am not discussing sociolinguistics, multilingualism, and the like, although I will touch lightly upon that very broad and encompassing subject called discourse analysis. I also do not deal in detail with various areas of applied linguistics.

There are many different ways of describing linguistic schools. Sampson provides a generally diachronic view beginning in the nineteenth century to the present.[4] Jeremy Thompson and Wendy Widder provide the only similar study for biblical studies, although their treatment problematically does not mention the most productive school in contemporary biblical studies (in my opinion), Systemic Functional Linguistics (SFL).[5] Robert Van Valin Jr. and Randy LaPolla differentiate between what they call the "syntactocentric perspective" and the "communication-and-cognition perspective"—in other words, basically Noam Chomsky and everyone else.[6] John Bateman has proposed a more nuanced categorization for the study of language focusing upon whether language is seen as in contexts, texts, heads, or groups. Chomskyans would locate language in texts, cognitivists would locate it in heads, and functionalists would locate it in contexts or groups.[7] An arguably more straightforward means is suggested by David Banks, who distinguishes between formal, cognitive, and functional theories of language.[8] I use this distinction in this chapter.

■ Traditional Grammar

Before I turn to the formalists, cognitivists, and functionalists, however, I include traditional grammar, as represented in the two major periods in language study before the rise of modern linguistics: the rationalist and comparative-historical schools. Many in New Testament Greek study still follow the

4. Sampson acknowledges that other schools might have developed since 1980, including cognitive linguistics, on which he has recently commented. Geoffrey Sampson, *The Linguistics Delusion* (Sheffield: Equinox, 2017), 77–87.

5. Jeremy Thompson and Wendy Widder, "Major Approaches to Linguistics," in *Linguistics and Biblical Exegesis*, ed. Douglas Mangum and Josh Westbury (Bellingham, WA: Lexham, 2017), 87–133.

6. Robert D. Van Valin Jr. and Randy J. LaPolla, *Syntax: Structure, Meaning and Function* (Cambridge: Cambridge University Press, 1997), 8–15.

7. John A. Bateman, "The Place of Systemic Functional Linguistics as a Linguistic Theory in the Twenty-First Century," in *The Routledge Handbook of Systemic Functional Linguistics*, ed. Tom Bartlett and Gerard O'Grady (London: Routledge, 2017), 11–12.

8. David Banks, *A Systemic Functional Grammar of English: A Simple Introduction* (London: Routledge, 2019), 1; cf. David Banks, *The Birth of the Academic Article: Le Journal des Sçavans and the Philosophical Transactions, 1665–1700* (Sheffield: Equinox, 2017), 7.

principles of these schools of thought, even though these principles have been superseded by forms of modern linguistic study.

"Traditional grammar" refers to an approach to language that is pre-linguistic. David Crystal defines its major features: the failure to recognize the difference between spoken and written language, emphasis upon restricted forms of written language, a failure to recognize various forms of language and how they are used, the tendency to describe language in terms of another language (often Latin), the appeal to logic as a means of describing and even assessing language, and the tendency to evaluate language as more or less logical or complex or primitive or beautiful or the like.[9] These traditional criteria grew out of a long history of discussion of language that dates back to the ancients and continued until the advent of modern linguistics. They were found in the two major periods of language study before the rise of modern linguistics: the rationalist and the comparative-historical.[10]

Rationalist Language Study

Rationalism, growing out of the Enlightenment, was characterized by rational thought, a shift from dogmatic to empiricist epistemology, an emphasis upon naturalism (as opposed to supernaturalism), and dissolution of the divide between secular and sacred. This desacralization included the Bible. The movement is perhaps captured best in the work of Baruch Spinoza (1632–77), a rationalist who believed in deduction from common knowledge.

The rationalist period of language study went hand in hand with the Enlightenment. This period extended from roughly the middle of the seventeenth century to the turn of the nineteenth century (1650–1800), with the rise of Romanticism (more precisely in 1798, with publication of *Lyrical Ballads* by William Wordsworth and Samuel Taylor Coleridge). Language study during the rationalist period was dominated by philosophers and linguists approaching language from a rationalist perspective, along with having historical concerns. Étienne Bonnot de Condillac (1714–80) believed that "abstract vocabulary and grammatical complexity developed from an earlier individual concrete vocabulary," and Johann Gottfried Herder (1744–1803) believed in the "inseparability of language and thought."[11] William Jones (1746–94), the British judge in India, opined that Sanskrit was "more perfect than the Greek,

9. David Crystal, *What Is Linguistics?*, 3rd ed. (London: Edward Arnold, 1974), 9–17.
10. See R. H. Robins, *A Short History of Linguistics*, 3rd ed. (London: Longman, 1990), 148–264, for the basic facts recounted in this chapter.
11. Robins, *Short History of Linguistics*, 165, 166.

more copious than the Latin, and more exquisitely refined than either,"[12] and James Harris (1758–1835) thought one could derive "grammar from ontology, since the verb, to him, denotes nothing less than existence itself."[13] The rationalist period was characterized by a philosophical orientation that logically deduced the nature of language from prior beliefs, usually grounded in one's understandings of reality. Hence there was the notion of better- and worse-formed languages, thought and language were inseparable, tense-forms indicated reality grounded in time, and more complex forms were developed from simpler ones.

Georg Benedikt Winer's (1789–1858) *Grammatik des neutestamentlichen Sprachidioms* (during his lifetime, editions were published from 1822 to 1855),[14] though not the first Greek grammar, fully represented the rationalist period. Winer was on the forefront of a new phase of New Testament Greek language study, even if he wrote in the rationalist mode as the period passed. Prior to Winer, study of Greek was dominated by the categories of Latin grammar, with a basic descriptivism verging on prescriptivism. Winer systematically applied the rationalist framework, with New Testament Greek seen as a logically based set of categories. Winer sees Greek as the "sure basis" for exegesis, with the Jewish writers of the Greek New Testament writing in a mixed Greek and Semitic language that represents a unified "single syntax." Winer specifically speaks of the "rational method" of Greek language study, equated with empiricism.[15] He follows these rationalistic principles throughout, finding consistency and regularity based upon empirical evidence (or his perception of empirical evidence). Hence Winer confines the meanings of the Greek tense-forms to temporal categories (he was a German, after all). He states: "Strictly and properly speaking no one of these tenses [of Greek] can ever stand for another," with the present tense-form being "used for the future in appearance only," because the label indicates that it must be only a present tense-form.[16]

Winer's grammar would otherwise be simply a curiosity of linguistic history were it not for the fact that the rationalistic approach is still widely found in New Testament Greek language study. The rationalistic approach is evidenced in many beginning Greek grammars, where tense-forms and temporal-

12. Robins, *Short History of Linguistics*, 149.
13. Hye-Joon Yoon, *The Rhetoric of Tenses in Adam Smith's "The Wealth of Nations"* (Leiden: Brill, 2018), 47.
14. Georg Benedikt Winer, *Grammatik des neutestamentlichen Sprachidioms* (Leipzig: Vogel, 1822); English translation: G. B. Winer, *A Treatise on the Grammar of New Testament Greek*, trans. W. F. Moulton, 3rd ed. (Edinburgh: T&T Clark, 1882).
15. Winer, *Treatise on the Grammar*, 3, 7.
16. Winer, *Treatise on the Grammar*, 331.

ity are equated as if there were an inherent logic in their meanings and names, reference is made to the "definite" article (Greek has no definite article), and other similar comments are made. The vast majority of elementary Greek grammars fall within this category, from J. Gresham Machen's (1923) to Daniel Zacharias's (2018), with that of William Mounce (1993; 4th ed., 2019) in between, and many others besides. More disturbing, perhaps, is the fact that intermediate-level Greek grammars continue to reflect rationalism as well. The most obvious examples of the rationalistic approach are Daniel Wallace's *Greek Grammar beyond the Basics* and, more recently, Andreas Köstenberger, Benjamin Merkle, and Robert Plummer's *Going Deeper with New Testament Greek*.[17] These grammars may not at first appear to be rationalistic grammars, as they seem to be familiar with the latest developments in Greek language study. Wallace, for example, accepts such apparently linguistic notions as "semantics and semantic situation," "synchronic priority," and "structural priority." However, he also relies upon the notion of "undisputed examples," reintroduces diachrony, has a nonsystemic view of structure, and maintains the strange belief in the "cryptic nature of language."[18] Köstenberger, Merkle, and Plummer don't even include as much linguistic information as the minimalist Wallace. They too define the meanings of the tense-forms in rationalistic terms (such as the "combinative aspect" of the aorist and present), utilize a traditional lexical-incremental morphology, and attempt to explain both the five- and eight-case systems.[19]

Comparative Historicism

Comparative-historical language study emerged in the nineteenth century, as languages were discovered and then studied in relation to each other under the influence of the dominant developmental hypothesis. This approach ended with the publication of Ferdinand de Saussure's *Course in General Linguistics* in 1916 and the rise of the Prague School. The comparative-historical approach was mostly influenced by the rise of Romanticism, with its emphasis upon the

17. Daniel B. Wallace, *Greek Grammar beyond the Basics: An Exegetical Syntax of the New Testament* (Grand Rapids: Zondervan, 1996); Andreas J. Köstenberger, Benjamin L. Merkle, and Robert L. Plummer, *Going Deeper with New Testament Greek: An Intermediate Study of the Grammar and Syntax of the New Testament* (Nashville: B&H Academic, 2016).

18. Wallace, *Greek Grammar beyond the Basics*, x–xvii.

19. By contrast, there are some intermediate grammars that are linguistic in orientation. Among others, these include Stanley E. Porter, *Idioms of the Greek New Testament*, 2nd ed. (Sheffield: Sheffield Academic, 1994); Robert A. Young, *Intermediate New Testament Greek: A Linguistic and Exegetical Approach* (Nashville: Broadman & Holman, 1994); and David L. Mathewson and Elodie Ballantine Emig, *Intermediate Greek Grammar: Syntax for Students of the New Testament* (Grand Rapids: Baker Academic, 2016).

self, subjectivity, and experience. The German poet and philosopher Friedrich Schlegel (1772–1829) formulated the term "comparative philology" (1808) to describe the comparisons of both derivational and inflectional morphology.

The Danish scholar Rasmus Rask (1787–1832) and the German Jacob Grimm (1785–1863) were major figures in the emergence of comparative historicism. Rask wrote grammars for Old Norse and Old English, and Grimm wrote the first Germanic grammar, developing terminology still used in linguistics ("strong/weak verbs," "ablaut," and "umlaut"). The high points were Franz Bopp's (1791–1867) major treatment on the conjugation system of Sanskrit, Greek, Latin, Persian, and German, and then his comparative grammar in three volumes. Wilhelm von Humboldt (1767–1835) defined the inner forms of languages as agglutinative, isolating, and flexional, and August Schleicher (1821–68) developed the comparative-philological tree diagram to describe the family of languages. The comparative-historical period reached its culmination in the New Grammarians, including Karl Brugmann (1849–1919) and Berthold Delbrück (1842–1922). The New Grammarians were an informal group of younger German linguists who took a scientific approach to language and believed that all sound changes followed exceptionless rules.

The three major reference grammars of New Testament Greek all reflect the comparative-historical perspective and were written during this period. These grammars are by Friedrich Blass, James Hope Moulton, and A. T. Robertson. Friedrich Blass (1843–1907) was not a comparative philologian but a classical philologian, as he acknowledges in the preface to the first edition of his Greek grammar, which appeared in 1896.[20] Nevertheless, he follows many of its principles by describing New Testament Greek in relationship to Attic Greek and Latin. For the fourth edition (1913), the Swiss comparative philologian Albert Debrunner (1884–1958) became the author. A number of further editions were made, and after Debrunner's passing, David Tabachowitz added supplementary volumes in 1965 and 1970, and then Friedrich Rehkopf took up the editorship in 1976 and continued to 2001. Robert Funk translated the ninth and tenth editions in 1961. The most important feature to note about the grammar, however, is that, no matter how many editions, the grammar is in its essentials the same, with its comparative-historical dimension becoming more explicit especially through the work of Debrunner.

James Hope Moulton (1863–1917), who was educated as a comparative philologian at Cambridge, acknowledges that he writes from this standpoint

20. Friedrich Blass, *Grammatik des Neutestamentlichen Griechisch* (Göttingen: Vandenhoeck & Ruprecht, 1896); English translation: Friedrich Blass, *Grammar of New Testament Greek*, trans. Henry St. John Thackeray (London: Macmillan, 1898).

in his preface to the second edition of his *Prolegomena*, the first volume of his projected three-volume grammar.[21] Whereas Adolf Deissmann made the discovery of the common vocabulary of the Greek New Testament and the Greek documentary papyri, Moulton emphasized the common grammar. His *Prolegomena* went through two further editions, in 1906 and in 1908, and then he began work on his accidence and word-formation. He wrote about two-thirds of this second volume before being killed crossing the Mediterranean in 1917. This work was completed by his student Wilbert Francis Howard (1880–1952).[22]

The culmination of the comparative-historical method in the study of the Greek New Testament, the grammar of A. T. Robertson (1863–1934), was published in 1914. Beginning by revising Winer's grammar, Robertson then realized that such a plan would not work because "so much progress had been made in comparative philology and historical grammar since Winer wrote his great book."[23] Robertson provides a twenty-four-page list of works most often cited, including two additional pages for the third edition, with the list full of comparative philologians. He notes the pre-Winer and then Winer periods, before referring to the "modern period," with its new tools, such as comparative philology. Robertson clearly recognizes that his grammar is an example of comparative philology. The comparative-historical perspective has continued in New Testament Greek grammatical study, in large part because of reliance upon these reference grammars.[24]

I note two important factors regarding both the rationalist and comparative-historical language schools. The first is that, no matter what developments may have occurred within linguistics (and some of those who persist in their rationalism and comparative historicism are aware of such developments), some continue to model these traditional forms of grammar in their work. The second is that these models of language, which arguably have been superseded in subsequent linguistic thought, remain foundational within New

21. James Hope Moulton, *Prolegomena*, vol. 1 of *A Grammar of New Testament Greek* (Edinburgh: T&T Clark, 1906).

22. James Hope Moulton and W. F. Howard, *Accidence and Word-Formation*, vol. 2 of *A Grammar of New Testament Greek* (Edinburgh: T&T Clark, 1929). The third and fourth volumes in the series, *Syntax* and *Style*, written by Nigel Turner, do not follow the same language theory.

23. A. T. Robertson, *A Grammar of the Greek New Testament in the Light of Historical Research* (New York: Hodder & Stoughton, 1914), vii.

24. E.g., Chrys C. Caragounis, *The Development of Greek and the New Testament: Morphology, Syntax, Phonology, and Textual Transmission* (Grand Rapids: Baker Academic, 2006); David S. Hasselbrook, *Studies in New Testament Lexicography: Advancing toward a Full Diachronic Approach with the Greek Language* (Tübingen: Mohr Siebeck, 2011).

Testament studies, providing most examples of beginning New Testament Greek grammars, several of the intermediate Greek grammars, virtually all of the advanced reference grammars, and occasional monographs. The fact that this situation exists should be a major concern for those who are in the field of New Testament Greek studies.

I turn now to the three categories of modern linguistic schools of thought— that is, those developed after the work of Saussure and the Prague School—in relationship to New Testament Greek language study. I treat them in the order of formalist, then cognitive, and finally functional schools.

Formalist Schools

The formalist schools of linguistics emphasize the forms of language, as opposed to its meaning or function. As Banks states concerning formalists, they "treat language as if it were no more than its form, a sort of linguistic algebra, with independent existence."[25] There are two major expressions of formalist linguistic schools within contemporary New Testament Greek study: Chomskyan formalism and construction grammar.

Chomskyan Formalism

The first linguistic school, and the most important so far as the wider field of linguistics is concerned, revolves around Chomsky and his followers. Chomsky's formalist linguistics was influenced by two teachers, Roman Jakobson (1896–1982) at Harvard University and Zellig Harris (1909–92) at the University of Pennsylvania. Jakobson promoted phonemic universalism, and Harris approached language in terms of the "formal" distribution of morphemes apart from meaning, along with the notions of generativity and transformations.[26] As a result, Chomsky's assumption is that there is an "autonomous cognitive faculty," a universal grammar that results in human internal grammar that follows linguistic universals. Such linguistics investigates not language use (performance) but the speaker's competence (Saussure's *langue* over *parole*), and especially the cognitive dimensions of language such as its acquisition. Chomsky therefore provides an analysis of grammar but not of language, if language is defined as what humans actually produce (*parole*).[27] All this can be described apart from meaning. As P. H. Matthews states, "A systematic

25. Banks, *Birth of the Academic Article*, 7.
26. Sampson, *Schools of Linguistics*, 130–31, 134–35.
27. Van Valin and LaPolla, *Syntax*, 9.

description of the 'internal structure' or 'expression' side of a language could, in principle, stand on its own."[28] Chomsky reflects this emphasis upon form rather than meaning in his phrase-structure grammar, with its transformations, as found in his first two major works, *Syntactic Structures* (1957) and *Aspects of the Theory of Syntax* (1965), what came to be known as his standard theory, later extended.[29] It was not until 1963 and later that semantics was explicitly introduced into transformational generative grammar—not by Chomsky but by others, such as George Lakoff—as generative semantics.[30] Semantics was included in subsequent versions of Chomskyan linguistics, including "government and binding" and then "principles and parameters," or the minimalist program. Chomsky has inspired a number of other linguistic schools—as well as cognitive linguistics, as I will note below—but, apart from cognitive linguistics, New Testament studies has not generally followed Chomskyanism.

The few Chomskyans to note within the sphere of New Testament Greek linguistics include Daryl D. Schmidt, J. P. Louw, Micheal Palmer, and, after a hiatus, Robert Crellin. Schmidt wrote a brief monograph on complementation using Chomsky's extended standard theory.[31] Louw utilizes his own form of constituent structure analysis, with the explicit admission that "meaning" is a prerequisite of analysis, a claim that Chomsky would not have made when Louw wrote.[32] Palmer draws upon later developments in Chomsky (later abandoned in the minimalist program), which resulted in X-bar theory or a theory of projection of elements, to describe phrase structure in Luke's Gospel.[33] Most recently, Crellin has studied the historical semantic development of the perfect tense-form using Chomskyan linguistics and neo-Davidsonian semantics, indebted to analytic philosophy.[34]

28. P. H. Matthews, *Grammatical Theory in the United States from Bloomfield to Chomsky* (Cambridge: Cambridge University Press, 1993), 23.

29. Noam Chomsky, *Syntactic Structures* (The Hague: Mouton, 1957), 93; Noam Chomsky, *Aspects of the Theory of Syntax* (Cambridge, MA: MIT Press, 1965), 3.

30. E.g., George Lakoff, "On Generative Semantics," in *Semantics: An Interdisciplinary Reader in Philosophy, Linguistics and Psychology*, ed. Danny D. Steinberg and Leon A. Jakobovits (Cambridge: Cambridge University Press, 1971), 232–96. See Randy Allen Harris, *The Linguistics Wars* (Oxford: Oxford University Press, 1993), 101–59.

31. Daryl Dean Schmidt, *Hellenistic Greek Grammar and Noam Chomsky: Nominalizing Transformations* (Chico, CA: Scholars Press, 1981).

32. J. P. Louw, *Semantics of New Testament Greek* (Atlanta: Scholars Press, 1982), 67–89. Cf. John Beekman, John Callow, and Michael Kopesec, *The Semantic Structure of Written Communication*, 5th ed., Semantic Structure Analyses Series (Dallas: Summer Institute of Linguistics, 1981), part of a series of semantic structural analyses to guide translators.

33. Micheal W. Palmer, *Levels of Constituent Structure in New Testament Greek* (New York: Peter Lang, 1995).

34. Robert Crellin, *The Syntax and Semantics of the Perfect Active in Literary Koine Greek* (Malden, MA: Wiley-Blackwell, 2016).

The small amount of significant research using Chomskyan linguistic theories is surprising, since the formalist descriptions are well suited to the limitations of knowledge of an ancient language. One reason may be that semantics (however it is defined) is always at play in linguistic description, even if the analysis does not readily concede this. How one identifies syntagmatic units and their constituents and relationships is as much semantic as syntactic. Another reason is that the functions of language are as important as the structures of language, even if related to each other in diverse ways. Theories that do not address the functions of language—especially in a discipline such as New Testament studies, which is attentive to the uses of language—have less attraction than those concerned with function. Analytic views of meaning, as in Crellin, do not aid this situation. A third reason is the relatively insignificant accomplishments of previous studies. In other words, the question "So what?" has not been answered.

Construction Grammar

A number of movements that shared Chomsky's perspective rejected major components of his developing grammar. Some might place construction grammar—of which there are many kinds—within cognitive linguistics, but since Chomskyan linguistics is the major dialogue partner of construction grammar, I place it here.[35] One of those who questioned Chomsky was Charles Fillmore (1929–2014), who finished his career at Berkeley. Fillmore was part of the mid-1960s reaction to Chomskyan formalism that resulted in an emphasis upon meaning. Fillmore first proposed what he called "case grammar" in an article titled "The Case for Case."[36] Case grammar, as opposed to grammatical case (with which most New Testament scholars are familiar), identifies semantic functions of noun phrases in relation to their verbs, such as agent, patient, instrument, and so on.[37] In New Testament studies, Simon Wong used case theory by Fillmore in his study of Paul,[38] but apart from a few articles by Wong (and one response to him), no more has been done in this area that I know of.

---

35. See Laura A. Michaelis, "Construction Grammar and the Syntax-Semantics Interface," in *The Bloomsbury Companion to Syntax*, ed. Silvia Luraghi and Claudia Parodi (London: Bloomsbury, 2015), 421–35. For example, William Croft is both a major figure in cognitive linguistics and the developer of what he calls radical construction grammar, one of the many forms of construction grammar.

36. Charles Fillmore, "The Case for Case," in *Universals in Linguistic Theory*, ed. Emmett Bach and Robert T. Harms (New York: Holt, Rinehart & Winston, 1968), 1–88.

37. See Matthews, *Grammatical Theory in the United States*, 179.

38. Simon S. M. Wong, *A Classification of Semantic Case-Relations in the Pauline Epistles* (New York: Peter Lang, 1997).

Fillmore, in conjunction with George Lakoff at Berkeley and Paul Kay at Stanford, developed the construction grammar adopted by the New Testament Greek scholar Paul Danove. Danove has been virtually alone in use of construction grammar, what he calls "case frame analysis." Danove himself, however, has been prolific. In virtually every monograph that he has written, case frame analysis has played a role.[39] Case frame analysis, according to Danove, is a descriptive, generative, and nontransformational theory concerned to describe predicators—that is, words that "license" other phrasal elements called arguments and adjuncts. A "valence description" is the fundamental descriptive mechanism, displaying predicators in terms of three strata: syntactic function (e.g., verbal subject, predicate, complement—there are three syntactic functions plus a function for adjuncts, called the C function), semantic function (based upon twenty-one thematic roles), and lexical information (realizations by various phrases, such as noun, verb, etc.).

This must be one of few areas in which other New Testament scholars have not developed an idea further, especially since Danove has been a tireless advocate for case frame analysis. However, the reasons are probably related to the fact that a number of features of the analysis are not readily apparent. The predicator is the unit of analysis, but the relationships among the levels of predicators are not obvious. Predicator is usually associated with a verb, but for case frame analysis, a predicator is any word that licenses other phrasal elements, and thus there is the potential for embedding and recursion. However, embedding and recursion are not adequately theorized in the model. There is also difficulty with the notion of function, since it is used of both syntax and semantics. More complex syntax is provided by Danove's C function (assigned to adjuncts), but that takes case frame analysis beyond its syntactical boundaries.

■ Cognitive Schools

I place cognitive schools of linguistics into their own category. This avoids the problem of deciding whether they should be placed with formalist theories

39. Paul L. Danove, *The End of Mark's Story: A Methodological Study* (Leiden: Brill, 1993); Paul L. Danove, *Linguistics and Exegesis in the Gospel of Mark: Applications of a Case Frame Analysis and Lexicon* (Sheffield: Sheffield Academic, 2002); Paul L. Danove, *Grammatical and Exegetical Study of New Testament Verbs of Transference: A Case Frame Guide to Interpretation and Translation* (London: T&T Clark, 2009); Paul L. Danove, *New Testament Verbs of Communication: A Case Frame and Exegetical Study* (London: Bloomsbury, 2015), 1–21. See also Paul L. Danove, *The Rhetoric of Characterization of God, Jesus, and Jesus' Disciples in the Gospel of Mark* (London: T&T Clark, 2005); Paul L. Danove, *Theology of the Gospel of Mark: A Semantic, Narrative, and Rhetorical Study of the Characterization of God* (London: Bloomsbury T&T Clark, 2019).

on the basis of their cognitive similarities with Chomskyan linguistics, as well as the fact that some of the important early advocates of these cognitive schools were educated by Chomsky or were highly influenced by him (e.g., Lakoff), or placed with functional theories as has been done by Van Valin and LaPolla.

Cognitive Linguistics

Cognitive linguistics is the fastest-growing and fastest-developing area within contemporary linguistics. As noted above, it shares a cognitive base with Chomskyan linguistics. However, the major difference is that, whereas Chomsky and his followers have traditionally argued for a universal grammar within the human brain, cognitive linguistics believes that language is used according to more general cognitive principles. Cognitive linguistics began to develop in the 1970s with the emergence of semantics in Chomskyan grammar and became more robust in the 1980s, and it continues to be an expanding area of linguistics.[40]

There are various definitions of "cognitive linguistics." For example, William Croft and Alan Cruse state that "three major hypotheses" guide cognitive linguistics. These are the following:

- Language is not an autonomous cognitive faculty.
- Grammar is conceptualization.
- Knowledge of language emerges from language use.[41]

One sees why cognitive linguistics is sometimes placed alongside functional schools, as it too is concerned with language use (although I would say that language use and language function may mean two different things in such definitions). Croft and Cruse note how the first principle distances cognitive linguistics from generative grammar and its autonomous language module (but without rejecting the idea that humans have innate language capacity), the second opposes truth-conditional semantics, and the third opposes reductionism in the first two on the basis of use.[42] As a result, linguistic knowledge

---

40. Vyvyan Evans and Melanie Green, *Cognitive Linguistics: An Introduction* (Edinburgh: University of Edinburgh Press, 2006), 3, state that it grew out of "dissatisfaction with formal [i.e., Chomskyan] approaches to language."

41. William Croft and D. Alan Cruse, *Cognitive Linguistics* (Cambridge: Cambridge University Press, 2004), 1.

42. Croft and Cruse, *Cognitive Linguistics*, 1. Ronald N. Langacker, *Cognitive Grammar: A Basic Introduction* (Oxford: Oxford University Press, 2008), 5, refers to grammar as working through symbolic relationships.

in cognitive linguistics becomes "conceptual structure," whether phonological, morphological, or syntactical. Further, cognitive language ability is similar to other kinds of cognitive ability.[43]

A second, arguably similar, definition is offered by Vyvyan Evans and Melanie Green. They contend that cognitive linguistics affirms two fundamental commitments, first articulated by Lakoff. These are the generalization commitment and the cognitive commitment. The generalization commitment assumes that "there are common structuring principles that hold across different aspects of language, and that an important function of linguistics is to identify these common principles."[44] Categorization is based upon family resemblances, polysemy, and metaphor, the last an immensely important topic in cognitive linguistics. The cognitive commitment holds "that principles of linguistic structure should reflect what is known about human cognition from other disciplines, particularly the other cognitive sciences (philosophy, psychology, artificial intelligence and neuroscience)."[45] The cognitive commitment relies upon language profiling using fuzzy boundaries, as well as metaphor. Evans and Green further identify a central notion in cognitive linguistics as the "embodied mind."[46] Rather than considering the mind distinct from the body (as per Descartes and his follower Chomsky), cognitive linguistics emphasizes embodied experience by an embodied mind.

Although there are many areas of cognitive linguistics, such as frame theory, that could attract New Testament scholars, scholars have tended to focus upon conceptual metaphor theory. One of the leading figures in this area is, again, Lakoff, who has worked with the philosopher Mark Johnson to develop notions of metaphor drawing upon human embodiment.[47] Conceptual metaphor theory contends that all of language is based on mapping semantic domains or conceptual spheres upon each other, especially more remote upon more familiar, such as the body. Conceptual metaphor theory, with some of its developments, including conceptual blending theory,[48] expands the range of metaphor by blending various metaphors together into

---

43. Croft and Cruse, *Cognitive Linguistics*, 2.
44. Evans and Green, *Cognitive Linguistics*, 28.
45. Evans and Green, *Cognitive Linguistics*, 40.
46. Evans and Green, *Cognitive Linguistics*, 44.
47. George Lakoff and Mark Johnson, *Metaphors We Live By* (Chicago: University of Chicago Press, 1980); George Lakoff and Mark Turner, *More Than Cool Reason: A Field Guide to Poetic Metaphor* (Chicago: University of Chicago Press, 1989).
48. Gilles Fauconnier and Mark Turner, *The Way We Think: Conceptual Blending and the Mind's Hidden Complexities* (New York: Basic Books, 2002). For a good history of the development of cognitive metaphor theory, see Zoltán Kövecses, *Metaphor: A Practical Introduction* (Oxford: Oxford University Press, 2002).

larger conceptual constructs within conceptual integration theory.[49] Significant works in conceptual metaphor and related theories within New Testament studies include studies by Bonnie Howe on 1 Peter, Beth Stovell on John's Gospel (although she also uses other linguistic theories, such as SFL), Jennifer McNeel on 1 Thessalonians and the infancy / nursing-mother metaphors, Frederick Tappenden on resurrection in Paul (plant and body-is-house metaphors), William Robinson on Romans 8 and "spirit-life is a journey," Erin Heim on adoption and sonship metaphors, and Gregory Lanier on a variety of Old Testament metaphors (e.g., horn, appearing, bird, stone), among others.[50] Most of these studies, with the exception of Stovell, are not readily concerned with the Greek language. Stovell's concern with Greek emerges from her use of SFL.

There has been much work in cognitive linguistics, but that work raises the question of whether this is in fact a school of linguistics. Evans and Green themselves state, "Cognitive linguistics is described as a 'movement' or an 'enterprise' because it is not a specific theory. Instead, it is an approach that has adopted a common set of guiding principles, assumptions and perspectives which have led to a diverse range of complementary, overlapping (and sometimes competing) theories."[51] An example of its limitations may be found in the failure of cognitive linguistics to develop a working model of grammar, at least as many if not most linguists would conceive of grammar. Ronald Langacker's notion that grammar is symbolic means simply—at least for him—that the relations between elements that form more complex structures are entirely symbolic. Sampson has criticized cognitive linguistics on several fronts. These include its making generalizations about human language on the basis of a limited array of evidence, primarily English. He notes that Chinese does not use metaphor in the same way, thus questioning whether conceptual metaphor theory follows general cognitive principles.

49. The notion of space is fundamental to conceptual integration theory, in which various concepts occupy space and are brought into relation with one another.

50. Bonnie Howe, *Because You Bear This Name: Conceptual Metaphor and the Moral Meaning of 1 Peter* (Leiden: Brill, 2008); Beth M. Stovell, *Mapping Metaphorical Discourse in the Fourth Gospel: John's Eternal King* (Leiden: Brill, 2012); Jennifer McNeel, *Paul as Infant and Nursing Mother: Metaphor, Rhetoric, and Identity in 1 Thessalonians 2:5–8* (Atlanta: SBL Press, 2014); Frederick S. Tappenden, *Resurrection in Paul: Cognition, Metaphor, and Transformation* (Atlanta: SBL Press, 2016); William E. W. Robinson, *Metaphor, Morality, and the Spirit in Romans 8:1–17* (Atlanta: SBL Press, 2016); Erin M. Heim, *Adoption in Galatians and Romans: Contemporary Metaphor Theories and the Pauline* Huiothesia *Metaphors* (Leiden: Brill, 2017); Gregory R. Lanier, *Old Testament Conceptual Metaphors and the Christology of Luke's Gospel* (London: Bloomsbury, 2018). Cf. Joel B. Green and Bonnie Howe, eds., *Cognitive Linguistic Explorations in Biblical Studies* (Berlin: de Gruyter, 2014).

51. Evans and Green, *Cognitive Linguistics*, 3.

That some languages might draw upon the world around them for their metaphors is hardly a deep or unique insight in any case. Sampson also points out that once one moves beyond the notion of "embodiment," the situation becomes less clear, especially as one moves into other languages.[52] Perhaps in that respect it is better to think of cognitive linguistics as an approach or orientation, one that is confined to English until we can establish its basis in other languages. Whatever value there may be in the works mentioned above, what is clear is that they are not really theories of linguistics so much as theories of cognition, arguably very different categories both definitionally and phenomenologically.

Relevance Theory

Related to this area of cognition is relevance theory. In 1957, Harvard philosopher H. Paul Grice (1913–88) published an article titled "Meaning," in which he laid the basis of inferential rather than code-based communication.[53] In 1975, Grice published an article on "Logic and Conversation."[54] This article outlined his theory of conversational implicatures that developed further inferential meaning. He categorized the implicatures under the "cooperative principle" and then laid out several subcategories related to quantity, quality, relation, and manner. According to Grice, these are the implicatures of successful conversation. At around the same time as Grice published his second article, Daniel Sperber and Dierdre Wilson began researching pragmatics and inferential communication. In 1986, they published a volume simply titled *Relevance*. Their stated goal is clear: "What is needed is an attempt to rethink, in psychologically realistic terms, such basic questions as these: What form of shared information is available to humans? How is shared information exploited in communication? What is relevance and how is it achieved? What role does the search for relevance play in communication?"[55] The result, relevance theory, is a cognitive theory that rejects code theories of language to argue for what is called a "principle of relevance"—that is, that "human cognitive processes . . . are geared to

52. Sampson, *Linguistics Delusion*, 77–87.

53. H. Paul Grice, "Meaning," in *Studies in the Way of Words* (Cambridge, MA: Harvard University Press, 1989), 213–23. This article was originally published in *The Philosophical Review* 66 (1957): 377–88.

54. H. Paul Grice, "Logic and Conversation," in *Studies in the Way of Words*, 22–40. This article was originally published in *Syntax and Semantics*, vol. 3, *Speech Acts*, ed. Peter Cole and Jerry L. Morgan (New York: Academic, 1975), 41–58.

55. Dan Sperber and Deirdre Wilson, *Relevance: Communication and Cognition*, 2nd ed. (Oxford: Blackwell, 1995), 38.

achieving the greatest possible cognitive effect for the smallest possible processing effort."[56] Relevance theory has become widely used in areas outside of New Testament studies, most notably in translation studies, including the Bible translation movement.[57]

Relevance theory has been applied to New Testament studies in a variety of ways. Stephen Pattemore applies relevance theory to the book of Revelation in two volumes.[58] Joseph Fantin uses relevance theory to treat the Greek imperative in one volume and the confession "Jesus is Lord" in another.[59] Margaret Sim has written a very basic introduction to the topic for use by biblical scholars in exegesis, along with an earlier work on the use of the Greek particles ἵνα and ὅτι.[60] Nelson Morales examines how the book of James uses the Old Testament on the basis of relevance theory's notion of metarepresentation.[61] As Fantin himself admits, however, it is highly questionable whether relevance theory is even a theory of linguistics, since it is arguably more a theory of communication.[62]

Despite the use of relevance theory in translation studies, the same kinds of questions arise as were asked above regarding cognitive linguistics. Relevance theory is perhaps better seen as an orientation than as a method or even a linguistic school. There is the further question of whether relevance theory has a sufficiently robust apparatus to answer the kinds of questions that linguists wish to ask of language. The generalizations that drive relevance theory—such as underdeterminacy and inference—may provide a foundation for pragmatic understanding, but questions remain whether these generalizations are sufficient without a more robust linguistic theory to provide suitable and sufficient linguistic description.

---

56. Sperber and Wilson, *Relevance*, vii.

57. See Ernst-August Gutt, *Translation and Relevance: Cognition and Context* (Oxford: Blackwell, 1991; repr., Manchester: St. Jerome, 2010).

58. Stephen Pattemore, *Souls under the Altar: Relevance Theory and the Discourse Structure of Revelation* (New York: United Bible Societies, 2003); Stephen Pattemore, *The People of God in the Apocalypse: Discourse, Structure and Exegesis* (Cambridge: Cambridge University Press, 2004).

59. Joseph D. Fantin, *The Greek Imperative Mood in the New Testament: A Cognitive and Communicative Approach* (New York: Peter Lang, 2010); Joseph D. Fantin, *The Lord of the Entire World: Lord Jesus, a Challenge to Lord Caesar?* (Sheffield: Sheffield Phoenix, 2011).

60. Margaret G. Sim, *A Relevant Way to Read: A New Approach to Exegesis and Communication* (Eugene, OR: Pickwick, 2016); Margaret G. Sim, *Marking Thought and Talk in New Testament Greek: New Light from Linguistics on the Particles* ἵνα *and* ὅτι (Eugene, OR: Pickwick, 2010).

61. Nelson R. Morales, *Poor and Rich in James: A Relevance Theory Approach to James's Use of the Old Testament* (University Park, PA: Eisenbrauns, 2018).

62. Fantin, *Greek Imperative Mood in the New Testament*, 333–34.

■ Functional Schools

A number of different functional schools of linguistics have flourished in the past, including Tagmemics and various forms of functionalism. At one time, Tagmemics was a major school of linguistics outside and within biblical studies. Kenneth Pike (1912–2000) developed Tagmemics as a stratified and unified theory of human behavior, including language.[63] Pike's major volume on the subject incited much subsequent work, especially by fellow SIL member Robert Longacre (1922–2014). Longacre developed his own linguistic model based upon Tagmemics but increasingly moved away from it.[64] I will instead focus upon two much more apparently active functional schools.

Cognitive Functionalism

The first school of linguistics that I will discuss is what has been called cognitive-functional linguistics. This approach could have been placed under cognitive schools, and perhaps should have been, but I place it here because it appears to be more functionalist in nature. I concentrate upon two major books that reflect this school. Neither of the books overtly uses the label "cognitive," but the first, by Stephen Levinsohn, often refers to a book that he wrote with an SIL colleague, where their method is referred to as "functional and cognitive."[65] The second volume, by Steven Runge, also defines and employs cognitive concepts.[66] Since these two works also fashion themselves as directed toward discourse, one might question whether this approach should instead be called "discourse functional" (as it is on the back cover of Runge's book) or whether such an approach to discourse should be included at all within the linguistic schools discussed here, as it draws upon such schools to formulate its discourse approach. A final consideration is that this approach is very light on theoretical foundations, with the major work by Levinsohn devoting only four (admittedly large) pages to establishing its

63. Kenneth L. Pike, *Language in Relation to a Unified Theory of the Structure of Human Behavior*, 2nd ed. (The Hague: Mouton, 1967).

64. Robert E. Longacre, *The Grammar of Discourse*, 2nd ed. (New York: Plenum, 1996). SIL has followed a number of different approaches to linguistics in its various educational centers (I owe this observation to Martin Culy), but most of these have not been developed into linguistic schools within NT Greek studies, apart from those noted in this chapter.

65. Robert A. Dooley and Stephen H. Levinsohn, *Analyzing Discourse: A Manual of Basic Concepts* (Dallas: SIL International, 2001), back cover and vii, although the volume also describes itself as a "'grab bag' of diverse methodologies" (vii).

66. See also Steven E. Runge, "The Greek Article: A Cognitive-Functional Approach" (paper presented at the Annual Meeting of the Evangelical Theological Society, Baltimore, MD, November 19–21, 2013).

linguistic foundation and the subsequent volume by Runge not containing much more information.

The approach of Levinsohn, followed in most significant respects by Runge, is found in his major book, *Discourse Features of New Testament Greek: A Coursebook on the Information Structure of New Testament Greek.*[67] Regarding his approach, Levinsohn refers to it as "descriptive linguistics."[68] This is a problematic term. Sampson devotes a chapter to what he calls "the descriptivists," where he focuses upon Franz Boas and Leonard Bloomfield, two major North American linguists who began their careers by describing indigenous Native American languages and continued this approach in their general linguistics. Bloomfield, influenced by the New Grammarians, took a behaviorist view or what he calls a mechanistic view of language. He defines meaning as "the situation in which the speaker utters it and the response which it calls forth in the hearer," a matter of stimulus and response.[69] I am sure that Levinsohn does not mean this, but his use of the term "descriptive" and his statement that he simply wishes to treat the Greek New Testament as he would any other text leave him open to misunderstanding.

Levinsohn offers several terms to describe his approach. Besides "descriptive," he also uses "eclectic." By this he means what one might imagine: he draws upon various linguistic theories in his descriptions—to the point of admittedly drawing opposite conclusions from these theories than their proponents did, specifically mentioning (in fact only mentioning, thus calling into question the notion of eclecticism) Talmy Givón, associated with West Coast Functionalism.[70] Levinsohn further calls his approach "functional" concerning the uses of linguistic structures and "structural" in his description of them (he does not call it cognitive). In relation to functionalism, Levinsohn notes that he ascribes to the principle that "choice implies meaning," indicating that when authors exercise choice, they are also expressing a difference in meaning.[71] He calls this a characteristic of functionalism, when it is actually a

---

67. Stephen H. Levinsohn, *Discourse Features of New Testament Greek: A Coursebook on the Information Structure of New Testament Greek*, 2nd ed. (Dallas: SIL International, 2000), vii–ix; Steven E. Runge, *Discourse Grammar of the Greek New Testament: A Practical Introduction for Teaching and Exegesis* (Peabody, MA: Hendrickson, 2010), 5–16.

68. Levinsohn, *Discourse Features*, vii.

69. Leonard Bloomfield, *Language* (New York: Holt, Rinehart & Winston, 1933), 139.

70. Levinsohn cites two works by Talmy Givón in his bibliography: *Topic Continuity in Discourse* (Philadelphia: Benjamins, 1983) and *Syntax: A Functional-Typological Introduction*, 2 vols. (Amsterdam: Benjamins, 1984, 1990).

71. This wording appears to be based on a reformulation of "meaning implies choice" in Charles Bazell, *Linguistic Form* (Istanbul: Istanbul Press, 1953), 51, endorsed in the latter form by numerous linguists; cf. Michael A. K. Halliday, *An Introduction to Functional Grammar* (London: Arnold, 1985), xiv, in which he states that SFL "is a theory of meaning as choice."

tenet of structuralism. If one were to take these characteristics—descriptive, eclectic, functional, and structural—one would probably conclude that this approach to linguistics has elements in common with the continental structuralists, such as the Prague Linguistics Circle, or possibly even the Copenhagen School. There is something to this, as Levinsohn then gives special attention to markedness, one of the legacies of the Prague School, and the differentiation between what he calls "semantic meaning" and "pragmatic effects," a distinction that has its place in many different linguistic schools, including Prague.

Runge, Levinsohn's closest follower, similarly states that his approach is "crosslinguistic," by which he presumably means eclectic. He states that he is interested in "how languages tend to operate rather than just focusing on Greek," a tendency seen in much recent discussion of typology, and that his approach is "function-based."[72] Runge states that he "presupposes three core principles." These are "Choice implies meaning," "Semantic or inherent meaning should be differentiated from pragmatic effect," and "Default patterns of usage should be distinguished from marked ones."[73] He then adds a feature not found in Levinsohn (the other three are from Levinsohn), that prominence and contrast capture a fundamental pragmatic implication.[74]

The major problem with the cognitive-functional approach—which does not really merit being called an approach—is that it is not a linguistic theory at all but is founded upon a relatively small set of generalizations and assertions mostly from structuralist linguistics, with very little that appears cognitive. Levinsohn treats a limited number of discourse features, all oriented to information structure. These include constituent order, sentence conjunctions, patterns of reference, backgrounding and highlighting, reporting of conversation, and boundary features. Runge is even more limited in the features of his discourse grammar. After treating conjunctions in a foundations chapter, he treats forward-pointing devices, information-structuring devices, and thematic highlighting devices. All the elements treated in both of these works are concerned with information structure or the textual dimension. In that sense, in a limited way both follow the pattern of the Prague School, which first developed markedness and information flow with its notions of

---

72. Runge, *Discourse Grammar*, xviii. He also states that his approach is not language specific but shows "how humans are wired to process language" (5), using the terminology of cognitive linguistics.

73. Runge, *Discourse Grammar*, 5.

74. Some have claimed that *The Greek Verb Revisited: A Fresh Approach for Biblical Exegesis*, ed. Steven E. Runge and Christopher J. Fresch (Bellingham, WA: Lexham, 2016), has presented a coherent approach to the matter of the Greek verb. However, at least six different schools of linguistics, as well as traditional grammatical approaches, are found in the volume.

theme and rheme and the Functional Sentence Perspective. The linguistic descriptions that Levinsohn and Runge provide often result in judgments being made that imply much more than a descriptive framework; there is nothing explicit in their approach that lays the foundation for such analysis (is this an implicit appeal to cognition?). This bottom-up approach seems to be fairly wooden in design, although the wide range of exegetical descriptions offered suggests that there are a number of unstated (and perhaps unrecognized or unassimilated) assumptions also at play.

Systemic Functional Linguistics

Systemic Functional Linguistics is the most well-developed model of what Sampson calls the London school of linguistics. The major inaugural figure in the London school was J. R. Firth (1890–1960), who developed ideas of the anthropologist Bronislaw Malinowski. One of Firth's students was Michael A. K. Halliday (1925–2018). In the 1960s, Halliday, who began his linguistic study by describing Chinese, first developed his scale and category grammar, which was based upon paradigmatic and syntagmatic axes. Under the influence of the functions of language as taught by Karl Bühler (1879–1963) of the Prague School, Halliday developed a stratal description that moved (reciprocally) from expression to content to context, with each stratum realizing the three (or four, depending upon Halliday's developing thought) metafunctions. SFL has continued to be further developed not only by Halliday (who recently died) but also by those of the Sydney school and the Cardiff school.

As a result, there are a variety of definitions of SFL available, but one of the best summaries of the theory is by Margaret Berry, which I draw upon but supplement here. There are seven important, relatively widely accepted notions: (1) SFL places a high emphasis upon the sociological or communicative aspects of language; (2) SFL sees language as a form of linguistic behavior rather than a form of knowledge of a language, thus viewing Saussure's *langue* as the language potential that is realized in *parole*; (3) SFL utilizes various matrices for describing language, including clines, ranks, strata, and levels, often reflecting degrees of delicacy; (4) SFL utilizes the notion of text as a semantic unit whose instances are used to verify the various linguistic hypotheses, often through corpus linguistics (the linking of the two has existed for some time, seen in Halliday's probabilistic grammar); (5) SFL recognizes the varying features of different languages and differentiates varieties of language according to situational use (the powerful notion of register); (6) SFL emphasizes the function of language in terms of three metafunctions that bisect the levels from context to expression; and (7) SFL recognizes two axes of system and structure, while emphasizing the system network as the primary means of modeling language.[75]

Since SFL was introduced in 1985 to New Testament studies,[76] a number of significant monographs have drawn directly upon it. I utilized system networks to describe the Greek verbal system in my first book and followed that with an intermediate Greek grammar utilizing SFL, a volume on linguistic analysis of the Greek New Testament with a number of chapters on SFL, and a linguistic commentary on the book of Romans using register discourse analysis.[77] Jeffrey Reed provided a summary of Hallidayan SFL organized by metafunction and drew SFL into discussion of the debate over literary integrity in Philippians.[78] Gustavo Martín-Asensio examined transitivity in Acts as a means of indicating foregrounding.[79] Stephanie Black treated conjunctions in Matthew, supplemented by relevance theory.[80] Ray Van Neste examined the cohesion of the Pastoral Epistles.[81] Todd Klutz offered what he called a sociostylistic reading of the exorcism stories in Luke-Acts.[82] Cynthia Long Westfall utilized a form of SFL discourse analysis to examine the form and meaning of Hebrews.[83] Matthew Brook O'Donnell utilized various elements

---

75. Margaret Berry, *Introduction to Systemic Linguistics*, 2 vols. (London: Batsford, 1975–77), 1:22–32; cf. Christopher S. Butler, *Structure and Function: A Guide to Three Major Structural-Functional Theories*, 2 vols. (Amsterdam: Benjamins, 2003), 1:43–48, whose definition, after nearly thirty years, is surprisingly similar: it emphasizes communication, function, semantics, and pragmatics as central, along with context, as well as raising questions about cognition and typology. Cf. Halliday, *Introduction to Functional Grammar*, xiii–xvi, but note that this volume does not include linguistic systems, added in subsequent editions. See Michael A. K. Halliday, *An Introduction to Functional Grammar*, 4th ed. (London: Routledge, 2014).

76. See Nigel J. C. Gotteri and Stanley E. Porter, "Ambiguity, Vagueness and the Working Systemic Linguist," *Sheffield Working Papers in Language and Linguistics* 2 (1985): 105–18.

77. Porter, *Verbal Aspect*; Stanley E. Porter, *Linguistic Analysis of the Greek New Testament: Studies in Tools, Methods, and Practice* (Grand Rapids: Baker Academic, 2016); Stanley E. Porter, *Letter to the Romans: A Literary and Linguistic Commentary* (Sheffield: Sheffield Phoenix, 2016), esp. 24–35.

78. Jeffrey T. Reed, *A Discourse Analysis of Philippians: Method and Rhetoric in the Debate over Literary Integrity* (Sheffield: Sheffield Academic, 1997).

79. Gustavo Martín-Asensio, *Transitivity-Based Foregrounding in the Acts of the Apostles: A Functional-Grammatical Approach to the Lukan Perspective* (Sheffield: Sheffield Academic, 2000).

80. Stephanie L. Black, *Sentence Conjunctions in the Gospel of Matthew: καί, δέ, τότε, γάρ, οὖν and Asyndeton in Narrative Discourse* (London: Sheffield Academic, 2002).

81. Ray Van Neste, *Cohesion and Structure in the Pastoral Epistles* (London: T&T Clark, 2004).

82. Todd Klutz, *The Exorcism Stories in Luke-Acts: A Sociostylistic Reading* (Cambridge: Cambridge University Press, 2004).

83. Cynthia Long Westfall, *A Discourse Analysis of the Letter to the Hebrews: The Relationship between Form and Meaning* (London: T&T Clark, 2005).

of SFL as a part of his study of corpus linguistics.[84] Ivan Kwong examined word order patterns in Luke's Gospel as a means of foregrounding.[85] Jae-Hyun Lee provided a discourse analysis of Romans 1–8, supplemented by some elements from Robert Longacre's Tagmemics.[86] Beth Stovell discussed metaphor in John's Gospel, in conjunction with conceptual metaphor theory.[87] Gregory Fewster drew upon grammatical metaphor as a means of treating creation language in Romans 8.[88] Wally Cirafesi revisited verbal aspect theory in parallel passages of the Synoptic Gospels.[89] Ronald Peters examined the Greek article in relation to relative pronouns.[90] David Lamb interpreted the community hypothesis in John's Gospel on the basis of theories of register and Halliday's notion of antilanguage.[91] Christopher Land utilized SFL to examine the cohesion and integrity of 2 Corinthians by examining different potential situations.[92] Bryan Dyer examined the notion of context of situation in Hebrews.[93] Finally, David Yoon has provided a discourse analysis of Galatians using SFL register theory.[94] Other works could also be included in this list. Their common factors are their incredible diversity and variety, yet all were written within the SFL framework. Some of them are very broad (such as Reed), while others are much more focused on individual elements (e.g., verbal structure, conjunction, the article). Some treat SFL as a theory of syntax or semantics, while others view it as a discourse analytic (e.g., Westfall in Hebrews, Porter in Romans). A number of studies have drawn upon the productive notion of register, a linguistic category to which SFL has given a particular definition.

---

84. Matthew Brook O'Donnell, *Corpus Linguistics and the Greek of the New Testament* (Sheffield: Sheffield Phoenix, 2005), esp. 30–33.

85. Ivan Shing Chung Kwong, *The Word Order of the Gospel of Luke: Its Foregrounded Messages* (London: T&T Clark, 2005).

86. Jae-Hyun Lee, *Paul's Gospel in Romans: A Discourse Analysis of Rom 1:16–8:39* (Leiden: Brill, 2010).

87. Stovell, *Mapping Metaphorical Discourse*, esp. 51–65.

88. Gregory P. Fewster, *Creation Language in Romans 8: A Study in Monosemy* (Leiden: Brill, 2013).

89. Wally V. Cirafesi, *Verbal Aspect in Synoptic Parallels: On the Method and Meaning of Divergent Tense-Form Usage in the Synoptic Passion Narratives* (Leiden: Brill, 2013).

90. Ronald D. Peters, *The Greek Article: A Functional Grammar of ὁ-items in the Greek New Testament with Special Emphasis on the Greek Article* (Leiden: Brill, 2014).

91. David A. Lamb, *Text, Context and the Johannine Community: A Sociolinguistic Analysis of the Johannine Writings* (London: Bloomsbury, 2014).

92. Christopher D. Land, *The Integrity of 2 Corinthians and Paul's Aggravating Absence* (Sheffield: Sheffield Phoenix, 2015).

93. Bryan R. Dyer, *Suffering in the Face of Death: The Epistle to the Hebrews and Its Context of Situation* (London: Bloomsbury, 2017).

94. David I. Yoon, *A Discourse Analysis of Galatians and the New Perspective on Paul* (Leiden: Brill, 2019).

Systemic Functional Linguistics, so far as I can determine, has been the most productive school of linguistics in New Testament Greek studies—apart from traditional grammar. Numerous monographs and journal articles have been written from this framework. This raises the question of why more scholars are not using it, or rather, how it is that so many have used it when SFL is, by all estimations, a very complex linguistic model to learn. There is no doubt that SFL is complex, especially as it was developed for English and hence does not readily encompass within its architecture issues regarding nonconfigurational or aspectual languages. The major reasons for its intensive utilization, however, appear to be its integrated model of meaning that encompasses the strata from expression to context. SFL is one of few linguistic models that has a robust concept of context. SFL also connects language with social context and hence models context in an explicit fashion, thus lending SFL to itself being a discourse analytic model.

■ Conclusion

There are many possible conclusions that one might draw from this survey. Some of these are that, on the one hand, a surprisingly large number of different linguistic schools are currently viable in New Testament Greek studies. Each one has had proponents, even though some of these schools have been more active than others. On the other hand, compared to the wider field of linguistics, the number of linguistic schools—if one can compare across fields—is relatively limited. There are numerous variations on Chomskyan formalism, many different nuances on cognitive linguistics, and quite a few functional models that have not been fully explored in New Testament Greek studies.

A perhaps even more important question concerns the relationship among these linguistic schools. There is a tendency in New Testament studies—one that I suspect has helped to dilute the effectiveness of the field—to practice widespread linguistic eclecticism. Scholars have tended—and not just in matters of language—to feel free to draw from a wide range of possibilities in their formulations of methods. In the survey above, we see those who practice more methodologically pure and more methodologically eclectic approaches. Cognitive functionalism is eclectic by definition, while Chomskyan formalism is much more purist. More to the point, however, is whether these various models are commensurable or incommensurable. In other words, must the lines between these various schools be rigorously maintained, or is there room for conceptual blending (to use a convenient term)? I think that this depends upon the schools of linguistics involved. If one is working within one of the major schools—formalist, cognitive, and functional—there is probably room for methodological interchange. For example, various cognitive models have a significant amount of overlap, and there is no reason to think that the same could not be true in New Testament Greek studies. The same argument might, at least to some extent, be made for formalist models, as well as functional models. I find it less easy to believe that one can cross these school boundaries so easily, and that is perhaps one of the reasons that I find it difficult to accept the cognitive-functional model. However, I suspect that even within these major school divisions there is limited commensurability. One may be able to tweak some of the extensions of a theory, but I doubt that many of the core principles of any method can be harmonized with other models. Thus, SFL may be able to debate over issues of stratification (as it indeed has), but stratification remains central to the model itself.

If we learn anything from this survey of models, it is that we must recognize that schools of linguistic thought are fundamental to our understanding and conceptualization of the Greek language. Those who think that they are simply examining the language probably hide much more than they reveal about their knowledge of Greek, almost assuredly adopting now outmoded traditional grammatical models. There is plenty of scope for further theoretical development within linguistics, including in the study of New Testament Greek, but those who are more explicit in their recognition of various linguistic schools at least show awareness that the study of the Greek New Testament demands that we attempt to think clearly and critically about major issues in language using the best available linguistic tools.

2

Aspect and Tense in New Testament Greek

CONSTANTINE R. CAMPBELL

Research of verbal aspect and tense has seen the most intense debate, scholarly engagement, and genuine advances in the study of Greek in the past thirty years. While it is virtually impossible to study Biblical Greek today without some awareness of the discussions and debates surrounding aspect and tense, the issues are still poorly understood. The linguistic complexities, jargon, and fierce differences among scholars have led many to remain unsure about what the real issues are, how to assess them, and much less how to apply any positive insights that have arisen.

This chapter will offer a summary of *some of* the recent scholarship on Greek aspect and tense before turning briefly to consider its relevance for exegesis. It is impossible to do justice to any of the topics addressed here, given space constraints, but it is hoped that this offering will provide a framework of understanding so that further detail may be pursued with profit.

■ Summary of Scholarship: Aspect

What Is Aspect?

In grammatical studies, the English word "aspect" derives from the French *aspect*, which means "point of view," or "viewpoint." While different definitions of "aspect" exist within grammatical and linguistic studies, this original meaning is most widespread in the study of Greek—"aspect" refers to "viewpoint."

But what viewpoint are we talking about? We are concerned with the way that Greek verbs present actions and states from a certain point of view. Every verbal process, such as an activity, action, or state, may be presented from one perspective or another, depending on one's point of view. A verb will be used to view an action either from *outside* the action or from *inside* the action. As Buist Fanning has described it, "The action can be viewed from a reference-point within the action, without reference to the beginning or end-point of the action, but with a focus instead on its internal structure or make-up. Or the action can be viewed from a vantage-point outside the action, with focus on the whole action from beginning to end, but without reference to its internal structure."[1] The external viewpoint (outside the action) is known as "perfective aspect"; the internal viewpoint (inside the action) is known as "imperfective aspect." Perfective aspect views an action as a whole and is often used to present an action in summary form. Imperfective aspect views an action from within it and is often used to present an action as unfolding or in progress.

An important illustration is often used to get at the difference between perfect and imperfective aspects. Imagine a reporter as she reports on a street parade. If she were to view the street parade from a helicopter, she would see the parade as a whole. She will describe the parade in a general, summarizing way, because she sees the whole thing. This viewpoint represents *perfective aspect*. But if that same reporter views the same parade from the street rather than the helicopter, her view of the parade will be different. From the street level, she will view the parade up close as it unfolds before her. Rather than viewing the parade as a whole from the helicopter, she now sees it from within. This viewpoint represents *imperfective aspect*.

All Greek scholars agree that the aorist is perfective in aspect, while the present and imperfect are imperfective in aspect. This means that the aorist is used to convey an action as a whole, often in summary fashion, while the present and imperfect convey an action as unfolding, often in progress or as a state. But debate remains concerning perfect, pluperfect, and future verbs.

Aktionsart

One attempt to answer the question of what distinguishes between two Greek past tenses has been the category of *Aktionsart*. This term literally

---

1. Buist M. Fanning, *Verbal Aspect in New Testament Greek*, Oxford Theological Monographs (Oxford: Clarendon, 1990), 27.

means "type of action" and refers to the ways that actions can unfold—the kinds of action. Some actions are punctiliar, some iterative, some ingressive, and so forth. A punctiliar action is something that happens in an instant, like a punch or a kick. An iterative action is something that is repeated over and over, like breathing. An ingressive action is one that is just beginning to unfold, like waking up.

There was once much confusion between *Aktionsart* and aspect, and sometimes those terms could be used interchangeably. But it is best to keep a clear distinction between them. While *Aktionsart* refers to a kind of action (how the action happens), "aspect" refers to viewpoint (how the action is viewed). There is a relationship between those two things, but we will return to that later.

Imagine me telling you that last night I cooked dinner. What actually happened as I prepared the meal? First, it took some time—about an hour, in fact. Second, cooking dinner actually involved several smaller actions, such as washing the potatoes and browning the ground meat. But if I just say, "I cooked dinner," none of those details are conveyed. The whole thing is simply summarized. This is an illustration of perfective aspect—the view of the whole (from the helicopter). *Aktionsart*, on the other hand, refers to what happened, rather than to how it is viewed and presented.

A Very Brief History

Now that we have set up some basic definitions, it is useful to understand how and why this discussion has evolved. Long before modern aspect discussions, nineteenth-century comparative philologists, such as Georg Curtius, discussed different kinds of actions represented by Greek verbs, distinguishing between, for example, durative and "quickly passing" actions. His label *Zeitart* (type of time) paved the way for other scholars to develop the concept of *Aktionsart* (type of action).[2]

From 1890 to 1910 there developed a productive period in which several scholars explored "aspect" and *Aktionsart* in Greek and other Indo-European languages, though these terms (and *Zeitart*) sometimes became confused and conflated. By the mid-1920s, however, these terms became more settled. *Aktionsart* would then refer to how an action actually occurs, influenced strongly by lexical considerations. "Aspect" was regarded as indicating the viewpoint from which an action is conveyed. This distinction is more or less

---

2. Georg Curtius, *Elucidations of the Student's Greek Grammar*, trans. E. Abbott, 2nd ed. (London: John Murray, 1875), 207–18.

the standard today within Greek studies, though some scholars and grammars still refer to aspect as though it is *Aktionsart*.

Through the middle of the twentieth century, some important contributions were made by scholars such as Jens Holt and Martín Ruipérez, but the main scholar who would exert the most influence over modern discussions was K. L. McKay. Working primarily within Classical Greek, and later with the Greek of the New Testament, McKay wrote about aspect from 1965 to 1994.[3] He argued that there were three or four aspects in ancient Greek, with present and imperfect tense-forms expressing imperfective aspect and the aorist expressing perfective aspect (he called it "aoristic" aspect). The perfect and pluperfect were regarded as stative in aspect (he called this "perfect" aspect), while the future represented a quasi-fourth aspect. Over the years McKay increasingly questioned the role of time in the Greek verb, eventually concluding that Greek verbs did not indicate temporal relationships directly but resulted from aspectual meaning in context.

Stanley Porter built on the work of McKay and others, publishing his doctoral dissertation on Greek verbal aspect in 1989.[4] Using linguistic principles derived mostly from Systemic Functional Linguistics, Porter was the first to apply a rigorous linguistic approach to the question of Greek aspect. As with McKay, Porter argued that Greek verbs are not tense-based but aspectual at their core. Temporal reference is created through the interplay between aspect, lexeme, and context. Porter also argued for three aspects in Greek: perfective, imperfective, and stative.

Fanning published his doctoral dissertation on Greek verbal aspect shortly after Porter in 1990.[5] Fanning, like Porter and McKay, affirmed the central importance of aspect for the Greek verbal system but, unlike them, also retained a place for tense. When a tense-form does not, however, express its expected time frame, this is largely because its aspect has overpowered it.

---

3. See, e.g., K. L. McKay, *A New Syntax of the Verb in New Testament Greek: An Aspectual Approach*, Studies in Biblical Greek 5 (New York: Peter Lang, 1994); K. L. McKay, "Aspectual Usage in Timeless Contexts in Ancient Greek," in *In the Footsteps of Raphael Kuhner*, ed. A. Rijksbaron, H. A. Mulder, and G. C. Wakker (Amsterdam: J. C. Gieben, 1988), 193–208; K. L. McKay, "Further Remarks on the 'Historical' Present and Other Phenomena," *Foundations of Language* 11 (1974): 247–51; K. L. McKay, "On the Perfect and Other Aspects in New Testament Greek," *Novum Testamentum* 23, no. 4 (1981): 289–329; K. L. McKay, "On the Perfect and Other Aspects in the Greek Non-Literary Papyri," *Bulletin of the Institute of Classical Studies* 27 (1980): 23–49; K. L. McKay, "The Use of the Ancient Greek Perfect Down to the Second Century A.D.," *Bulletin of the Institute of Classical Studies* 12 (1965): 1–21; K. L. McKay, "Time and Aspect in New Testament Greek," *Novum Testamentum* 34, no. 3 (1992): 209–28.

4. Stanley E. Porter, *Verbal Aspect in the Greek of the New Testament, with Reference to Tense and Mood* (New York: Peter Lang, 1989).

5. Fanning, *Verbal Aspect in New Testament Greek*.

Also, in contrast to Porter and McKay, Fanning argued for two aspects (not three), rejecting stative aspect.

Porter and Fanning became the two main protagonists of the modern era of Greek aspect studies, with the contributors who followed positioning themselves in relation to them both—either positively or negatively. Mari Broman Olsen followed Fanning in recognizing only two aspects and partially followed both Fanning and Porter with respect to tense, arguing that some tense-forms have consistent temporal references and that others do not.[6] Rodney Decker followed Porter in the number of aspects and in rejecting the notion of tense in the indicative mood.[7]

Trevor Evans's work on the verbal syntax of the Greek Pentateuch led him to retain the notion of tense in the indicative mood and affirm only two aspects.[8] Instead of stative aspect, Evans suggested that the Greek perfect is in fact imperfective in aspect. As Evans's student, I follow him in my own work on that issue, arguing for the imperfective aspect of the Greek perfect and pluperfect, while rejecting stative aspect.[9] With the exception of the future indicative, I have argued against the notion of tense in Greek indicative verbs (contra Evans), preferring a spatial system of remoteness and proximity that works in concert with aspect to produce predictable *Aktionsart* functions and temporal reference.

Following Porter most closely have been David Mathewson, working on aspect in Revelation;[10] Wally Cirafesi, working on aspect and the Synoptic Problem;[11] and Douglas Huffman, working on aspect and prohibitions in the Greek New Testament.[12]

6. Mari Broman Olsen, *A Semantic and Pragmatic Model of Lexical and Grammatical Aspect*, Outstanding Dissertations in Linguistics (New York: Garland, 1997).

7. Rodney J. Decker, *Temporal Deixis of the Greek Verb in the Gospel of Mark with Reference to Verbal Aspect*, Studies in Biblical Greek 10 (New York: Peter Lang, 2001).

8. T. V. Evans, *Verbal Syntax in the Greek Pentateuch: Natural Greek Usage and Hebrew Interference* (Oxford: Oxford University Press, 2001).

9. Constantine R. Campbell, *Verbal Aspect, the Indicative Mood, and Narrative: Soundings in the Greek of the New Testament*, Studies in Biblical Greek 13 (New York: Peter Lang, 2007), 161–237; Constantine R. Campbell, *Verbal Aspect and Non-Indicative Verbs: Further Soundings in the Greek of the New Testament*, Studies in Biblical Greek 15 (New York: Peter Lang, 2008), 8–9; Constantine R. Campbell, *Basics of Verbal Aspect in Biblical Greek* (Grand Rapids: Zondervan, 2008), 46–52.

10. David L. Mathewson, *Verbal Aspect in the Book of Revelation: The Function of Greek Verb Tenses in John's Apocalypse*, Linguistic Biblical Studies 4 (Leiden: Brill, 2010).

11. Wally V. Cirafesi, *Verbal Aspect in Synoptic Parallels: On the Method and Meaning of Divergent Tense-Form Usage in the Synoptic Passion Narratives*, Linguistic Biblical Studies 7 (Leiden: Brill, 2013).

12. Douglas S. Huffman, *Verbal Aspect Theory and the Prohibitions in the Greek New Testament*, Studies in Biblical Greek 16 (New York: Peter Lang, 2014).

Following the so-called Perfect Storm—a debate between Porter, Fanning, and me on the aspectual nature of the Greek perfect at the 2013 Society of Biblical Literature annual conference—a group of scholars led by Steven Runge addressed various questions regarding the Greek verbal system at a conference in Cambridge in 2015. This led to the publication of *The Greek Verb Revisited*—a collection of essays addressing tense, aspect, mood, and voice in the Greek verbal system.[13] While not all contributors were completely uniform, the volume taken as a whole argued for tense within the indicative mood, and two aspects—rejecting stative aspect but arguing for "combinative" aspect for the perfect and pluperfect forms. These forms represent a combination of perfective and imperfective aspects that allows the perfect to retain a more or less traditional expression of perfective (past) action with an imperfective (present) resulting state.

Debated Points

Before we explore various areas of debate concerning verbal aspect in Greek, it is worth noting the considerable breadth of agreement among Greek scholars. First, all scholars agree on the central significance of aspect for the Greek language. Aspect is not some kind of passing fad for understanding Greek; it is here to stay and represents a far superior approach to the verbal system than previous approaches.

Second, we are not talking about "aspect or tense" when we discuss verbal aspect. Those categories are not in competition as though students must choose whether they will accept aspect or tense as the correct way to understand Greek verbs. Everyone agrees about the importance of aspect. Yes, the question of tense is one area of ongoing debate, but it is not "aspect or tense." It is yes to aspect, and maybe to tense—depending on whom you ask.

Third, all agree that aspect is essential for exegesis and translation of Greek text. Grasping what aspect is and why it matters is not negotiable for Greek New Testament studies, and anyone who wants to handle the text in a responsible way must grapple with, understand, and apply the insights gleaned from aspect studies.

Fourth, while various definitions of aspect exist within the wider linguistic world, Greek aspect studies has more or less kept in line with the original understanding of aspect, which is *viewpoint*. Another major understanding of aspect originated with Bernard Comrie in 1976, which has to do with internal temporal relationships, but this approach has rightly been critiqued

---

13. Steven E. Runge and Christopher J. Fresch, eds., *The Greek Verb Revisited: A Fresh Approach for Biblical Exegesis* (Bellingham, WA: Lexham, 2016).

for resorting to temporal understandings of a spatial concept.[14] Since aspect is about viewpoint, it is a spatial concept, viewing activities and actions either internally or externally.

Fifth, all scholars agree that Greek exhibits at least two aspects: perfective and imperfective. The Greek aorist is perfective in aspect, while present and imperfect tense-forms are imperfective in aspect. But the other tense-forms are debated, so to that debate we now turn.

The most significant area of disagreement concerns the number of aspects within the Greek verbal system. There are at least two (perfective and imperfective) that are agreed upon. But is there also a third, known as stative aspect? As with much of the discussion, this particular debate can be defined with respect to Porter and Fanning. Porter, following McKay and others, endorses this third stative aspect as a way of explaining perfect and pluperfect meaning and function. The chief advantage of this view is that it does account for the apparent stativity of much perfect and pluperfect usage. It also may account for the different verbal stem of these forms as compared to aorist and present stems. As mentioned previously, several scholars have followed Porter on this issue, such as Decker, Mathewson, and Huffman.

On the other hand, Fanning has argued against stative aspect, claiming that it is out of step with wider linguistic understanding and that stativity is properly understood as an *Aktionsart* value rather than an aspect.[15] I agree with Fanning on this point and have made my own arguments against stative aspect.[16] But while Fanning argues that the Greek perfect represents a combination of perfective aspect, stative *Aktionsart*, and present tense, I argue that it is imperfective in aspect. At the 2013 Perfect Storm debate, Porter, Fanning, and I debated these issues at length.

The aspect of the future tense-form is also contested. Some, such as Porter, argue that the future is unaspectual.[17] Some, such as I, argue that it is perfective in aspect.[18] And others, such as Ernest de Witt Burton, regard the future as a combination of perfective and imperfective aspects.[19]

But perhaps the most (in)famous area of debate concerns the place of temporality and tense in the Greek verbal system. As mentioned above, this question is *not* about whether Greek has an aspectual or tense-based verbal

14. Bernard Comrie, *Aspect: An Introduction to the Study of Verbal Aspect and Related Problems*, Cambridge Textbooks in Linguistics (Cambridge: Cambridge University Press, 1976).

15. Fanning, *Verbal Aspect in New Testament Greek*, 117.

16. Campbell, *Verbal Aspect, the Indicative Mood, and Narrative*, 166–75.

17. Porter, *Verbal Aspect*, 410.

18. Campbell, *Verbal Aspect, the Indicative Mood, and Narrative*, 139–51.

19. Ernest de Witt Burton, *Syntax of the Moods and Tenses in New Testament Greek*, 3rd ed. (Chicago: University of Chicago Press, 1900; repr., Grand Rapids: Kregel, 1976), 31–33.

system. All agree that it is an aspectual system. But not all agree as to the place of tense alongside aspect: *Does* it exist alongside aspect (and subordinate to it), or does it not exist at all? With that, we turn now to the next section, addressing tense.

■ Summary of Scholarship: Tense

What Is Tense?

First, when we discuss tense, we are not referring to verbal morphology. This can be confusing because we are often used to referring to verbs as "tenses"—the present tense, the past tense, the future tense, and so forth. With those labels "tense" really refers to the morphological forms of present, past, and future. But we are talking not about verbal morphology but about one facet of verbal function.

Second, as we discuss tense, we are not referring simply to temporal reference. Temporal reference can occur in a number of ways. Words such as "now," "later," "today," and "tomorrow" can all help to establish temporal reference. These are deictic markers that indicate the time frame. "Tense," however, is a very specific way of referring to time. It concerns the ways in which verbs indicate time—specifically, the time at which verbal actions take place. So, the present tense indicates that an action is to be understood as occurring at the time of speaking (or writing). The past tense indicates that an action is to be understood as occurring before the time of speaking (or writing).

Third, tense always indicates time in relation to something else—usually the time of speaking or writing. So if an action is conveyed with a present tense, it does not mean that it is happening "now"—perhaps two thousand years after it was written about. The action is "present" only in its temporal reference with respect to the author or speaker's portrayal of the event, not in relation to actual reality. Talking about time can be confusing in that way: there really is no such thing as absolute time in language, only relative time. For example, a speaker may use the future tense to say that they will travel tomorrow, but if that tomorrow was two thousand years ago, in what sense is the travel in the future? It was only in the future in the past. Now, it is all actually in the past. But the future tense still points to a future event—but only from the perspective of the speaker at the time.

So, the question here is: Does the Greek verbal system express tense? In other words, when we encounter a Greek present verb form, does it indicate present temporal reference, or is its temporal reference flexible? When we encounter an aorist, will it necessarily refer to the past?

Debate concerning Tense

While Curtius laid the groundwork for Greek aspect studies in the nineteenth century, he also made significant advances in understanding tense in the Greek verbal system. The most significant advance was to demonstrate that tense does not exist outside the indicative mood.[20] Prior to Curtius, the common assumption had been that all the Greek moods conveyed tense—the subjunctive, imperative, and optative, as well as participles and infinitives. This assumption was derived from Latin, which conveys tense across all its moods, and Latin was the lens through which Greek (and other languages) was studied after the Renaissance period. Curtius's claim that tense existed only within the indicative mood was a radical suggestion at the time but is now the standard understanding. No one today considers tense to be a factor within non-indicative Greek moods.

But what about the indicative mood? For some scholars, Curtius did not go far enough. Not only does tense not play a role within non-indicative moods, but it does not play a role in the indicative mood either. The first scholar to move in this direction was McKay, who as early as 1965 asserted that tense was less of a factor in the Greek verbal system than aspect.[21] His assertions about tense in the indicative mood became progressively stronger, to the point at which in 1994 he denied that tense existed in that mood.[22] But before McKay had evolved fully to this point, Porter had already defended this position in 1989.

Porter argued that the Greek indicative mood conveys aspect only, without tense, and any verb's temporal reference comes about through the combination of aspect and context.[23] In other words, aorist indicatives often refer to "past" events because of the nature of perfective aspect (which is particularly apt for conveying completed past actions) and because aorists are often used in contexts that are already past-referring, such as narratives that are by nature set in the past. An explanation of indicative verbs that relies on aspect only, and not tense, would then account for the high number of exceptions to the rule—presents that refer to the past, aorists that refer to the present, perfects that do not refer to a past action, and so forth.

Fanning, on the other hand, in line with typical approaches to the Greek verb since Curtius, argued that tense remains a feature of the indicative mood

20. Georg Curtius, *Die Bildung der Tempora und Modi im Griechischen und Lateinischen sprachvergleichend dargestellt* (Berlin: Wilhelm Besser, 1846), 148–52.
21. McKay, "Use of the Ancient Greek Perfect," 1–21.
22. McKay, *New Syntax of the Verb*, 39–40.
23. Porter, *Verbal Aspect*, 76–83, 98–102.

alongside aspect.[24] Since aspect is the dominant category, it could overpower tense so that certain verb forms would not always indicate the temporal reference they are supposed to. Fanning was also sensitive to the features of certain lexemes, acknowledging that some verbal lexemes buck their tense's temporal reference for reasons related to their diachronic development through the evolution of the Greek language.

And so the first (in)famous clash between these two new Greek aspect scholars (at the 1991 Society of Biblical Literature conference) was focused on tense in the Greek indicative mood. Both agreed that aspect was primary, but Fanning maintained tense alongside aspect, while Porter rejected tense. Porter's position was certainly the controversial one, though it ought not to have been as controversial as it was. Curtius had done the same thing with all the other moods 120 years earlier, and McKay had been chipping away at tense in the indicative mood for a couple of decades already. Moreover, there are other languages that do not encode tense in their verbal system.

While some students and scholars gravitated to the radically linguistic approach of Porter, others found Fanning's work more in line with the trajectories of previous Greek studies. Most of the academic contributors following Porter and Fanning would position themselves, once again, in relation to these two on the question of tense. Olsen mediated between the two, accepting tense for some indicative forms and rejecting it for others.[25] Decker followed Porter.[26] Evans followed Fanning.[27] I followed Porter (with modifications).[28] Mathewson, Cirafesi, and Huffman followed Porter.[29] Runge and his collaborators followed Fanning.[30]

While tense is not the most important question to consider, in my opinion, it nevertheless remains a fraught one. There are really two issues to evaluate. First is the obvious fact that many Greek verbs do not conform to their expected temporal reference. The statistics are quite overwhelming for some tense-forms, such as the so-called present indicative, which refers to the present only about 70 percent of the time. The aorist, Greek's default "past" tense, refers to the present or the future about 15 percent of the time. The Greek perfect, which is supposed to refer to a past action with present consequences, does this less than half the time. In fact, the only Greek tense-form that consistently refers to the time it is supposed to is the future.

24. Fanning, *Verbal Aspect in New Testament Greek*, 198–324.
25. Olsen, *Semantic and Pragmatic Model of Lexical and Grammatical Aspect*, 201–2.
26. Decker, *Temporal Deixis*, 149–55.
27. Evans, *Verbal Syntax*, 40–51.
28. Campbell, *Verbal Aspect, the Indicative Mood, and Narrative*, 84–91.
29. Mathewson, *Verbal Aspect in the Book of Revelation*, 17–18; Cirafesi, *Verbal Aspect in Synoptic Parallels*, 14–15; Huffman, *Verbal Aspect Theory*, 69–74.
30. Runge and Fresch, *Greek Verb Revisited*, chaps. 4 (122–60), 11 (353–78), and 12 (379–415).

The second issue to evaluate, however, is why the Greek indicative tense-forms *do* nevertheless have default temporal expressions. In other words, before we jettison tense altogether, we must ask, Why then *does* the aorist refer to the past 85 percent of the time? Why does the present refer to the present 70 percent of the time? Any conception of the inner workings of Greek tense-forms must account for these patterns. So, an important question to ask is this: Can a "non-tense" understanding of Greek verbs account for the ways in which verbs are actually used?

Semantics and Pragmatics

In order to address these questions about tense, it is necessary to introduce the important linguistic distinction between "semantics" and "pragmatics." While these terms can mean different things in various linguistic discussions, the most common way they have been used in Greek verbal studies is as follows. "Semantic values" are features that are encoded at the morphological level—that is, a semantic feature of the aorist tense-form will be something that every aorist has in common because the aorist form, or morphology, conveys that feature. "Pragmatic values," on the other hand, refer to the variable functions of morphological forms. When a verb is used in relation to different lexemes and the vicissitudes of context, it performs different functions—that is, any aorist can be used in a variety of ways, depending on the other elements of language that interact with it. Thus, the distinction between semantics and pragmatics can be summarized as the difference between form and function. What does a form mean, and what can a form do? The two things are of course closely related, and sometimes it's not possible to tease them apart clearly. Nevertheless, the distinction between semantics and pragmatics remains highly useful and plays directly into the question of tense in the Greek indicative mood.

As for aspect and *Aktionsart*, it is generally agreed that aspect is a semantic value, while *Aktionsart* is a pragmatic category.[31] The Greek aorist, for example, is perfective in aspect down to its morphology—it semantically encodes perfective aspect. But the aorist is capable of several different functions in context, or kinds of action—that is, *Aktionsarten*. An aorist may function as punctiliar, or iterative, or ingressive, depending on the lexeme and the context. But every aorist will always express perfective aspect. Aspect is semantic; punctiliar function is pragmatic. But what about tense?

---

31. E.g., Fanning, *Verbal Aspect in New Testament Greek*, 29–50 (Fanning uses the phrase "procedural characteristics" instead of *Aktionsart*); Olsen, *Semantic and Pragmatic Model of Lexical and Grammatical Aspect*, 17–22, 202–17 (Olsen uses the phrase "lexical aspect" instead of *Aktionsart*); Constantine R. Campbell, *Advances in the Study of Greek: New Insights for Reading the New Testament* (Grand Rapids: Zondervan, 2015), 120–24.

The question about tense in the Greek indicative mood comes down to the distinction between semantics and pragmatics. If that theoretical distinction is held, we must ask if temporal expression is semantically encoded in indicative verbs, or if it is a pragmatic expression of verbs in context. For those who deny the existence of tense in the Greek indicative mood, it is chiefly because temporal reference is not a semantic value of the morphological form. This is why so many verbs behave in ways that are contrary to their supposed tense—temporal reference is not semantic, and it is therefore flexible to some degree. Temporal reference, rather, is regarded as a pragmatic feature of verbs in context.[32]

For others, however, temporal reference is regarded as semantic in spite of the many exceptions to the rule. They are therefore comfortable with the claim that tense exists alongside aspect in the indicative mood, because both are regarded as semantic features of verbal morphology.[33] But how, then, do they account for the many exceptions to the rule? In Fanning's case, for example, he does not regard the distinction between semantics and pragmatics to be a tight one. There is some blurring at the edges between semantics and pragmatics, or, at least, semantic values can be rubbed out in certain contexts. This means, for Fanning, that while tense is a semantic value of Greek indicative verbs, in certain instances a verb's semantic temporal reference may be overpowered by other factors, such as aspect.[34]

Thus, in the end, one's position on tense in the Greek indicative mood largely depends on the methodological presuppositions one holds. If a clear distinction between semantics and pragmatics is held, it is almost inevitable that temporal reference will not be accepted as semantic. If the distinction is less tightly held, there is room to accept temporal reference as semantic without exceptions to the rule carrying much weight. The debate about tense, therefore, is actually a debate about linguistic methodology.

Time and Space

There is a third position that sits somewhere between the "aspect-only" and "aspect + tense" positions. This involves spatial metaphors that stand alongside aspect as semantic values. In our literature, the concept of remoteness

---

32. McKay, *New Syntax of the Verb*, 39–40; Campbell, *Advances in the Study of Greek*, 114–17.

33. Fanning, *Verbal Aspect in New Testament Greek*, 323–24; Christopher J. Fresch, "Typology, Polysemy, and Prototypes: Situating Nonpast Aorist Indicatives," in Runge and Fresch, *Greek Verb Revisited*, 379–415.

34. Fanning, *Verbal Aspect in New Testament Greek*, 185–90, 194–96, 221–40, 265–82, 299–305, 308–9.

was first suggested by McKay and was later developed further by Porter.[35] This was posited as an alternative understanding of the meaning of the Greek augment and as a way to distinguish tense-forms that share the same aspect, such as the present and imperfect.

The Greek augment has long been regarded as an indicator of past temporal reference, adorning the Greek aorist, imperfect, and pluperfect indicative tense-forms. Though there are several examples of aorists dropping their augment while still referring to the past, in Homeric poetry, this was most likely for purposes of style and meter. But the augment could indicate the spatial metaphor of remoteness rather than past temporal reference.

While it is perhaps a little difficult for modern English speakers to wrap their minds around the concept of remoteness, it is actually quite a natural concept, especially for ancient cultures. Actions are perceived as being "distant" from the speaker. They are remote compared to actions that are nearer. We might normally think of actions in the past as opposed to the present, but this is a very temporal way to conceive of actions, while many ancient cultures leaned toward more spatial ways of thinking.

In truth, our conceptions of time are overlaid on spatial realities. A day is measured by the rotation of the earth on its axis, a month by the orbit of the moon around the earth, and a year by the orbit of the earth around the sun. These are spatial realities that determine our major divisions of time. But how we break a day up into twenty-four hours is arbitrary. Breaking up an hour into sixty minutes is arbitrary. Having a seven-day week is arbitrary (well, the seven-day week has a biblical precedent). And there is nothing special about ten years constituting a decade, or one hundred years constituting a century. The point is that our major measurements of time are determined by physical, spatial realities. And our minor measurements of time are arbitrary divisions within those larger measurements.

Moreover, as cognitive linguists have demonstrated, it is naturally human to think first in spatial categories before developing more abstract notions such as time.[36] This is easily observed in the development of infants. Long before they understand what time is, they are already navigating their worlds through spatial reasoning. It is also observed culturally; human cultures tend

---

35. McKay, "Use of the Ancient Greek Perfect," 19n22; Porter, *Verbal Aspect*, 95.

36. E.g., H. H. Clark, "Space, Time, Semantics, and the Child," in *Cognitive Development and the Acquisitions of Language*, ed. T. E. Moore (New York: Academic Press, 1973), 61; H. Grimm, "On the Child's Acquisition of Semantic Structure Underlying the Wordfield of Prepositions," *Language and Speech* 18 (1975): 110; Martin Haspelmath, *From Space to Time—Temporal Adverbials in the World's Languages* (Munich: Lincom Europa, 1997), 140.

to be much more spatially oriented early in their development before abstract notions such as time become more prevalent.

Thus, there is a natural relationship between space and time, and space is actually the more natural of the two. The concept of remoteness fits into this broader sense in which people may regard their world more spatially than we do today. And the beauty of remoteness is that it does not nullify the possibility of past temporal reference. Indeed, past time is simply one expression of remoteness.

This means that if, say, the Greek aorist is regarded as perfective in aspect and spatially remote at the semantic level, this will account for the 85 percent of aorists that refer to the past—since past time is a temporal expression of remoteness. But it will also account for the 15 percent of aorists that do *not* express past temporal reference, since there are other ways in which remoteness may function. In other words, the spatial value of remoteness is more easily regarded as a semantic feature of the aorist than as past temporal reference since it does not yield exceptions.

I have developed the concept of spatial metaphors beyond Porter and McKay to include the opposite of remoteness—namely, proximity.[37] While the aorist and imperfect indicatives convey remoteness, the present tense-form conveys proximity. This explains why the majority of present indicatives express present temporal reference, which is a natural expression of the spatial value of proximity. And proximity is also able to explain the uses of the present indicative that do *not* convey present temporal reference, since there are other pragmatic expressions of proximity besides temporal reference.

■ Relevance for Exegesis

We turn now to consider how these issues impact our reading of the Greek New Testament. There are several ways in which understanding verbal aspect may shape our reading of Greek text. First, it will correct certain mistakes that are commonly made in interpretation. For instance, the claim that the aorist indicative in Romans 5:6 ("For while we were still weak, at the right time Christ *died* [ἀπέθανεν] for the ungodly," NRSV) proves the once-off nature of Christ's death is mistaken. The aorist does not prove the "punctiliar" nature of Christ's death since it conveys a summary of the event, from an external perspective. A similar mistake has been made concerning the aorist imperative in John 17:17 ("*Sanctify* [ἁγίασον] them in the truth; your word is truth,"

---

37. Campbell, *Verbal Aspect, the Indicative Mood, and Narrative*, 48–57.

NRSV), claiming that the aorist proves that sanctification is an instantaneous event. But the perfective aspect of the aorist imperative conveys a specific command, not an instantaneous one. And there are many other such examples.

Second, several positive insights into the Greek text are possible through a competent understanding of aspect. Apart from the obvious importance of reading each aorist as perfective in aspect, each present as imperfective, and so forth, we will focus on two major advances. One is the interaction between aspect and *Aktionsart*. The other is the way in which aspect is used to help structure narrative texts.

Aspect and Aktionsart *Interactions*

While older approaches to Greek verbs focused on their type of action—their *Aktionsart*—aspect focuses on the viewpoint through which each action is portrayed. However, it is still useful to reflect on the nature of each action. Aspect does not operate alone within a text but interacts with lexeme and context to create *Aktionsart* expressions or implicatures.[38] For instance, an aorist is not, in and of itself, punctiliar in nature, but its perfective aspect may combine with a punctiliar lexeme to create a punctiliar *Aktionsart*. In other words, *some* aorists may be punctiliar in function, even though aorists are not punctiliar in their semantic nature.

Every aspect is capable of expressing a variety of functions within a context, depending on the pragmatic features at work in any given text. Alongside punctiliar *Aktionsart*, the perfective aspect of the aorist can express, for example, summary, ingressive, and gnomic *Aktionsarten*, depending on the lexeme used and the context. The aorist indicative can also express present and even future temporal reference.

The imperfective aspect of the present indicative is able to express, for example, progressive, stative, iterative, and gnomic *Aktionsarten*, depending on lexeme and context. It also often conveys past temporal reference as the so-called historical present. The imperfective aspect of the perfect indicative is able to express stative and arguably progressive *Aktionsarten*, depending on lexeme and context, and can be used in parallel to the historical present as an historical perfect, referring to a simple past action. Similar patterns of usage apply to the imperfect, pluperfect, and future tense-forms.

The chief advantage of relating aspect to *Aktionsart* through such predictable patterns is that the exegesis of Greek verbs may be approached with a more objective methodology than older attempts. Instead of the somewhat

---

38. Fanning, *Verbal Aspect in New Testament Greek*, 29–50; Campbell, *Advances in the Study of Greek*, 120–24.

subjective intuition of the interpreters of yesteryear, this approach relies on recognizing established patterns of aspect-*Aktionsart* interactions and allows scrutiny of the process and its results. Thus, the study of aspect offers a superior methodology for exegesis.

Aspect and Narrative Structure

Aspect functions in a predictable manner within narrative texts. This can be useful to understand in observing how larger units of narrative text are constructed and how they function. The most fundamental distinction within narrative is between narrative proper and discourse—event-based story versus reported speech or thought. Within narrative proper—event-based story—we find mainline and offline strands. Mainline strands include sequential events that outline the development of the story, while off-line strands supplement the mainline by offering commentary, explanation, and background to narrative events.[39]

While these distinctions are universal within narrative texts of any language, Greek maps such narrative strands through the use of its indicative verbs. In general, mainline material is conveyed by use of the aorist indicative, since its perfective aspect is especially suited to outlining narrative events. Off-line material is generally conveyed by imperfect and pluperfect indicatives, since their imperfective aspect and remoteness is suited to commentary, explanation, and background information. Discourse material is dominated by present and perfect indicatives, since their imperfective aspect and proximity is suited to the reporting of speech and thought.

Recognizing these patterns within narrative texts allows us to account for a key reason why certain tense-forms are used. Their aspectual nature functions to structure and shape narrative material so that it can convey its various types of information in an effective manner. This helps us to understand the function of aspect, as well as the inner workings of narrative.

■ Conclusion

Aspect and tense remain controversial topics in Greek research today, but many insights have already been gained from the discussions and debates concerning them. While some confusion may still exist for budding students and experienced teachers alike, the worst mistake would be to remain disengaged

---

39. Campbell, *Verbal Aspect, the Indicative Mood, and Narrative*, 239–47; Campbell, *Advances in the Study of Greek*, 124–26.

from the issues. Many, if not most, areas of scholarship exist in a state of flux, with their own significant debates and differences of scholarly opinion. But this does not mean that students ought to avoid them while teachers ignore them. The study of Greek verbal aspect is here to stay, which means that Greek verbs simply must be understood in light of it.

The application of aspectual insights presents its own challenges, but there is an increasing number of tools to aid in this endeavor. The beginner may start with the foundational insight that verbs convey actions through *viewpoint*—some an external viewpoint, others an internal viewpoint. Temporal considerations are secondary to this important point. Understanding the interaction between aspect, lexeme, and context is the next step toward careful exegesis. And finally, consideration of viewpoint enables the assessment of verbal function in wider units of text.

3

The Greek Perfect Tense-Form

Understanding Its Usage and Meaning

MICHAEL G. AUBREY

■ Introduction

A strange thing happens as a student finishes year one of New Testament Greek and begins year two. It is perhaps a little confusing, maybe a lot confusing, as for some reason all the definitions and explanations of the various grammatical categories become more complicated.

Of course, some of this is natural to the learning process: when you first began your journey into the Greek language, so many new things were happening all at once. You had a brand-new alphabet and pronunciation to remember. Every class brought new vocabulary terms to memorize. Hopefully most of them were Greek! Some of them were terms for concepts that were brand new to you, words like "aorist" and "imperfect" or "case," "number," and "gender." Ideally, some at least sounded familiar: "noun" and "verb," certainly, but also probably "present" and "perfect." Though at the same time, the way your teacher talked about these more familiar words still might have been a bit foreign and taken some getting used to. In order to help you process all this new information, the definitions of these words in class were likely concise and simple. That first semester of Greek, especially, can feel a little overwhelming at times. If you look past that first year, though, many of those concise definitions almost assuredly grew a bit in their complexity. Language is a vast and often complicated system. It is only natural that as you learn the content, the material you are learning grows with you.

Yet, for some reason, the Greek perfect in particular seems to become more difficult in intermediate Greek than other areas of grammar. That difficulty is not the student's fault but ours. We, the grammarians and language scholars who have devoted our careers to studying Greek, well, we do not always agree with one another. Because of that, there is a sense that we have failed the students, who are trying to learn. Our books and articles sometimes have the tendency to make the Greek perfect *more complicated* where it perhaps should not be.

If you took a second-year Greek class, you almost certainly had an intermediate textbook. It might have been Daniel Wallace's *Greek Grammar beyond the Basics*, Stanley Porter's *Idioms of the Greek New Testament*, or David Alan Black's *It's Still Greek to Me*.[1] Perhaps you read Constantine Campbell's *Basics of Verbal Aspect in Biblical Greek* as well.[2] Those who were particularly industrious (or particularly perplexed and seeking answers!) might even have gone to the library to see what other grammars say. That probably made things worse rather than better. The diversity of labels and definitions in textbooks and grammars makes a student's job unfairly hard.

This larger grammatical context has led me to take a slightly different approach in this chapter. Rather than merely summarizing the different definitions and explanations (which I will certainly do!), I desire to equip students with the tools to evaluate alternative approaches on their own. It is my belief that even a small understanding of how grammarians and linguists go about the task of analyzing a grammatical category like the perfect will go a long way toward helping students navigate through disagreements in grammars. Ideally, we can do this without reducing the choice of one perspective over another to a popularity contest.

■ Competing Definitions

Back when I studied my first year of New Testament Greek, our class used Clayton Croy's *Primer of Biblical Greek*.[3] Since then I have learned to ap-

---

1. Daniel B. Wallace, *Greek Grammar beyond the Basics: An Exegetical Syntax of the New Testament* (Grand Rapids: Zondervan, 1996); Stanley E. Porter, *Idioms of the Greek New Testament*, 2nd ed. (Sheffield: Sheffield Academic, 1994); David Alan Black, *It's Still Greek to Me: An Easy-to-Understand Guide to Intermediate Greek* (Grand Rapids: Baker, 1998).

2. Constantine R. Campbell, *Basics of Verbal Aspect in Biblical Greek* (Grand Rapids: Zondervan, 2008).

3. Clayton Croy, *A Primer of Biblical Greek* (Grand Rapids: Eerdmans, 1999).

preciate it for its use of both New Testament and Septuagint examples. Many of you likely used William Mounce's *Basics of Biblical Greek Grammar*. Or maybe your professor assigned you Rodney Decker's *Reading Koine Greek*.[4] Croy gives the following definition for the perfect:

> The Greek perfect tense denotes an action completed in past time with an effect that continues into the present. The tense thus has two foci: a completed past action and a present effect. To say in the Greek perfect tense, "I have filled the cup," is equivalent to saying, "I filled the cup and it is now full."[5]

Contrast that definition with Decker's description in his own first-year grammar:

> The aspect of the perfect is stative: it describes a state/condition rather than an action—a situation described with no reference to change or expenditure of energy. This "state" refers to the state of the grammatical subject of the sentence, not the object.[6]

These are both first-year grammars. One says the perfect denotes an action as completed. The other says the perfect describes a state and not an action. The first-year Greek student has the pleasure of having only one grammar, but second-year students and beyond no longer have the luxury of not needing to deal with such contradictions. To make matters worse, intermediate textbooks likely do not improve the situation.

If you look in Wallace's *Greek Grammar beyond the Basics*, this is the definition of the perfect you will find:

> The unaffected meaning is a combination of the external and internal aspects: The *action* is portrayed *externally* (summary), while the *resultant state* proceeding from the action is portrayed *internally* (continuous state).[7]

Black's grammar is similar but phrased quite differently:

> The **perfect tense** describes an action as completed at the time of writing or speaking. While dealing with the past to some extent, the perfect tense is primarily concerned with present time. An action has occurred in the past whose

4. William D. Mounce, *Basics of Biblical Greek Grammar*, 2nd ed. (Grand Rapids: Zondervan, 2003); Rodney J. Decker, *Reading Koine Greek: An Introduction and Integrated Workbook* (Grand Rapids: Baker Academic, 2014).
5. Croy, *Primer of Biblical Greek*, 83.
6. Decker, *Reading Koine Greek*, 329.
7. Wallace, *Greek Grammar beyond the Basics*, 501.

results are still apparent. Thus τέθνηκε (the perfect of ἀποθνῄσκω) does not mean "he died" but "he is *now* dead." Similarly, γέγραφα (the perfect of γράφω) means "[it is *there* on paper, because] I wrote [it]." There is no exact English equivalent to the Greek perfect. The so-called English perfect, formed by the auxiliary verb *have*, is the nearest equivalent that can be given, but it will not always serve to translate a Greek perfect.[8]

Additionally, in Porter's intermediate grammar, you encounter a third definition:

> *The perfect and pluperfect tense-forms occur in contexts where the user of Greek wishes to depict the action as reflecting a given (often complex) state of affairs.* The stative aspect carries the most semantic [*sic*; weight?] conveyed by the tense-form *by itself* (without reference to contextual factors) than by any other tense-form. This has long been recognized, but when it comes to defining what the meaning of the tense is, there has been disagreement. The definition enshrined for centuries regarding continuance of completed action must now be replaced. This definition was never without problems, as an examination of the grammars shows, where various categories must be introduced to cope with major conceptual difficulties (e.g., discussions of so-called intensive, extensive, and completed perfects). The force of the stative aspect is that the grammatical subject of the verb is the focus of the state of affairs. Thus the perfect οἶδα means "I know" or "I am in a knowledgeable state," not "I know and the fact remains known"; and ἤλπικα means "I am in a hopeful state."[9]

These three definitions are quite different but do have some things in common. Wallace's and Black's definitions are in basic agreement: Wallace's "external (summary)" corresponds to Black's "completed," and Black's "results are still apparent" corresponds to Wallace's statement that "the *resultant state* proceeding from the action is portrayed *internally* (continuous state)." Further, note that both definitions are like Croy's definition above. Comparably, Decker's and Porter's definitions also correspond to each other. The attentive reader might also recognize that the definition Porter declares "must now be replaced" is the one preferred by Croy, Wallace, and Black.

Finally, one other discussion of the perfect that you might encounter in a first- or second-year class is from Campbell's *Basics of Verbal Aspect in Biblical Greek*. Campbell provides a very helpful survey of the numerous positions and proposals that have been put forward for the perfect in recent

---

8. Black, *It's Still Greek to Me*, 107–8 (emphasis original).

9. Porter, *Idioms of the Greek New Testament*, 39–40 (emphasis original). Given Porter's discussion of aspect on p. 22, I believe the word "weight" was lost between pp. 39 and 40.

decades in the advanced grammatical literature, under the aptly titled chapter "The Problem of the Perfect."[10] Campbell's own proposal is that the perfect is another *imperfective* aspect with the additional heightened proximity for the perfect proper and heightened remoteness for the pluperfect, which he describes as focusing closer in on the event, noting, "The effect of this close-up view is that it concentrates the action by zooming in on it."[11]

All these different options likely seem difficult to evaluate. Everyone mentioned above is a thoughtful and seasoned scholar, and there are even more in the more advanced grammatical literature who are making the case for one of these views or another. How shall we decide who is right and who is wrong? Or perhaps that is the wrong way to approach the question entirely. All these grammarians have endeavored to think seriously about the language. They have each come to slightly different conclusions. We can only assume that each of them is endeavoring to account for the patterns they see. To that end, perhaps the most beneficial thing we can do is to provide students with some basic tools for finding the grammatical patterns of the Greek perfect and pluperfect.

■ Practical Advice on Verbs and the Perfect Verb Forms

There are two concepts that will help form a foundation not only for evaluating what is stated in grammars but also for developing some basic skills for analyzing grammar yourself. The first of these is *event structure*, the conceptual underpinning of both *Aktionsart* and "aspect," two words that perhaps you have only just learned for the first time in Campbell's chapter on tense and aspect earlier in this book. I say event structure is *conceptual* because it exists only in your mind; it is part of your capacity for imagination.

Imagine you are mugged. You experience the mugging in the regular flow of time without a well-defined beginning, middle, or end. When you report back to friends and family, you make choices, conscious and subconscious, about the structure of the event. How do you elaborate it? Perhaps you just say, "I was mugged," or "I got mugged today"—one salient participant and one completed event. Or maybe you say, "Some guy mugged me"—two participants and one event. You could even say, "I was walking to the store and someone jumped out in front of me and demanded my wallet." Now you have two participants and three events, the first presented as incomplete and

10. Campbell, *Basics of Verbal Aspect*, 46–52.
11. Campbell, *Basics of Verbal Aspect*, 51. See chap. 2 of the current volume for more on Campbell's position.

two as completed. In each case, depending on your audience, your social comfort, and other circumstances, you choose where you begin your story and where you end your story. None of the objective events of the mugging obligates you to say one thing rather than the other. Understanding this fact about event structure gives you the space to consider how writers of Greek texts are making choices to present their own stories.

The second concept for thinking about the grammar of the perfect is *transitivity*. Campbell notes there are more nuanced models of what it means for a clause to be transitive or intransitive. Campbell suggests that a clause's transitivity, rather than being defined merely by whether a clause has an object, must also be affected by the action of the event.[12] I would like to take that idea and move it one step further: transitivity is itself a scalar concept.[13] We can organize clauses that have an object alone on a scale from those that are high in transitivity (*Rachel shattered the window*) to those that are low in transitivity (*Rachel remembered her mother*). We will examine each of these concepts, event structure and transitivity, in turn.

Verbs and Events as Miniature Stories

In the 2006 film *Stranger than Fiction*, Will Ferrell's character, Harold, discovers that he is living out in real time the novel-writing process of Emma Thompson's character, a novelist. Hearing Thompson narrating that the innocuous act of adjusting the time on his wristwatch would result in his immanent death, Harold seeks the help of a professor of English literature, Jules Hilbert (Dustin Hoffman). Professor Hilbert helps Harold determine what kind of story he is in with the hope of saving his life. In one scene, Hilbert explains to Harold how narrative works: "Some plots are moved forward by external events and crises. Others are moved forward by the characters themselves. If I go through that door, the plot continues. The story is me through the door. If I stay here, the plot can't move forward, the story ends. Also, if I stay here, I'm late."

That short statement by Professor Hilbert is a surprisingly apt description of *event structure*. The larger story shares the structure of its constituent sentences. Just as stories have an instigation or a beginning state (Hilbert is on one side of the door), a central process or a change (Hilbert moves through the door), and completion or a result state (Hilbert is on the other side of the door), language users can use aspect to present events from particular perspectives (see fig. 3.1).

---

12. Campbell, *Basics of Verbal Aspect*, 55–56.
13. Gilbert Lazard, "Transitivity Revisited as an Example of a More Strict Approach in Typological Research," *Folia Linguistica* 36 (2003): 141–90.

Figure 3.1
Event Structure

> ***Internal Event Structure***
>
> **Instigation—Process—Completion**

Adapted from Masayoshi Shibatani, "On the Conceptual Framework for Voice Phenomena," *Linguistics* 44, no. 2 (2006): 221.

In turn, a speaker may use aspect to view event structure as an undifferentiated whole (perfective/aorist), as in figure 3.2. Here the speaker is viewing an event in terms of its entirety, without reference to how the internal process unfolded. It simply happened.

Figure 3.2
Perfective Aspect

> ***External Event Structure***
>
> **Perfective:**
>
> **An event happened.**

Professor Hilbert went through the door.

Here the speaker's choice provides no reference to the initiation, internal process, or conclusion of the event. The event's internal structure is entirely ignored, with just the bare assertion that it took place. Alternatively, a speaker could also draw attention to the internal progress of the event, using the imperfective aspect, as in figure 3.3. In this example, the focus of attention is on the process portion of the event structure, without any reference to its instigation or completion.

Figure 3.3
Imperfective Aspect

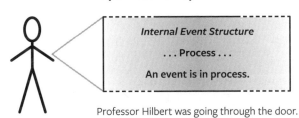

> ***Internal Event Structure***
>
> **. . . Process . . .**
>
> **An event is in process.**

Professor Hilbert was going through the door.

Did Hilbert get through the door? Perhaps he did. Or maybe he was interrupted, was called in another direction and stopped part way through. The speaker has left the boundaries of the action open ended. The imperfective aspect, by itself, makes no claim about whether the event reaches a conclusion.

While the perfective and imperfective are the two most common forms aspect takes in languages, there are others. Languages might provide their speakers the means of construing any phase of an event as an aspect, such as any of the following in figure 3.4.

Figure 3.4
Possible Phases of an Event

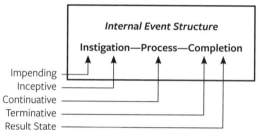

Adapted from Shibatani, "On the Conceptual Framework for Voice Phenomena," 221.

Languages with such aspects exist. Manipuri, a Tibeto-Burman language, has a large set of aspects its speakers use for structuring events as phases. Consider the sentences provided in example 1 below.[14]

EXAMPLE 1

a. Inceptive: This aspect uses the *-gət* suffix.

Sentence:	məhak-nə	phu-***gət***-li
Word for word:	he-NOMINATIVE	beat-**START**-NONFUTURE
Translation:	He **began** to beat.	
Meaning:	The *-gət* aspect suffix communicates that an action has started.	

b. Continuative: This aspect uses the *-rì* suffix.

Sentence:	məhak	hoytup	ca-***rì***
Word for word:	he	apple	eat-**CONTINUATIVE**
Translation:	He **is eating** an apple.		
Meaning:	The *-rì* aspect suffix communicates that an action is continuing.		

14. Examples are taken from D. N. S. Bhat and M. S. Ningomba, *Manipuri Grammar* (Munich: Lincom Europa, 1997), 251–67.

c. Change: This aspect uses the -*re* suffix.

Sentence:	əŋaŋ	əsi	caw-_**re**_
Word for word:	child	this	big-CHANGE
Translation:	This child **has grown big**.		
Meaning:	The -*re* aspect suffix communicates that action produced a change in the subject.		

d. Terminative/Cessative: This aspect uses the -*rəm* suffix.

Sentence:	yumthək	ədu	yu-_**rəm**_-mì
Word for word:	roof	that	leak-STOP-DURATIVE
Translation:	That roof had been leaking (but it **stopped**).		
Meaning:	The -*rəm* aspect suffix communicates that an action has stopped.		

Speakers of the Manipuri language may present an event in terms of a particular *phase*. In sentence 1a, the speaker has chosen to draw attention to the *start or inception* of the event. In 1b, the focus is on a man whose action of eating is *ongoing/continuing*, and similarly in 1c, on the *change* from not-big to big. In sentence 1d, the speaker has chosen to focus on the *cessation* or *termination* of the leak. This illustrates the large number of ways aspect might function. Though the English language has no grammatical aspect for these, English speakers can express these same phases, but we do so with lexical items—"begin," "become," "stop"—rather than aspect markers.

All of this provides us with a set of questions to ask about how the event structure is being used:

- How is the speaker depicting the event's structure?
- How many participants are there?
- Does a participant experience or undergo a change?

These last two questions (the number of the participants and the question of change) take us directly to our next topic: transitivity.

Transitivity: From Subject to Object

Grade-school English classes teach that a *transitive* clause is a clause with an object (Rachel kicked the ball) and that an *intransitive* clause is one without an object (Rachel walked around). The use of "transitive" is no accident for talking about actions that have two participants, since the concept of *transfer* from one participant to another is central to the formulation of transitivity. The six clauses in examples 2–5 each have an object (see below). Yet the manner in which action moves from subject to object changes as we move from example 2 to example 5. "Shattering" and "tapping," in 2a–b, denote a transfer of kinetic energy from (and by) the subject to the object.

EXAMPLE 2

a. Subject → Object (high energy transfer): Rachel shattered the window.

b. Subject → Object (low energy transfer): Rachel tapped her glass.

Sentences such as these are what most of us would immediately think of if we were asked to give an example of a transitive clause—they are *prototypically* transitive. Prototypical transitive clauses have the following traits:[15]

• The subject and the object are maximally distinct (i.e., they are separate people/things).
• The agent subject volitionally instigates the event.
• The patient object alone is affected.

Of course, there are other kinds of transitive clauses that do not obey these rules. For example, consumption events are a little strange in that both the subject and the object are affected.

EXAMPLE 3

Subject ↔ Object (consumption transfer): Rachel ate an apple.

Here the object, "an apple," is totally affected by the event, but the action of eating involves the agent subject, "Rachel," transferring the apple into herself. Thus, Rachel is an *affected* agent.[16] Verbs like "eat" sit on the threshold between transfer of the action toward the object and transfer of the action toward the subject. Additionally, the event shifts the distinctiveness of the subject and object from a state of maximal distinctiveness (both Rachel

---

15. Åshild Næss, *Prototypical Transitivity*, TSL 72 (Amsterdam: Benjamins, 2007), 44–46.

16. Næss, *Prototypical Transitivity*, 72–81. Many reciprocal verbs (e.g., "fight," "converse," "embrace") also involve an affected agent. See Suzanne Kemmer, *Middle Voice* (Amsterdam: Benjamins, 1993), 102–8.

and the apple exist separately) to minimal distinctiveness (the apple is now internal to Rachel).

Similarly, the distinctiveness of the subject and the object may be reduced with verb classes involving dressing and grooming. Thus, in example 4, Rachel is a volitional agent, but the subject and object share a whole-part relationship. Rachel is not maximally distinct from her hands, which naturally results in Rachel also being an affected agent subject.

EXAMPLE 4

Subject ↔ Object (transfer): Rachel washed her hands.

The transfer could also go in the opposite direction, as in example 5. While reading certainly involves Rachel acting volitionally, she does not act upon the book. Since reading is a cognitive event (opening a book and turning pages, by itself, is not reading), the cognitive effect of the book's information upon the reader is central.

EXAMPLE 5

a. Subject ← Object (cognitive transfer): Rachel read the book.

b. Subject ← Object (perception experience): Rachel saw a buffalo.

A verb like "see," in 5b, similarly involves a transfer to the subject. Additionally, while Rachel has some control over what she *looks at* (volitional), she has less control over what she *sees* (nonvolitional). Here Rachel is not an agent subject acting on an object or instigating the event. Instead, she merely experiences an object, without affecting that object in any way. Only one transitivity trait remains: "Rachel" and "a buffalo" are maximally distinct from each other.

So, we can add a few more questions to ask when we are looking at clauses.

- Who/what is instigating the event?
- Who/what is affected by the event?
- To what degree are the subject and object distinct from each other?

Aspect, event structure, and transitivity are all central for understanding the linguistic context for looking at the Greek perfect.

■ The Perfect in Use

When we encounter examples of the perfect, whether in grammars or in the wild, it is essential to understand something: *not all verbs have the option of the perfect as an inflectional form.* In fact, most verbs whose primary sense is stative never form perfects. See table 3.1 for some representative examples. You might recognize some from the New Testament.

Table 3.1 Stative Verbs

ἀδημονέω	be anxious	μακροθυμέω	be patient
ἀθυμέω	be discouraged	μένω	remain
ἄπειμι	be absent	μεσόω	be in the middle
ἀρκέω	be sufficient	ὁμοιάζω	be like
ἀστατέω	be homeless	ὀφείλω	be obligated
γέμω	be full	παραφρονέω	be beside oneself
δειλιάω	be cowardly	πάρειμι	be present
εἰμί	be	πενθέω	mourn
εἰρηνεύω	be at peace	περίκειμαι	be around
ἐκθαμβέω	be alarmed	περισσεύω	abound
ἐλεάω	have mercy on	πυρράζω	be red
ἔξειμι	be permitted	σπλαγχνίζομαι	have compassion
εὐλαβέομαι	have respect	στίλβω	shine
εὐχαριστέω	be thankful	στυγνάζω	be gloomy
ζάω	live	τύφω	smoke; smolder
ζέω	be enthusiastic	ὑπονοέω	be suspicious
ἠχέω	sound; ring	χολάω	be angry
θορυβάζω	be distracted	χρηστεύομαι	be kind

Similarly, nonstative verbs that *do not* effect a change of state in a participant (whether the subject or the object) likewise demonstrate a clear avoidance of the perfect. "Activity verbs" involve energy and duration (unlike the stative verbs above; see table 3.2), and those that do not require duration are called "semelfactive verbs" (table 3.3).[17]

17. A semelfactive is an event that happens instantaneously, without anyone or anything undergoing a change of state. In English, these are often intransitive—e.g., "The thunder clapped," "The headlights flashed," or "The jewel glinted." See Carlota S. Smith, *The Parameter of Aspect*, 2nd ed. (Dordrecht: Kluwer Academic, 1997), 17–38. The verbs in table 3.3, when they involve duration, necessarily convey repetition or iteration: "Light flashed for an hour" can only refer to repeated flashing over the course of that hour.

Table 3.2 Activity Verbs

ἀγαθοποιέω	do good	κλαίω	weep; cry
ἀγρεύω	hunt, fish, catch	μαγεύω	practice magic
ᾄδω	sing	μαστίζω	whip; scourge
ἀθλέω	compete	μυκτηρίζω	ridicule; sneer
ἀλαλάζω	wail; clash	ὀρχέομαι	dance
ἀλήθω	grind	περιπατέω	walk; lie
ἀμάω	reap	πέτομαι	fly
ἀνέω	winnow	ποιμαίνω	shepherd
ἀροτριάω	plow	προσεύχομαι	pray
βόσκω	feed; herd	σαλπίζω	blow a trumpet
βρύχω	grind one's teeth	στενάζω	sigh; groan
γελάω	laugh/ridicule	συζητέω	debate; argue
γεωργέω	cultivate; till	τεκνογονέω	bear children
γογγύζω	complain, grumble	τεκνοτροφέω	parent children
δυσφημέω	slander; defame	τελεσφορέω	produce ripe fruit
κακοποιέω	do evil	τρώγω	eat
καλοποιέω	do what is right	ψάλλω	sing praise

Table 3.3 Semelfactive Verbs

ἅλλομαι	leap; spring up
ἀστράπτω	flash; gleam
διστάζω	doubt; waver
κατασείω	motion; make a sign
νυστάζω	nod
ὀκνέω	hesitate; delay
ῥαπίζω	strike, slap

I do not claim that the perfect is an impossibility with these verbs. At the very least Greek speakers did not find the perfect useful for them. This lack of use is likely semantically motivated.

The remaining verbs, those that *do* inflect a perfect, nearly all involve a change of state: one participant is in a different state at the end of the event. It could be physical (κλάω, "break"), a position (ἵστημι, "set, make stand"), a location (ἀποστέλλω, "send," or ἔρχομαι, "come/go"), cognitive (διδάσκω, "teach," or μανθάνω, "learn"), or some kind of status (κρίνω, "judge"). There are also still a few stative verbs like ἀγαπάω, "love"; ἐλπίζω, "hope"; πιστεύω, "believe, trust"; and, of course, the infamous οἶδα, "know." By organizing these verbs along the transitivity scale, we can use our questions about event structure and transitivity to understand how the perfect functions.

High-Transitivity Verbs

At the high end of the transitivity scale are events where an agent subject causes a physical change in a wholly different object. One of the most prominent of these verbs is ἵστημι, "set, make stand." Below in example 6 is a three-way contrast between the perfective aorist, imperfective present, and the perfect.[18]

EXAMPLE 6

a. Perfective aorist: λαβὼν παιδίον **ἔστησεν** αὐτὸ ἐν μέσῳ αὐτῶν.
   Taking a child, **he made** him **stand** among them. (Mark 9:36)
b. Imperfective present: **ἵστημί** σοι πάντα τὰ ἀφαιρέματα.
   I set before you all the tribute. (1 Macc. 15:5)
c. Perfect[19]: Ἡ μήτηρ σου καὶ οἱ ἀδελφοί σου **ἑστήκασιν** ἔξω.
   Your mother and your brothers **are standing** outside. (Luke 8:20)

This three-way contrast helps illustrate how a given perfect cannot be treated separate from its paradigm. The *perfective* aorist and the *imperfective* present are both highly transitive events. There are two participants: an agent subject effecting a change of state in the object. There's a transfer of energy from the subject that produces a standing position for the object: subject → object. The perfect of this otherwise transitive verb shifts the perspective of the verb's lexical semantics (see fig. 3.5).

Figure 3.5
Perfect ἑστήκασιν in Luke 8:20

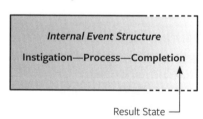

Result State

18. Throughout the following examples, all translations are mine.
19. I use the term "perfect" here to refer to the aspect of both the perfect and the pluperfect tenses. This is primarily because of the general lack of consensus as to the best single label for its meaning.

We can make a few observations about this perfect. First, the perfect reduces the number of participants from two to one. The one participant left is the one that is the *affected object* in the other two aspects. Second, the logic of why some grammars talk about completed events and other grammars talk about states is clear. There is no event, completed or otherwise, in Luke 8:20, only the state of standing—Jesus's mother and brothers were not previously sitting outside. From that perspective, the description of the perfect as stative aspect seems reasonable. On the other hand, there is still a *paradigmatic contrast* between the change-of-state event denoted by both the perfective aorist and imperfective present as compared with the perfect here. The speaker chose the perfect relative to those two other options. In the paradigm, the specific phase of the event being presented is also a *completed state*.[20]

The third observation worth noting for the perfect ἕστηκα ("I am standing") is that this perfect is *active-only*. There is no middle form. This is akin to how some verbs are *middle-only*, as Jonathan Pennington will discuss in his chapter. Likewise, some perfects are middle-only. Consider another highly transitive verb, κλάω ("I break"), in example 7.

EXAMPLE 7

a. Perfective aorist: λαβὼν ὁ Ἰησοῦς ἄρτον καὶ εὐλογήσας **ἔκλασεν**.
   Jesus, taking bread and giving thanks, **broke** it. (Matt. 26:26)

b. Imperfective present: τὸν ἄρτον ὃν **κλῶμεν** . . .
   The bread that **we break** . . . (1 Cor. 10:16)

c. Perfect: ἡ δὲ κώπη **κέκλασται**.
   The oar **is broken**. (Plutarch, *Against Colotes* 2)

The perfective aorist and imperfective present have two participants: an agent subject acting upon a patient object. The object undergoes a change of state. The perfective and imperfective are *active*, but the perfect is *middle*. If we search across Greek literature, we find no use of κέκλακα ("I have broken something").[21] I call this usage the "result-state reading." Most highly transitive

---

20. We could add a third view. Campbell suggests the perfect is *imperfective*, which has a logic to it since the state of Jesus's mother and brothers *persists* at the time of speaking. Campbell, *Basics of Verbal Aspect*, 52.

21. In very early Greek, active-only perfects like ἕστηκα ("I am standing") were the only kind of perfect. Originally the perfect made no distinction in voice, but eventually the perfect endings grew to be associated with the active voice like the other aspects. As the Greek voice system developed, middle perfect performed this function for other verbs. See Edith Claflin, "Voice and the Indo-European Perfect," *Language* 15 (1939): 155–59; Andreas Willi, *Origins of the Greek Verb* (Oxford: Oxford University Press, 2018), 210–19.

verbs demonstrate this pattern in the perfect. Whether active-only or middle-only, they denote the result state relative to the other aspects. Table 3.4 lists some common New Testament verbs and their perfect forms that follow this pattern.

Table 3.4 High-Transitivity Verbs

Active-Only Perfects			
ἀνοίγω	open	ἀνέῳγα	am open
ἀπόλλυμι	destroy	ἀπόλωλα	am destroyed
ἐγείρω	cause to wake	ἐγρήγορα	am roused
πείθω	persuade	πέποιθα	am persuaded
Middle-Only Perfects			
δικαιόω	justify; declare righteous	δεδικαίωμαι	am vindicated
δουλόω	enslave	δεδούλωμαι	am enslaved
θλίβω	afflict; oppress	τεθλίμμαι	am afflicted
χωρίζω	separate; divide	κεχώρισμαι	am separated

Mid-Transitivity Verbs: Physical Domain

When we shift slightly down the transitivity scale, the way the perfect is used also shifts. Included in this group are caused-motion verbs, transference verbs, labor/production verbs, and finish/achieve verbs. These verbs have subjects that are *affected agents*. For instance, in example 8, δίδωμι ("give") is a transference verb. The object is the primary affected participant. It undergoes a change of state from being in the subject's possession to being in the possession of the dative recipient. The nature of "giving" also means that the subject and the dative recipient each undergo their own change of state: from being a possessor to not being a possessor and vice versa.

EXAMPLE 8

a. Perfective aorist: ἐκβαλὼν **ἔδωκεν** δύο δηνάρια τῷ πανδοχεῖ.

Taking out two denarii, **he gave** them to the innkeeper. (Luke 10:35)

b. Imperfective present: Ὁ θεὸς ὑπερηφάνοις ἀντιτάσσεται, ταπεινοῖς δὲ **δίδωσιν** χάριν.

God opposes the proud, but **gives** grace to the humble. (James 4:6)

c. Perfect: κἀγὼ τὴν δόξαν ἣν **δέδωκάς** μοι **δέδωκα** αὐτοῖς.

The glory which **you have given** me I **have given** them. (John 17:22)

Here the perfect continues to have two participants—there is no reduction. Second, the perfect usage continues to profile the final or *completive* end of the event's internal structure, which we can label the "event-completion reading." Third, whether there is attention upon the final state of the subject or that of the object seems to depend primarily upon larger discourse issues; in John 17:22 above, a case can be made that the Father-as-giver is salient and the disciples-as-receivers is also salient. The most attention is on the *completed transfer* of God's glory to Jesus and from Jesus to the disciples—the completed phase of the event, represented in figure 3.6.

Figure 3.6
Perfects with Affected Agents

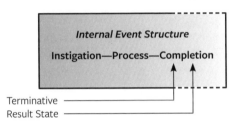

With labor and finish/achieve verbs, the subject is also an affected agent: the subject participates in the entire process of the event and benefits from the event's completion.

EXAMPLE 9

a. Perfective aorist: ἐτέλεσεν ὁ Ἰησοῦς τοὺς λόγους τούτους.
Jesus **finished** these words. (Matt. 7:28)

b. Imperfective present: ἀμφότεροι οὖν τὸ ἔργον **τελοῦσιν**.
They both, then, **are carrying out** their work. (Herm. Sim. 2.7)

c. Perfect: τὸν δρόμον **τετέλεκα**.
I have completed the race. (2 Tim. 4:7)

As with caused-motion verbs, the perfect retains both its participants in the active voice and denotes that the process of the event is fully achieved. The perfect and the perfective aorist with verbs like these often demonstrate semantic overlap when examined merely from English translation. However, they tend toward discourse-level distinctions. The perfective aorist in sentence 9a is part of the narrative discourse, while the perfect in sentence 9c is direct discourse. The aorist is used for sequencing narrative, but speakers tend to avoid using the perfect for this. Conversely, the aorist does not get used in direct discourse in the manner of the perfect here in sentence 9c.[22] Paul uses the perfect to make a strong assertion about the completion of an event in order to highlight the achievement of the subject.

For these mid-transitivity verbs, if the speaker wants to talk about only one participant as with the high-transitivity verbs, the middle voice is used. Note how αἴρω ("take away, remove") functions in the perfect active, versus the perfect middle in example 10.

EXAMPLE 10

a. Active: ἦρκεν χεῖρας ἐναντίον τοῦ κυρίου.
   He has lifted his hand against the Lord. (Job 15:25 LXX)
b. Middle: ἀπὸ γὰρ προσώπου ἀδικίας ἦρται ὁ δίκαιος.
   From the face of injustice the righteous person **is removed.** (Isa. 57:1 LXX)

Both perfects convey event completion. Job 15:25 (the perfect active) presents the completed event as the reason for why a person is being punished, but the perfect middle describes a state without reference to action at all, concerned with only the result state. Also, notably, from the perspective of the raw data, verbs that can have two participants in the perfect active still show a frequency preference for the perfect middle, referring to the state of the subject.

Mid-Transitivity Verbs: Cognitive Domain

This next group of mid-transitivity verbs contains two-participant verbs where the object undergoes a cognitive change, not a physical one. But the pattern is basically the same. Since communication and cognition involve the mental state of the subject, it continues to be an *affected agent*.

EXAMPLE 11

a. Perfective aorist: ἐλάλησαν αὐτῷ τὸν λόγον τοῦ κυρίου.
   They spoke to him the message of the Lord. (Acts 16:32)
b. Imperfective present: ὃν γὰρ ἀπέστειλεν ὁ θεὸς τὰ ῥήματα τοῦ θεοῦ λαλεῖ.
   For he whom God sent **speaks** the words of God. (John 3:34 NASB)
c. Perfect: Ταῦτα λελάληκα ὑμῖν παρ᾽ ὑμῖν μένων.
   These things I have spoken to you while I remain with you. (John 14:25)

22. For a discussion of the perfect in discourse, see Steven E. Runge, "Discourse Function of the Greek Perfect," in *The Greek Verb Revisited: A Fresh Approach for Biblical Exegesis*, ed. Steven E. Runge and Christopher J. Fresch (Bellingham, WA: Lexham, 2016), 458–85.

The perfect retains the same number of participants as the perfective aorist and imperfective present but also continues to place its attention upon the final phase of the event. Jesus's words in sentence 11c reference speech already completed.

Often perfects with communication verbs leave out the accusative object and include only the speaker and audience. This is a natural result of the fact that the perfect is being used immediately after communicating the content, as in example 12.

EXAMPLE 12

ὅτι ζῶν ἐγὼ καὶ τὸ κράτος τῆς βασιλείας μου, **λελάληκα** καὶ ποιήσω ταῦτα ἐν χειρί μου.

Because I live and by the power of my kingdom, **I have spoken** and I shall do these things by my hand. (Jdt. 2:12)

The author of Judith presents Nebuchadnezzar as using the perfect λελάληκα to conclude a royal command to his general Holofernes. Pragmatically, in such a context, the perfect has the effect of tying the completion of the speech to the completion of its purpose—as a servant might reply: "To hear is to obey." John seems to leverage this pragmatic effect to break up Jesus's long monologues in his Gospel.[23]

Writing verbs involve a physical artifact and share features of the physical and cognitive types.

EXAMPLE 13

a. Perfective aorist: **ἔγραψεν** δὲ καὶ τίτλον ὁ Πιλᾶτος.
   Pilate also **wrote** a notice. (John 19:19)
b. Imperfective present: Ταῦτά σοι **γράφω** ἐλπίζων ἐλθεῖν πρὸς σὲ ἐν τάχει.
   These things **I am writing** to you, hoping to come to you soon. (1 Tim. 3:14)
c. Perfect: ἀπεκρίθη ὁ Πιλᾶτος, Ὃ **γέγραφα, γέγραφα.**
   Pilate replied, "What **I have written, I have written.**" (John 19:22)

In John 19:22, the Pharisees want Pilate to change the notice above the head of Jesus that declares him King of the Jews, but Pilate refuses to change it, saying simply: "What I have written, I have written." The attention is upon the finality of the act: the notice exists as written, and neither Pilate, nor the

---

23. See John 14:25; 15:3, 11; 16:1, 4, 6, 25, 33.

cognitive state of Pilate, nor the status of the writing is changing again. Result states are often interpreted as *persistent* states.

Still in the appropriate discourse context, a speaker might place primary attention upon the subject of the clause rather than the object, even with a mid-transitivity perfect. In example 14, in the Fragments of Papias, the author describes the historical tradition that Mark wrote the Gospel of Mark on the basis of Peter's recollections.

EXAMPLE 14

ἀναγκαίως νῦν προσθήσομεν ταῖς προεκτεθείσαις αὐτοῦ φωναῖς παράδοσιν, ἣν περὶ Μάρκου τοῦ τὸ εὐαγγέλιον **γεγραφότος**.

For the present purpose we must add to his statements, already quoted above, a tradition which is about Mark, the **author** of the Gospel. (FPap 3.14)

The discourse context shows that the relevant affected participant is the subject, not the object, because Mark-as-author is the new information for the audience, not the gospel-as-written state. Both alternatives, either a completed writing or the subject as an author, are discourse-motivated versions of the event-completion and result-state readings of the perfect.

Low-Transitive and Agentive-Intransitive Verbs

This last set of action verbs has the lowest transitivity, where direction of transfer between the two participants is reversed. Rather than moving from subject to object, the event's energy moves from the object to the subject. Since these verbs do not have affected objects, the perfect necessarily refers to the state of the subject. A good example is μανθάνω ("learn"), in example 15.

EXAMPLE 15

a. Perfective aorist: οὐδεὶς γνησιώτερον **ἔμαθεν** ἀπ᾽ ἐμοῦ λόγον.
   No one has ever **learned** from me a more reliable word. (Barn. 9.9)

b. Imperfective present: νῦν **μανθάνω** δεδεμένος μηδὲν ἐπιθυμεῖν.
   Now **I am learning**, as a prisoner, to desire nothing. (Ign. *Rom.* 4.3)

c. Perfect: **μεμάθηκεν** ἡ γλῶσσα αὐτῶν λαλεῖν ψευδῆ.
   Their tongue **has learned / knows** how to speak lies. (Jer. 9:4 LXX)

While the other two aspects present the process of learning either as a whole (aorist/perfective) or incomplete (present/imperfective), the perfect denotes learning's result state: knowing.

One-participant intransitive-action verbs are similar. Πταίω ("stumble, fall") has two senses. One refers to a change from upright to fallen, the other just the momentary wavering, a stumble.

EXAMPLE 16

a. Perfective aorist: μὴ ἔπταισαν ἵνα πέσωσιν; μὴ γένοιτο.

Did **they stumble** such that they fell? Absolutely not. (Rom. 11:11)

b. Imperfective present: πολλὰ γὰρ **πταίομεν** ἅπαντες.

For **we** all **stumble** in many ways. (James 3:2)

c. Perfect: εἶδον παῖδες Ἀδραάζαρ ὅτι **ἐπταίκασιν** ἀπὸ προσώπου Ισραηλ.

The sons of Hadraazar saw that **they had fallen** before Israel. (1 Chron. 19:19 LXX)

Both the perfective aorist and the imperfective present use either sense, but the perfect denotes only the completed fall. This distinction makes sense only if the perfect is not merely stative *by itself* but specifically refers to the result-state phase of the event.

Intransitive-motion verbs behave in two ways. With some, both the completed motion and the resulting location may be in focus, as in example 17, while others make no reference to the motion, as in example 18.

EXAMPLE 17

a. Perfective aorist: ὁ δὲ ἀποβαλὼν τὸ ἱμάτιον αὐτοῦ ἀναπηδήσας **ἦλθεν** πρὸς τὸν Ἰησοῦν.

Throwing off his cloak and jumping up, **he came** to Jesus. (Mark 10:50)

b. Imperfective present: Τρίτον τοῦτο **ἔρχομαι** πρὸς ὑμᾶς.

This the third time **I am coming** to you. (2 Cor. 13:1)

c. Perfect: λέγω ὑμῖν ὅτι καὶ Ἠλίας **ἐλήλυθεν**.

I tell you that Elijah certainly **has come / is** certainly **here**. (Mark 9:13)

EXAMPLE 18

a. Perfective aorist: **ἤγγισαν** εἰς τὴν κώμην οὗ ἐπορεύοντο.

They drew near to the village where they were traveling. (Luke 24:28)

b. Imperfective present: ὅλως εἰς συναγωγὴν ἀνδρῶν δικαίων οὐκ **ἐγγίζει**.
He never **comes near** an assembly of righteous men. (Herm. Mand.
11.13).

c. Perfect: **ἤγγικεν** ἡ βασιλεία τοῦ θεοῦ.
The kingdom of God **is near**. (Luke 10:11)

Finally, be aware that these low-transitive and intransitive verbs have
idiosyncratic voice alternations. As with the highest-transitivity verbs, some
are middle-only and others are active-only. For example, μανθάνω ("learn")
above from example 15 is an active-only verb in all tenses, except the future,
where it is middle-only.

Stative Verbs

We finally return to stative verbs. Recall from earlier that most stative verbs
do not form perfects at all. What about those that do? Thus far, we have seen
that the concepts of event completion and result state are integral to the perfect's usage. Yet the basic idea of stativity is contrary to the very concepts of
completion and result. States lack energy consumption, transfer, and change,
so what happens when a perfect is used with such a verb? The speaker has two
options to form a perfect with a state verb. Each involves analogical extension.[24]
Speakers can convert the state and retain the change-of-state semantics, or they
can convert the change-of-state semantics and retain the stativity of the verb.
Both occur when stative verbs form perfects. The perfect of some cause-of-state
verbs already shares semantic correspondence with a normal stative verb, such
as πείθω, "persuade; make trust," and πιστεύω, "believe, trust," in example 19.

EXAMPLE 19

καταβάτω νῦν ἀπὸ τοῦ σταυροῦ καὶ **πιστεύσομεν** ἐπ᾽ αὐτόν. **πέποιθεν** ἐπὶ τὸν
θεόν, ῥυσάσθω νῦν εἰ θέλει αὐτόν.

Let him now come down from the cross and **we will believe** in him. **He
believes** in God, so let God deliver him now if he wants him. (Matt.
27:42–43)

Often simply adding a change to the beginning of the stative verb makes
it possible for that stative verb to have a perfect form. This is an *inchoative*

---

24. Analogy drives diachronic change. Raimo Anttila, "Analogy: The Warp and Woof of
Cognition," in *Handbook of Historical Linguistics*, ed. Brian Joseph and Richard Janda (Oxford: Wiley-Blackwell, 2003), 425–40.

usage. Thus in John 6:66–69, the perfect of πιστεύω ("believe, trust") and γινώσκω ("know") may be used to express the meaning *come to believe* and *come to know* in example 20.

EXAMPLE 20

εἶπεν οὖν ὁ Ἰησοῦς τοῖς δώδεκα, Μὴ καὶ ὑμεῖς θέλετε ὑπάγειν; ἀπεκρίθη αὐτῷ Σίμων Πέτρος, Κύριε, πρὸς τίνα ἀπελευσόμεθα; ῥήματα ζωῆς αἰωνίου ἔχεις, καὶ ἡμεῖς **πεπιστεύκαμεν** καὶ **ἐγνώκαμεν** ὅτι σὺ εἶ ὁ ἅγιος τοῦ θεοῦ.

Jesus then said to the twelve, "Don't you also want to leave?" Simon Peter answered him, "Lord, to whom would we go? You have words of eternal life, and we have **come to believe** and **know** that you are the Holy One of God." (John 6:67–69)

In the larger discourse, Jesus's teaching is difficult for some to accept. Jesus asks the Twelve if they want to leave too. Peter replies that they have come into a state of belief and knowledge about Jesus that is too significant to ignore: he is the Holy One of God. Similarly, ἔχω ("have") may be used to express the meaning *come to have*, as in Romans 5:2 in example 21.

EXAMPLE 21

δι᾽ οὗ καὶ τὴν προσαγωγὴν **ἐσχήκαμεν** τῇ πίστει εἰς τὴν χάριν ταύτην . . .

Through whom also **we have come to have / have obtained** access by faith into this grace . . . (Rom. 5:2)

The other option is to adapt the meaning of the perfect to the stative verb like this: normal perfects refer to event completion or result state (see fig. 3.7).

Figure 3.7
Perfect Usage

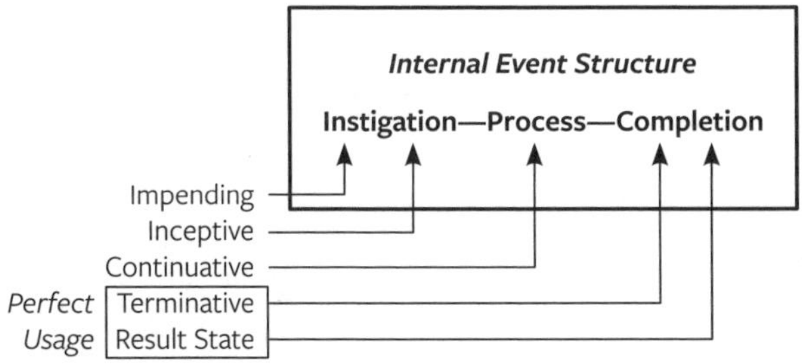

Some types of states may be construed as scalar, without any discrete boundary (see fig. 3.8).

Figure 3.8
Scalar State

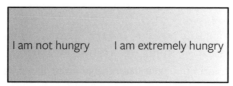

I am not hungry   I am extremely hungry

The result state denoted by the perfect is treated analogically as the highest degree of a state by mapping the event's structure over the scale of states.[25] Indeed, some English aspectual adverbs also share this function, as in example 22. This is an *intensive* usage.

EXAMPLE 22

a. "I'm hungry" versus "I'm **completely** famished."

b. "John is exhausted" versus "John is **totally** exhausted."

The adverbs "totally" and "completely" normally refer to the final phase of an event, but when used with a state they also refer to the highest degree of a state. We find comparable usage with ἀσθενέω ("be sick") in example 23, βδελύσσομαι ("abhor") in example 24, and πιστεύω ("believe") in example 25. This is an *intensive* usage.

EXAMPLE 23

a. Perfective aorist: ἠσθένησα καὶ ἐπεσκέψασθέ με.
   I was sick and you cared for me. (Matt. 25:36)

b. Perfect: κατὰ ἀτιμίαν λέγω, ὡς ὅτι ἡμεῖς **ἠσθενήκαμεν.**
   To my shame, I say, that we **were too weak!** (2 Cor. 11:21)

EXAMPLE 24

a. Perfective aorist: ἐμίσησαν ἐν πύλαις ἐλέγχοντα, καὶ λόγον ὅσιον **ἐβδε-λύξαντο.**

---

25. Grammarians have recognized this pattern. Albert Rijksbaron notes, "In the case of verbs whose present stem forms [i.e., non-past, imperfective] already to some degree express a state, the perfect expresses the highest degree of that state (so-called intensive perfect)." Albert Rijksbaron, *The Syntax and Semantics of the Verb in Classical Greek*, 3rd ed. (Chicago: University of Chicago Press, 2003), 38.

They hated the barrister at the gates, and a pious word **they abhorred.**
(Amos 5:10 LXX)

b. Perfect: ἐβδελυγμένα δὲ ἐναντίον ἐμοῦ χείλη ψευδῆ.

[Because my throat will practice truth,] lies **are utterly disgusting**
before my lips. (Prov. 8:7 LXX)

EXAMPLE 25

ἐγὼ **πεπίστευκα** ὅτι σὺ εἶ ὁ χριστὸς ὁ υἱὸς τοῦ θεοῦ.

[Jesus said to her, "I am the resurrection and the life. Whoever believes in me,
even if they die, will live. Everyone who lives and believes in me will never
die. Do you believe this?" She answered him, "Yes, Lord.] I **most certainly
believe** that you are the Messiah, the Son of God." (John 11:25–27)

Other stative verbs that allow intensive readings in the perfect are included
in table 3.5.

Table 3.5 Stative Verbs

ἀγαπάω	love
διψάω	be thirsty
ἐλπίζω	hope
ἐπιθυμέω	desire
θαυμάζω	be amazed
θέλω	want, wish
θυμόομαι	be angry
κάμνω	be tired
μεθύω	be drunk
μεριμνάω	be anxious; care for (someone)
μισέω	hate
πάσχω	suffer; experience
πλουτέω	be rich
φοβέομαι	be afraid

However, because both these uses (the inchoative and the intensive) are
analogically motivated, they run the risk of semantic bleaching. This is a
process of language change by which a construction is used with such a high
frequency that its meaning grows weaker.[26] It has already affected perfects

---

26. Bernd Heine, *Auxiliaries: Cognitive Forces and Grammaticalization* (Oxford: Oxford
University Press, 1993), 54.

like οἶδα, "know," which was a lexicalized perfect already in Homer.[27] The nature of such language-change processes requires us to be cautious to avoid overinterpreting perfects formed from stative verbs.

■ Summary

Organizing verbs by transitivity and asking some questions about the number of participants illustrates a few important points about the perfect. First, perfects have a clear preference for change-of-state verbs. In practice this means that the perfect is used to present situations as involving event-completion and result-state phases of aspect structure. Second, there is a clear preference for the subject to be the experiencer of that state, whether through transitivity shifts or voice alternations in the perfect.

The highest-transitivity verbs have *only* intransitive perfects.

- The subject of the perfect exists in a result state.
- That result-state perfect exists paradigmatically alongside the *transitive* non-perfects.
- The object of the transitive non-perfect is the subject of the intransitive perfect.
- Since the perfect is intransitive, some are active-only, and others are middle-only.

The mid-transitivity verbs have transitive perfects.

- The subject is an agent that is still affected by the event.
- The object is in a resultant state relative to the event's completion.
- Perfects are *transitive* in the active voice and *intransitive* in the middle voice.
  ἀπέσταλκα ("I have sent [a messenger]") ↔ ἀπέσταλμαι ("I am sent")
  γεγράφα ("I have written [a letter]") ↔ γεγράπται ("It is written")

The low-transitivity and intransitive verbs have low-transitivity and intransitive perfects.

- The subject is the affected participant.
- Both event-completion and result-state readings are effectively indistinguishable.

27. See K. L. McKay, "On the Perfect and Other Aspects in New Testament Greek," *Novum Testamentum* 23, no. 4 (1981): 289–329.

- Transitivity and voice alternations have lexical idiosyncrasies.

  μεμάθηκα ("I have learned" = I know [+ acc.] ↔ [*active-only*])

  ἠγώνισμαι ("I have fought to the end" [+ acc.] ↔ [*middle-only*])

Stative verbs, generally, do not form perfects. When they do, they follow two possible patterns. One extends the semantics of the stative verb to adapt to the perfect. The other extends the perfect to adapt to the semantics of the stative verb.

- πιστεύω ("believe") → πεπιστεύκα ("have come to believe")
- μεθύω ("be drunk") → μεμεθύσμαι ("be completely drunk")

In summary, the usage of the perfect, while affected by other features of grammar and lexicon, does maintain consistency in meaning. By paying attention to how many participants there are in a clause, how participants are affected by the event, and how energy is transferred from one to another, you have all the skills and information you need for evaluating on your own how the perfect is used in the New Testament or even why one grammar says one thing and another sounds completely different.

4

The Greek Middle Voice

An Important Rediscovery and Implications for Teaching and Exegesis

JONATHAN T. PENNINGTON

■ **The Voice of the Traitors**

There's an Italian proverb, "Traduttore traditore," which we translate into English (somewhat ironically and treasonously) as "Translator, traitor."[1] In either language this proverb can be read and applied in sundry ways, one of which is to highlight something that all bilingual people know: different languages map reality in different ways. Therefore, while communication between speakers of different languages is possible and happens all the time, in translation there is always some degree of transformation, some mismatch, some remainder, and some plus, which can playfully (and sometimes more seriously)[2] be described as treachery or treason. Of course, one of the many

---

1. This informs the insightful chapter by Moisés Silva, "Are Translators Traitors? Some Personal Reflections," in *The Challenge of Bible Translation*, ed. Glen Scorgie, Mark Strauss, and Steven Voth (Grand Rapids: Zondervan, 2003), 37–50. There is a comparable Hungarian saying, "Fordítás: ferdítés," roughly translated, "Translation is distortion."

2. A couple of famous international examples from the mid-twentieth century are (1) when Nikita Khrushchev's Cold War response to the American government was rendered as "We will bury you" instead of the better "We will outlast you"; and (2) when just days before the bomb was dropped on Hiroshima, the prime minister of Japan Kantaro Suzuki responded to Harry

ironies of such an assertion is that what an Italian thinks of as "treachery" or "treason" will never be identical to what an English speaker reading this sentence thinks of, thereby proving the proverb!

Pondering the complexities of translation and thinking of translation as some kind of inevitable and playful "treason" is nothing new; it is a problem as old as post–Tower of Babel human existence.[3] But scholars continue to discover ways in which this treason has occurred that we didn't previously realize, situations where we have assumed we understood what a text is saying, but its meaning was lost in translation. This is especially frequent in the study of ancient texts, which come from languages and cultures very different from our own. Unlike during simultaneous translations at the United Nations or with an English teacher and her ESOL students, no immediate feedback is available to indicate that a misunderstanding has occurred. Quite the opposite: these ancient texts are passive. They speak but cannot respond to or clarify later readers' misunderstandings of what they are saying. Thus it is frighteningly easy for later readers, even sincere scholarly interpreters, to misunderstand what a text is saying because of an unrecognized mismatch between the cultures and languages that produced a text and the later receivers.[4]

Such mismatches of language and culture that lead to misunderstandings are legion and are born from many sources. Sometimes the language mismatches are lexical (different word concepts), sometimes they are syntactical (different ways languages structure words together), and sometimes they are grammatical (different ways languages communicate through word forms). One area of inevitable mismatch between Koine-era Greek and modern English is the grammatical category of voice. Generally in linguistics, "voice" refers to the relationship of the action of a verb and its participants, whether the patient or the agent. The reason there is an inevitable and unavoidable

---

Truman with "mokusatsu," which means, "No comment. We need more time," but which was instead translated as "silent contempt." For further reflections, see Mark Polizzotti, "Why Mistranslation Matters," *New York Times*, July 28, 2018, https://www.nytimes.com/2018/07 /28/opinion/sunday/why-mistranslation-matters.html.

3. For some helpful explorations of the history and philosophy of translation theories, see Umberto Eco, *Mouse or Rat? Translation as Negotiation* (London: Phoenix, 2003); Charles Taylor, *The Language Animal: The Full Shape of the Human Linguistic Capacity* (Cambridge, MA: Harvard University Press, 2016); Rainer Schulte and John Biguenet, *Theories of Translation: An Anthology of Essays from Dryden to Derrida* (Chicago: University of Chicago Press, 1992).

4. Language is embedded in culture, in what Umberto Eco calls the "cultural encyclopedia" of each culture, with its narratives, assumptions, evocations, sensibilities, and resonances. Therefore, translation across time and space inevitably involves many layers of "treason." Umberto Eco, *A Theory of Semiotics* (Bloomington: Indiana University Press, 1976); Umberto Eco, *Kant and the Platypus: Essays on Language and Cognition* (New York: Harcourt, Brace, 1997), 224–79.

mismatch between these two languages is seen in the most basic issue that Greek and English have a different system of voices. English has two voices: active and passive. Greek has three: active, middle, and passive. This does not mean that the translation of voice between Greek and English is impossible, of course, but it does mean that the mismatch will easily go beyond mere inconvenience to outright treason. Or to speak less dramatically and more technically, this difference in the voice structure will often cause some confusion when translating from Greek into English, and sometimes, worse than confusion: translators and interpreters will often not even recognize that a mismatch has occurred. This latter state is in fact what has been occurring in English translations and exegesis of New Testament Greek texts for many generations. This lack of recognition has been perpetuated by a number of misrepresentations of the Greek voice system meant to be helpful but based on the misstep of interpreting Greek through the lens of other languages, particularly Latin and then later, English. In this chapter we will explore this misstep (called "deponency") and offer the rediscovered genius of the Greek middle voice, concluding with some suggestions for how this rediscovery might help our exegesis of Greek texts.

Employees Must Wash Hands

In one of my favorite examples of linguistic vandalism, some clever souls defaced the instructions on the ubiquitous public bathroom hand dryers. The normal sign, reading "Employees Must Wash Hands," was modified with the addition, "Or you can do it yourself if they're not available." The brilliance of this little bit of cleverness is that it plays on the ambiguity of the English verb "to wash," which, like many English verbs, can be used transitively or intransitively, with no morphological distinction. The pun functions well because the assumption in the command to "wash" is that it will be understood intransitively—that employees must wash *their own hands*—but with the additional instructions, the verb is being interpreted transitively, creating the mentally jarring, funny scenario of employees washing each customer's hands for them. Such is language, and such is the possibility of misinterpretation, often with humorous results.

This example serves well for our discussion here of the differences between the English voice system and the Greek system, which has a middle voice. First, although for native English speakers the idea that the verb is to be interpreted intransitively is so assumed that the other morphologically possible option is not even considered (hence the effectiveness of the joke), imagine a non-native speaker from the present or the future trying to interpret the hand dryer sign: it takes something more than knowledge of language to interpret the command; understanding of cultural customs will inevitably influence the interpretation. Is this a responsibility or expectation of twenty-first-century United States culture that employees of a business wash customers' hands? It's not impossible, and the command itself does not clarify apart from knowledge of cultural customs and sensibilities. Language is embedded in culture, and different languages map reality in different ways in a chicken-and-egg relationship, mutually informing and creating such that "Which came first?" is impossible to definitively discern. Applying this to our discussion at hand (no pun intended), we must start with an acknowledgment that the way English speakers conceive of and use the verbal voice system does not necessarily correspond well to the usage in the Greek system, reflecting different ways to conceptualize certain relationships and embodied activities.

Second, our hand-washing jest is appropriate to the misinterpretation of the Greek voice system in the Anglophone world because a common misunderstanding and misassumption about the Greek middle voice has been that it is functioning reflexively. Thus, one will often find explanations in elementary Greek grammars that the Greek middle is the form used to express reflexivity. This is an understandable attempt to make sense of an entirely foreign voice form by connecting it to something familiar in English. Examples such as the Greek middle form being used when Judas "hanged himself" are common. From an English perspective this gives a handhold desperately needed when climbing the sheer rock face of Greek learning, especially at the impasse of the voice system. The problem is that this use of the Greek middle is not actually functioning as a reflexive. This usage is appropriate for Judas hanging himself, for other reasons—namely, as we will see below, because a subject-affected/focused voice form is appropriate for such a self-affected action. When Greek wants to communicate reflexivity (in a comparably English sense), it does so frequently by a means other than the middle voice, with the Greek reflexive pronoun.

The Recent Discussion of the Greek Middle Voice (with Some Indulgent Autobiography)

A lot has been happening in our understanding of Koine Greek in the last twenty-five years, with many of the leaders of these changes contributing to the present volume. Many of these changes have centered on the Greek verb—how it functions and what it communicates (or doesn't) through its morphology. Most of this discussion and debate has focused on the complex issues of tense and aspect (see chap. 2).

But another, secondary element of our reevaluation and growth in understanding of the Greek verbal system has to do with voice and, especially, the trickiest and most unfamiliar part of the Greek voice system, the middle voice. This chapter will survey the recent discussion of the Greek middle voice and suggest some ways forward. My survey here will be somewhat autobiographical because I have had the privilege to be present at the river source of these discussions and to float along with them over the last fifteen years, occasionally putting my paddle in the water and suggesting which fork to take as we proceed.

In *Advances in the Study of Greek*, Constantine Campbell provides a brief survey of recent developments regarding the middle voice and, particularly, the topic of debate, whether Greek middle verbs should ever be classified as "deponent."[5] As noted, I have been involved in this discussion and have continued to argue against using the category of "deponent" to describe and understand the Greek middle voice. To explain my own views and arguments I will survey my own journey of inquiry and understanding that has evolved over time. Starting back in 1998, I was working on a vocabulary list for audio recordings of Greek words in frequency order.[6] As I compiled this list, looking up every Greek word in various lexicons to determine the best and most frequent English glosses, I began to notice some inconsistency in how lexical headword forms (the form of the verb used for the lexicon entry) were given. This inconsistency related to the voice in which the headword forms were provided. In modern grammars verbs that were called "deponent" were classified as such because they existed in middle forms only, supposedly having "laid aside" (Latin, *deponere*) their active forms. This is what I had been taught and had taught others. However, I noticed two inconsistencies. First, there were many words whose headword form was given in the middle voice (-ομαι, indicating that these words must be deponent and therefore always, or mostly, occur in middle forms). However, actual occurrences of some of these verbs show that the usage was mixed—sometimes middle, sometimes active. Second, the opposite phenomenon also occasionally occurred: verbs whose headword form was given in the active voice (-ω) but whose actual usage was consistently middle. Moreover, the lexicons were often inconsistent in whether they presented a word in the active or middle forms. For example, for the word φοβέω / φοβέομαι ("I fear"), some lexicons and grammars list this in the simple active indicative form (-εω) while others list the middle/passive

---

5. Constantine R. Campbell, "Deponency and the Middle Voice," in *Advances in the Study of Greek: New Insights for Reading the New Testament* (Grand Rapids: Zondervan, 2015), 91–104.

6. Jonathan T. Pennington, *New Testament Greek Vocabulary* (Grand Rapids: Zondervan, 2001).

φοβέομαι (thereby communicating deponency). The same is true for σέβω / σεβέομαι ("I worship") and several others. All these inconsistencies revealed some confusion and caused me to begin to ask how the classification of "deponency" was determined. Is this purely a matter of extant morphological forms? If so, what corpus of literature do we use to determine this? How does the grammatical understanding of deponency relate to these decisions?

As I began to dig deeper into the subject of the grammar of deponency, I found comments that expressed some degree of uncertainty regarding our understanding of deponency. This uncertainty was surprising to me as one who had been taught deponency as a basic (if somewhat confusing) component of Greek grammar. For example, Stanley Porter wrote, "There is room for much more work in areas related to Greek voice. One of those areas is deponent verbs."[7] Similarly, Dan Wallace commented that "the criteria for determining deponency still await a definitive treatment."[8] Going back to earlier grammarians, I was surprised to find an even stronger sentiment, typically expressed in disparaging remarks about the whole category of deponency. James Hope Moulton called the idea of Greek deponency "unsatisfactory."[9] Even more stoutly, A. T. Robertson, who always puts "deponency" in scare quotes, wrote: "The truth is that [the term] should not be used at all."[10] This only served to pique my interest even more. How could it be that something so standard as deponency was so profoundly questioned by the leading grammarians?

So I did what any overly eager MDiv student would do: I pursued an independent study with my mentor, Professor Robert Yarbrough, exploring the question of deponency. By the end of that semester, I determined that something was awry. This became my first published article[11] and my first paper presentation at the Biblical Greek Language and Linguistics section of the Society of Biblical Literature (SBL), the same place where all the discussion about verbal aspect was happening. Through my connections with Zondervan, I met and struck up a friendship with the delightful Bernard Taylor, an older scholar who had been working in Greek lexicography for a long time

7. Stanley E. Porter, *Idioms of the Greek New Testament*, 2nd ed. (Sheffield: Sheffield Academic, 1994), 63.

8. Daniel B. Wallace, *Greek Grammar beyond the Basics* (Grand Rapids: Zondervan, 1996), 430n65.

9. James Hope Moulton, *Prolegomena*, vol. 1 of *A Grammar of New Testament Greek*, 3rd ed. (Edinburgh: T&T Clark, 1908), 153.

10. A. T. Robertson, *A Grammar of the Greek New Testament in the Light of Historical Research*, 4th ed. (Nashville: Broadman, 1923), 332; see also pp. 811–13.

11. Jonathan T. Pennington, "Deponency in Koiné Greek: The Grammatical Question and the Lexicographical Dilemma," *Trinity Journal* 24 (Spring 2003): 55–76.

and had come to similar conclusions through his lexical work.[12] We met, shared notes, and realized we were on to something important: deponency is problematic. In that SBL paper and subsequent article, I laid out my thesis:

> Deponency is a grammatical category that has been misapplied to Greek because of the influence of Latin grammar and our unfamiliarity with the meaning of the Greek middle voice. Most if not all verbs that are traditionally considered "deponent" are truly middle in meaning. Therefore, the use of the category of deponency—"verbs that are middle-passive in form but active in meaning"—needs to be minimized at least, and possibly rejected all together.[13]

After explaining how deponency has been defined, I proceeded to examine the history of the Greek verb voice system, which originally had no passive voice (this was a later development) but consisted of a binary mode between verbs that were active and middle (that's our later English term, not the Greeks'). In the active voice, the subject does the action of the verb, and in the middle, the subject also does the action of the verb but in some way that entails a greater subject-affectedness or involvement. This is not so much reflexivity but action on, for, or toward oneself. Many verbs are natural candidates for this type of action, such as shaving, giving an answer, walking (as opposed to traveling by horseback or ship), and receiving. Indeed, many of these Greek verbs are middle-only in form, not because they have somehow lost or laid aside their active forms but precisely because they are subject-affected in some way, a conceptualization that the Greek language is aware of and tends to distinguish with the middle voice form. I discovered that, even though these works are typically off the radar of biblical scholars, there had already been robust discussion of the middle voice in multiple languages, including in Greek. Scholars like Suzanne Kemmer had long identified this large category of middle-only verbs that included verbal ideas such as the actions just described, and also including other subject-affected/subject-focused concepts such reciprocity, intellectual activities, emotional states, volitional activities, sensory reception, and various states and involuntary conditions.[14]

---

12. While I was wrestling with these same issues, unbeknownst to me, Bernard Taylor was already formulating his thoughts as they related to producing his lexicon. (See Bernard Taylor, "Deponency and Greek Lexicography" [paper presented to the joint session of the International Organization for Septuagint and Cognate Studies and the Biblical Lexicography section, at the Annual Meeting of the Society of Biblical Literature, Denver, CO, November 17–20, 2001]). This became a chapter by the same name in Bernard Taylor, ed., *Biblical Greek Language and Lexicography: Essays in Honor of Frederick W. Danker* (Grand Rapids: Eerdmans, 2004), 161–76.

13. Pennington, "Deponency in Koiné Greek," 61.

14. Suzanne Kemmer, *The Middle Voice* (Amsterdam: Benjamins, 1993). Also, an early attempt to rethink this issue can be found in Neva Miller, "A Theory of Deponent Verbs," in

In this article I went on to suggest that the reason we had lost this Greek self-understanding and replaced it with the notion of such middle-only verbs being somehow defective (deponent) is twofold. First is the undue influence of Latin grammar and usage on our understanding of Greek, beginning especially in the Renaissance, when Greek was reintroduced to the West. Not coincidentally, Latin has a group of verbs that appear in the passive form but are active in meaning, which came to be labeled as "deponent." This ready-to-hand description proved too convenient and easy as a way to (mis)understand what was happening in these seemingly odd Greek middle-only verbs. The same thing was happening in the way in which the Greek verbal system was understood during this time period in regard to tense, time, and aspect, a misstep that has only begun to be corrected in the last thirty years. Latin's dominance and on-the-surface similarity to Greek proved overly influential, resulting in the introduction of a Latin term to explain the Greek middle verbs, a weapon at the scene that indicated foul play may have occurred.[15]

The second, comparable wrong turn that resulted in the creation of the category of Greek deponency was that of examining and teaching Greek from the perspective of English grammar. As with Latin or any other language, one inevitably begins with one's native conceptualization to first understand and then explain the foreign language being learned. Because English does not have a verbal form that encodes or marks for the idea of subject-affectedness, it was natural and easy for English speakers to misunderstand these Greek oddities as again somehow defective, borrowing that mistaken Latin term "deponency." Thus the genius of the Greek middle was killed; though it was not done maliciously, in the linguistics courts it would be deemed Involuntary Voiceslaughter.

I then turned to address a couple of potential problems with my evaluation: phenomena within Greek that seem to imply something like deponency is indeed happening. In the cases of both "future middles" and "passive deponents," I suggested that these seeming supporting bits of evidence for deponency can and should be easily explained in another way.[16] In the case of future middles, where an active form in the present stem appears as a middle in the future stem,[17] I follow the lead of other linguists who observe that this

---

Analytical Lexicon of the Greek New Testament, ed. Barbara Friberg, Timothy Friberg, and Neva F. Miller (Grand Rapids: Baker Academic, 2000), 423–30.

15. Pennington, "Deponency in Koiné Greek," 62–64.

16. Pennington, "Deponency in Koiné Greek," 67–68.

17. Examples include ἀναβαίνω → ἀναβήσομαι; ἐσθίω → φάγομαι; λαμβάνω → λήμψομαι; πίνω → πίομαι. Note that many of these are suppletive as well (i.e., they use forms from different cognates).

makes sense within the Greek middle conceptualization because by nature the future tense-form is an imagined mental reality, thus fitting well into the middle category. In the case of passive deponents, we find verbs that are middle-only in the present tense-form but when they appear in the aorist form take on the passive rather than middle endings.[18] For those interpreting the verbal system through deponency, this appears to be evidence for some kind of loss of form, but there is a linguistic and historic explanation that makes much more sense within the Greek system. Simply, over time the more familiar productive form for producing aorist passive endings (the strong θη) was encroaching into the aorist middle space. This encroachment was especially likely when a (non-native) speaker was faced with creating the aorist form of a middle-only verb whose stem ends in a liquid or nasal, thus requiring knowledge of how to handle the aorist middle's sigma-tense formative that must drop and be compensated for within the lexeme. It was simply much easier to use the aorist passive forms in this situation, with no loss of understanding to the hearer. Indeed, we find that in such verbs (such as ἀποκρίνομαι) some speakers use the technically proper aorist middle form while most instead use the technically improper aorist passive (ἀπεκρίθη). Thus, once again, the so-called passive deponents are not evidence for the existence of Greek deponency but instead reflect basic linguistic borrowing and speech patterns within the sophisticated Greek middle system.

Finally, in the article I came back around to what initially piqued my inquiry into this whole issue: how to handle the middle voice in Greek lexicons. I examined the problem and suggested that we need to broaden the literary corpus beyond Biblical Greek to make such decisions. We should then consistently use the middle form of the headword if that is the consistent usage within this corpus. I also suggested that with some words, the lack of understanding of the Greek middle system has created a confusion with the sense of some lexemes, namely, in the case where the stems of two different verbs are homographs—that is, spelled the same way. For example, it could be that ἅπτω ("to light") and ἅπτομαι ("to touch") or ἄρχω ("to rule") and ἄρχομαι ("to begin") are not actually the same word in two different voices but are in fact two distinct words, one that is active and the other a middle-only verb, with stems that are homonyms (cf. the different English words that are identified only by their pronunciations, "lead"/"lead"; "resent"/"re-sent"; "recover"/"re-cover"; "putting"/"putting").[19]

18. Note that it is only in the future and aorist tense-forms in the Hellenistic period that one can distinguish between middle and passive. In the present, imperfect, and perfect stems, the middle and passive forms have collapsed together. These are sometimes referred to as medio-passive.

19. Pennington, "Deponency in Koiné Greek," 69–75.

The result of my initial foray into rediscovering the middle voice was that Porter, who was the convener of the Biblical Greek Language and Linguistics group at SBL, invited me to further explore this topic in an edited volume titled *The Linguist as Pedagogue*.[20] In my chapter in this book, I rehearse some of the same arguments but also provide a more extensive discussion informed by crosslinguistic studies of other languages that also code for subject-affectedness, including Sanskrit, Icelandic, and Mohave. Also, in accord with the volume's title, I offer some suggestions for how to teach the Greek middle voice and let it have a voice, while not writing off the seemingly odd middles as deponent and also being aware that these rediscovered middles are not necessarily exegetically significant. They may be simply an embedded aspect of the language whose nuances must be taken on a case-by-case basis.

As mentioned, though I was early in the public discourse and questioned deponency in publications, I was certainly not the first or the most knowledgeable to write about these issues. Taylor continued to reflect on this issue and published some of his work. Also, my senior in insight and stature was Carl Conrad, who had long before offered an alternative understanding of the Greek middle voice on the old B-Greek website.[21] Additionally, the world of New Testament Greek started listening to the broader linguistic discussion of Greek outside of biblical studies, as with the important work of Rutger Allan.[22]

As a result, steam was building, resulting in two sessions at SBL dedicated just to the topic of the Greek middle voice. In 2010 we convened a session that included papers by Porter, Taylor, Campbell, and me. There was general consensus that it was time to significantly revise the way we have conceived of the Greek voice system, including a rejection of deponency as a category.[23]

---

20. Jonathan T. Pennington, "Setting Aside 'Deponency' and Rediscovering the Middle Voice for New Testament Studies," in *The Linguist as Pedagogue: Trends in the Teaching and Linguistic Analysis of the Greek New Testament*, ed. Stanley Porter and Matthew Brook O'Donnell (Sheffield: Sheffield Phoenix, 2009), 183–205.

21. See Carl Conrad, "New Observations on Voice in the Ancient Greek Verb" (unpublished paper, Washington University in St. Louis, November 19, 2002), https://pages.wustl.edu/files/pages/imce/cwconrad/newobsancgrkvc.pdf, 6–7. See also the complementary discussion in E. J. W. Barber, "Beyond the Passive," in *Proceedings of the First Annual Meeting of the Berkeley Linguistics Society* (Berkeley: Berkeley Linguistics Society, 1975), 19–21. Visit B-Greek at ibiblio.org/bgreek/forum.

22. Rutger J. Allan, *The Middle Voice in Ancient Greek: A Study in Polysemy*, Amsterdam Studies in Classical Philology 11 (Amsterdam: Gieben, 2003).

23. Around this same time one of Dan Wallace's students at Dallas Theological Seminary, Ludwig Stratton, was working on a dissertation arguing *for* the importance and retention of the category of deponency. Those of us involved in the discussion eventually read this dissertation, which, while providing some insights, was not found to be convincing or persuasive.

For my paper, I took the next step beyond conceptualization and tried to apply the revised understanding of the Greek middle to actual texts to see what could be learned. While writing my "Test-Driving the Theory—Middle Voice Forms in Matthew," I continued to grow in my understanding and appreciation of the work of Conrad and others, adopting his terminology of MP1 and MP2 forms. Conrad helpfully categorizes the voice system into two different medio-passive forms, the -μαι/-σαι/-ται pattern (MP1) and the -θη pattern (MP2).[24] On the practical side, I worked through many middle verbs and forms in the Gospel of Matthew, noting the difficulty of determining at points which occurrences are middles and which passives. I also noted several examples of words that may have some nuanced differences between their active and middle forms (αἰτέω), some middle-only verbs whose headword forms are incorrect (εὐαγγελίζομαι, σεβέομαι, φοβέομαι), and some examples of MP2 forms encroaching on MP1 forms (ἀποκρίνομαι, φοβέομαι, πορεύομαι). I concluded this paper with an appeal for more work to be done in a number of areas related to the Greek middle: standardization for lexical headword forms, improvement in the morphological tagging with regard to the middle in our Greek digital databases, and reexamination of text-critical decisions with these new insights into the importance of the middle.

Three years later we convened yet another Biblical Greek Language and Linguistics session to drive home the issue of the Greek middle, under the rather violent-sounding banner "We've Killed Deponency. Where Next?" Invited papers were once again given by me, Taylor, and, to our great honor and pleasure, the classicist Allan, whose work has become the definitive statement on the middle voice.[25] My own small contribution to this discussion reflected my own growing understanding, including much help from my former student Bobby Jamieson, who co-wrote the paper with me. The two biggest areas where we explored the importance of the Greek middle voice were transitivity and markedness.

Transitivity

First, a word about the relationship of voice and transitivity. How does middle voice relate to transitivity? Some scholars have argued that the middle voice is valency-reducing; that is, it reduces the number of a verb's "arguments" or verbal adjuncts. On this view, the middle voice de-transitivizes a

24. See Carl Conrad, "Active, Middle, and Passive: Understanding Ancient Greek Voice" (unpublished paper, Washington University in St. Louis, December 16, 2003), https://pages.wustl.edu/files/pages/imce/cwconrad/undancgrkvc.pdf.
25. Allan, *Middle Voice in Ancient Greek*.

prototypical active, transitive verb, rendering it intransitive.[26] However, again following Allan, it seems to me that with respect to transitivity the middle voice is a marked coding of a departure from the prototypical transitive verb event, while not rendering the verb "intransitive" per se.[27]

To unpack this concept we need to back up a bit and first establish the prototype. Recent linguistic studies have established that transitivity is not an absolute category but a relative one; that is, transitivity occurs along a spectrum rather than as a binary on-off switch.[28] In their seminal article, Paul Hopper and Sandra Thompson list a number of features that define a prototypical transitive clause: two participants; the action is telic, punctual, and volitional; the agent is high in potency; and the object is highly affected.[29] Building on Hopper and Thompson, Talmy Givón has argued that the two most salient properties determining transitivity are agency and affectedness. In a prototypical transitive sentence, there is a visible, volitional, controlling agent (or cause) and a clearly visible result-registering patient (or effect).[30] And, of course, in the prototypical transitive clause, the agent is coded by the grammatical subject, the patient is coded by the direct object, and the verb is in the active voice.[31]

Seen in this light, the middle voice encodes a departure from prototypical transitivity in that the agent and grammatical subject of the verb in some way undergoes the effect of the event. As Allan notes, "This effect can be of a physical or a mental nature, and it can be direct or indirect (in that it involves an external object)."[32] In other words, even where a middle verb involves an object external to the subject/agent, the action is conceived as affecting the subject, not merely the external object—that is, the agent is also in some sense the patient.

For example, Matthew 27:35 reads, σταυρώσαντες δὲ αὐτὸν διεμερίσαντο τὰ ἱμάτια αὐτοῦ ("After crucifying him they divided his clothing"). The middle διεμερίσαντο does take τὰ ἱμάτια as an external object, but the action is not prototypically transitive. Before the soldiers (the plural subject of the verb) divide the clothes, the clothes are in an unspecified state and, saliently, not in the possession of the soldiers. But after the soldiers have divided his clothes,

26. See discussion in Allan, *Middle Voice in Ancient Greek*, 53–56.
27. Allan, *Middle Voice in Ancient Greek*, 19.
28. See, e.g., the seminal study Paul J. Hopper and Sandra A. Thompson, "Transitivity in Grammar and Discourse," *Language* 56 (1980): 251–99.
29. Hopper and Thompson, "Transitivity in Grammar and Discourse," 252.
30. Talmy Givón, *Syntax: A Functional-Typological Introduction*, vol. 1 (Amsterdam: Benjamins, 1984), 20. Cited in Allan, *Middle Voice in Ancient Greek*, 8.
31. Cf. Allan, *Middle Voice in Ancient Greek*, 14.
32. Allan, *Middle Voice in Ancient Greek*, 19.

the clothes themselves have been parceled out and are now in the possession, variously, of each of the soldiers. In other words, the action represented by διεμερίσαντο does not finally terminate upon the clothes, which are the external object, but terminates upon the group of soldiers, in that the goal and end point of their action is their new subject-affected state of possessing a portion of Jesus's clothing. This is to say that the action of dividing the clothing results in a benefit and a change of state for the soldiers. Before the action, they did not possess Jesus's clothing, but after dividing his clothing they did. Compare this with what would have been the case if the soldiers had simply "divided" his clothing by tearing it to pieces and leaving it on the ground.[33] This action would have altered the clothing itself—thus constituting a prototypically transitive action—but would not have affected the subjects of the action in any notable way.

Again, I should reiterate that understanding the middle voice as a departure from prototypical transitivity does not entail the conclusion that all active verbs are transitive or that all middle verbs are intransitive. Instead, transitivity is a spectrum, and the active verb voice is one component of a high-transitive clause. Thus, the middle "de-transitivizes" a verb event in that it in some sense "bends" the action back toward the subject/agent.[34] E. J. W. Barber's work on the middle in Attic Greek nicely summarizes and pictorially represents what I have argued for here (see fig. 4.1).[35]

Figure 4.1
How Active and Middle Voice Direct Action

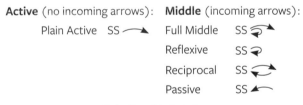

Barber, "Beyond the Passive," 21.

Barber points out that the active verb is the only Greek verbal phrase in which *no* arrows point back toward the subject (called the "surface subject"

---

33. Given the semantic nuances of διαμερίζω, Matthew would likely have used a different verb to describe an action like this. Yet there are examples of an active sense of διαμερίζω in, e.g., Deut. 32:8 LXX.

34. Here I am following the language of my colleague Peter Gentry in his Advanced Greek Grammar class notes on the middle voice.

35. See a broader discussion in Barber, "Beyond the Passive," 19–21. "SS" refers to "surface subject," which is to say "grammatical subject."

[SS]). In what she calls the "full middle," there is action that affects an external object (the outgoing arrow), which also impacts the agent (the looped arrow). A reflexive verb is an action, as the looped arrow indicates, in which the sentence subject acts in some manner upon itself. A reciprocal action is one in which multiple agents (subjects and objects) perform some action upon each other. And a passive verb event is one in which the subject undergoes an action performed by an external agent. Thus, Barber rightly views the Greek passive as a subspecies of middle. The point to note here is that all the verbal actions in the right column have an arrow pointing toward the grammatical subject. On the other hand, the active is the only verbal action in which no arrow points toward the subject. This, Barber rightly argues, encapsulates the basic polarity between the active and middle voices, and it does so in categories that manifestly entail a difference in transitivity.[36]

One final note on transitivity: the degree of transitivity of any verb phrase is determined in part by the degree of transitivity inherent in the verbal lexeme—that is, transitivity is in part lexeme-specific. Some verbs are inherently more transitive than others, and some are inherently intransitive, or stative, and so on. Yet, as we've noted, when a verb is employed that is capable of a range of transitivity, the middle voice de-transitivizes the verb phrase in some measure by identifying the agent with the undergoer of the action.

What is the cash value of this idea of the middle voice as a departure from prototypical transitivity? Simply this: particularly for speakers of a language such as English, which does not morphologically encode middle action, transitivity provides a useful lens to clarify the basic conceptual significance of the middle. In other words, the concept of transitivity, specifically a departure from prototypical (high) transitivity, clarifies that the difference between the active and middle voices resides in the end point or goal of the action. Prototypically, in the active voice the end point of the action is an object external to the agent, which we typically call a direct object. But in the middle voice, the end point of the action is in fact the subject, who is the agent of the verb. In the middle the action always "aims at" the subject in some sense, even when it also affects an external object.

The one exception to this in Koine Greek is the passive voice. Here I would briefly repeat that the passive, as Allan, Barber, Conrad, and others have argued, is in fact simply one species of middle; that is to say, the Greek middle

---

36. Barber also perceptively notes that in English, each of these types of action, except for the passive, is encoded by the active voice (Barber, "Beyond the Passive," 21). Thus, the English voice system marks subject agency versus nonsubject agency, an active-passive dichotomy, whereas the Greek voice system marks subject-affectedness and operates on an active-middle dichotomy.

voice encodes subject-affectedness. For the ancient Greeks, the distinction between subject agency and nonsubject agency was not deemed worthy of a categorical morphological distinction.[37]

MARKEDNESS

The other issue worthy of exploration is the relationship of the middle voice to markedness—that is, indicating some meaning by lexical form. I came to understand that the middle voice doesn't just encode subject-affectedness but is marked for it, as compared to the unmarked active voice. The Greek voice system is a binary encoding of active versus middle, the latter encoding subject-affectedness. In terms of marking, the active voice is non-marked, while the middle is marked as subject-affected.[38] This is significant because the default, non-marked active forms are indicating nothing explicitly about subject-affectedness, thus allowing there to be potentially subject-affected ideas in an active form, even though they are not marked as such. In other words, the middle forms are indicating some sense of subject-affectedness (even if historically that is now not easily discernible), while the active forms are not speaking to this issue either way. As a result the idea of middle subject-affectedness is in no way challenged by pointing to active forms that we would expect to be in the middle because they seem to be subject-affected notions. A subject-affected verb usage is not *required* to be in the middle voice, while middle forms are indicating some sense of subject-affectedness. Finally, Bobby Jamieson and I suggested that in teaching the Greek middle voice we should adopt the categories of MP1 and MP2 as well as the language of middle-only verbs rather than deponent. We also articulated a general rule of thumb to teach students when wrestling with middle and passive forms: when one sees a medio-passive form, begin with the assumption of subject-affected markedness, then ask whether the subject is the agent of the action or not, and then

---

37. See Conrad, "New Observations on Voice," 7–8.

38. See Allan, *Middle Voice in Ancient Greek*, 29. His conclusions regarding the markedness of the middle voice are worth reproducing in full: "Since the active voice can occur in environments in which the subject is affected (contextual neutralization), it can be concluded that the active is unspecified as to the semantic feature *subject-affectedness*. Conversely, the middle voice is semantically marked with respect to affectedness of the subject. As a consequence, event types that do not involve subject-affectedness cannot be expressed by a middle verb." See further Allan's discussion of apparently synonymous active-middle pairs on pp. 203–5 and the conclusion on pp. 246–47. Thanks are due to Mike Aubrey, whose post on this question drew my attention to material in Allan's work that I had not previously taken full account of. See Mike Aubrey, "Clarifying Allan & Kemmer on Middle Voice: Markedness," Koine Greek: Studies in Greek Language & Linguistics, January 16, 2011, http://evepheso.wordpress.com/2011/01/16 /clarifying-allan-kemmer-on-middle-voice-markedness.

translate into English appropriately as an English active (subject is agent) or an English passive (subject is not the agent).

This survey of developments in our understanding of the Greek middle over the last fifteen years has been largely autobiographical in part because of my ongoing involvement at the heart of these discussions, but more importantly, as a reflection of my own limits as a Greek scholar. I am no trained linguist, and my own areas of scholarly research and writing over the last fifteen years have been rather removed from the study of Koine Greek, focusing instead on literary, hermeneutic, and reception-history issues of the Gospels. As a result, my survey above speaks primarily from what I have come to understand about the Greek middle. Others, such as Liz Robar, Steve Runge, Dan Maketansky, and Mike and Rachel Aubrey, whose works on the subject I gladly recommend, have greater expertise in these areas and continue to work and write to improve our understanding.

■ Reading Biblical Greek Wisely

Based on the preceding survey, and with the suggestion for my readers to pursue other works on the Greek middle as well, I conclude this chapter with a few suggestions on how the rediscovery of the middle may have a positive impact on our reading of Biblical Greek. Overall, my suggestion is analogous to what I teach students about the complex and ongoing issues of Greek verbal aspect: Be wise and humble, and don't overstate opinions about the impact of any particular verb form. Be wary of any simplistic arguments based myopically and narrowly on a view of Biblical Greek verbs as alchemy that promises to turn lead into gold. This is not how languages work; they are replete with exceptions, subtleties, frozen forms, and inexplicable and mysterious habits.

With this humility and qualification in place, we can offer some potential insights that rediscovering the middle voice may provide in our reading of the biblical texts. First, with sensitivity to Greek's usage of a subject-affected encoded set of verbs, we may be able to discern nuances in certain verbs, especially in groups of words that share a semantic domain that contains both active-passive and middle-only verbs. For example, utilizing J. P. Louw and Eugene Nida's semantic-domain approach, we can examine the range of words that they classify in the categories of "hostility," "strife" (39.1–39.61), and "military activities" (55.1–55.25).[39] In these categories we find fifty-three words for fighting or struggling, twenty-nine of which are active verbs and

---

39. J. P. Louw and Eugene Nida, *Greek-English Lexicon of the New Testament: Based on Semantic Domains*, 2 vols., 2nd ed. (New York: United Bible Societies, 1989).

twenty-four of which are middle-only. There do seem to be some nuanced distinctions between the active verbs that communicate such ideas as waging war, persecuting, attacking, triumphing, conquering, overpowering, and instigating rebellion. By comparison, the sense of the middle-only verbs appears to be much more personal and psychological—personally opposing someone, contending for something, rising up in pride, struggling against or for a person or thing, joining in a verbal attack. Again, because an active verb is unmarked for subject-affectedness, relative to a middle-only verb, this analysis does not *require* the active verbs *not* to indicate subject-affectedness. Nevertheless, the middle-only verbs for fighting and struggling do seem to indicate a greater degree of this sense. The implications for non-native readers of these Greek texts is an openness to the interpretation and translation of these words in ways that indicate the same (as much as possible) in English.

Another potential implication of rediscovering the significance of the Greek middle is increased sensitivity to nuanced distinctions that may occur when a particular lexeme appears in both the active and middle forms. I stated above that a common mistake for English speakers in interpreting the Greek middle has been to take it as reflexive, as opposed to nonreflexive in the active. While this English-centric reading of the Greek voice system is not accurate, this does not mean that all active versus middle distinctions are nonexistent. Rather, with verbs that function with both active and middle forms there may be a kind of subject-affectedness that is inherent in the middle version of the lexeme. One such example is the verb "to ask, to request," the Greek lexeme αἰτε-, which can function as an active verb (αἰτέω) or as a middle (αἰτέομαι). Both voice forms existed in Classical Greek, the Septuagint, and the New Testament.[40] Over the course of the verb's development it appears that active forms were on the rise relative to the middle usage, but this could reflect the widespread usage of Greek as a secondary and tertiary language, resulting in the loss of such nuances as subject-affected middles, especially for speakers whose other tongues do not encode this way. BDF observes a distinction in Classical Greek, with the active αἰτέω being used for a request in general and the middle for asking for a loan or in a situation of commerce, a distinction that can be understood as subject-affected.[41] BDF suggests that the same distinction is up and running in the New Testament; BDAG disagrees.[42] My own study of the occurrences of αἰτέω / αἰτέομαι in the New Testament provides mixed results, making it difficult to generalize or be definitive. There

---

40. LXX (93): 55 middle, 37 active, 1 passive. NT (70): 32 middle, 38 active.

41. BDF §316, 2. They go on to say that, in general, in the NT the middle is used of requests in commerce and the active for requests addressed to God.

42. BDAG, 30.

·are several texts where the active and middle forms of the verb occur together, providing an interesting case for testing the theory.[43] In most of these, however, it is difficult to discern what differences are at play. This does not mean they are not there; it means only that whatever subtleties or ironies may be functioning are lost on non-native speakers (or at least this one). One text, James 4:2–3, is particularly interesting because of its alternation between the active and middle forms:

ἐπιθυμεῖτε καὶ οὐκ ἔχετε, φονεύετε καὶ ζηλοῦτε καὶ οὐ δύνασθε ἐπιτυχεῖν, μάχεσθε καὶ πολεμεῖτε, οὐκ ἔχετε διὰ τὸ μὴ **αἰτεῖσθαι** ὑμᾶς, **αἰτεῖτε** καὶ οὐ λαμβάνετε, διότι κακῶς **αἰτεῖσθε**, ἵνα ἐν ταῖς ἡδοναῖς ὑμῶν δαπανήσητε.

You desire and do not have, so you murder. You covet and cannot obtain, so you fight and quarrel. You do not have, because you do not **ask**. **You ask** and do not receive, because **you ask** wrongly, to spend it on your passions. (ESV)

Commentators often do not know what to do with this, providing various interpretations.[44] Joseph Mayor suggests that there is a distinction at work between the active and middle forms of the verb, with the active αἰτεῖτε referring here to using only the words of request, in distinction from the middle αἰτεῖσθε, which is asking in the proper spirit of prayer. When put into contrast with each other, the middle form highlights the inner, dynamic, subject-affected, prayerful request in contrast to the flat and generic asking.[45] He seems to be alone in this interpretation. Other commentators observe the connection with Matthew 7:7, interpreting James 4:3a as a direct allusion to Matthew 7:7, a reasonable interpretation in light of the deep connections between James and the Sermon on the Mount. The significance here is that James, whose Greek shows some sophistication, is using the middle forms, but he switches to the active to signal the connection to and source of Matthew 7:7, which uses the active.[46] This may indeed be enough of an explanation for the otherwise odd shift between forms in such a short text. Nonetheless, our

43. Matt. 20:20–22 // Mark 10:35–38; Mark 6:22–25; John 16:23–26; James 4:2–3; 1 John 5:14–16.

44. For a summary of the various views, see Ralph Martin, *James*, WBC (Waco: Word, 1988), 146–47; and Peter Davids, *The Epistle of James*, NIGTC (Grand Rapids: Eerdmans, 1982), 160.

45. Joseph B. Mayor, *The Epistle of St. James: The Greek Text with Introduction, Notes, Comments and Further Studies in the Epistle of St. James* (1913; repr., Grand Rapids: Zondervan, 1954), 137–38.

46. This is the suggestion that Dale Allison offers as well: "The switch from the middle to the active back to the middle may, then, be a sign of James' indebtedness to tradition, and perhaps evidence that he wished at least Christian readers to note his indebtedness." Dale C. Allison Jr., *James*, ICC (London: T&T Clark, 2013), 605.

rediscovery of the middle at least opens us up to ponder whether some other distinction may be at play.

Another text that may be revealing intended differences between the active and middle forms of αἰτέω is Mark 6:22–25. Once again, we have both voice forms appearing in one passage. In the dialogue recorded in John the Baptist's beheading, Herod uses the active form twice, while Herodias's daughter uses the middle form.[47]

> [22]καὶ εἰσελθούσης τῆς θυγατρὸς αὐτοῦ Ἡρῳδιάδος καὶ ὀρχησαμένης ἤρεσεν τῷ Ἡρῴδῃ καὶ τοῖς συνανακειμένοις. εἶπεν ὁ βασιλεὺς τῷ κορασίῳ αἴτησόν με ὃ ἐὰν θέλῃς, καὶ δώσω σοι [23]καὶ ὤμοσεν αὐτῇ [πολλὰ] ὅ τι ἐάν με **αἰτήσῃς** δώσω σοι ἕως ἡμίσους τῆς βασιλείας μου. [24]καὶ ἐξελθοῦσα εἶπεν τῇ μητρὶ αὐτῆς· τί **αἰτήσωμαι**; ἡ δὲ εἶπεν· τὴν κεφαλὴν Ἰωάννου τοῦ βαπτίζοντος. [25]καὶ εἰσελθοῦσα εὐθὺς μετὰ σπουδῆς πρὸς τὸν βασιλέα **ᾐτήσατο** λέγουσα θέλω ἵνα ἐξαυτῆς δῷς μοι ἐπὶ πίνακι τὴν κεφαλὴν Ἰωάννου τοῦ βαπτιστοῦ.

> [22]For when Herodias's daughter came in and danced, she pleased Herod and his guests. And the king said to the girl, "**Ask** me for whatever you wish, and I will give it to you." [23]And he vowed to her, "Whatever **you ask** me, I will give you, up to half of my kingdom." [24]And she went out and said to her mother, "For what **should I ask**?" And she said, "The head of John the Baptist." [25]And she came in immediately with haste to the king and **asked**, saying, "I want you to give me at once the head of John the Baptist on a platter." (Mark 6:22–25 ESV)

It is possible to see the Classical Greek distinction between asking generally (active) versus asking contractually (middle) at work here; that is, Herod, who has all the power, offers to grant this young girl any request she makes, up to half of his kingdom—a rash offer indeed! He makes this drunken and foolish offer generally, but the girl, led by her scheming mother, Herodias, seizes upon the opportunity to bind him to his word by using language that is more contractual in nuance. Would all of Mark's hearers, or today's readers, catch this nuance? Not necessarily, but many likely would, depending on their sensitivity to such Greek nuances.

◼ Returning to Work

The point of this chapter has been to rehearse what has been happening in our developing rediscovery of the importance of the Greek middle voice. It has been not comprehensive or definitive but suggestive, inviting students

---

47. The Greek text here is from NA[28].

and teachers of the Greek Bible to reconsider and reframe how we think and talk about the Greek voice system. It is an exciting time to be working with a network of scholars as we grow in our understanding of the subtleties and beauties of the Greek verbal system. To do so, however, we must first wash our hands of an only-English understanding of voice before returning to the work of reading the Greek Bible.

5

Discourse Analysis

Galatians as a Case Study

STEPHEN H. LEVINSOHN

D iscourse analysis (or "text-linguistics," to use the European term) takes into account factors that are not treated in most Greek grammars (questions of morphology or syntax). In particular, it concerns features of the larger context than the individual sentence. It may simply focus on how the contents of the previous sentence affect the way the current sentence is structured. However, it also looks for ways in which the author's *purpose* influences the way the information in each sentence is presented.

■ Discourse Insights from Other Linguists

This presentation begins with a brief review of my journey to my current position as a discourse linguist. My wife and I became members of Wycliffe Bible Translators in 1965 and began work with the Inga (Quechuan) people of Colombia (South America) three years later. Before leaving the UK, we spent two summers at what was then called the Summer Institute of Linguistics (now SIL International), receiving training in field linguistics. The model we learned was one devised by John Bendor-Samuel called Syntagmatics or, simply, Structure-Function,[1] and it served us well during our first four years with the Ingas.

We returned to the UK in 1972 for me to study for an MA in linguistic science at the University of Reading. One course introduced the three linguistic schools that were then in vogue: Noam Chomsky and followers' Transformational Generative Grammar, Kenneth Pike and Robert Longacre's Tagmemics, and Michael Halliday's Systemics, with the lecturer pointing out the strengths and weaknesses of each.

However, when I started working on my thesis on discourse features of the Inga language, my supervisor, Peter Matthews, took one look at my corpus and said, "You need to use a Prague School approach." This led, among other things, to my rejecting the counterintuitive Hallidayan two-way division of every sentence into a theme (the initial constituent) and a rheme. Instead, I followed Eduard Beneš[2] in treating initial adverbial constituents as what he called "points of departure," with the rest of the sentence maintaining the theme and rheme (topic/comment) division. The following English sentences illustrate the difference between the two approaches.

Both Halliday and Beneš divide example 1 in the same way.

EXAMPLE 1

Sentence: The younger son set off for a distant country.
Theme (topic): the younger son
Rheme (comment): set off for a distant country

However, their division in example 2 differs markedly.

EXAMPLE 2A (HALLIDAY)

Sentence: Not long after, the younger son set off for a distant country.
Theme (topic): not long after
Rheme (comment): the younger son set off for a distant country

EXAMPLE 2B (BENEŠ)

Sentence: Not long after, the younger son set off for a distant country.
Point of Departure: not long after

1. John T. Bendor-Samuel, "The Structure and Function of the Verbal Piece in the Jebero Language" (PhD diss., University of London, 1958).
2. Eduard Beneš, "Die Verbstellung im Deutschen, von der Mitteilungsperspektive her betrachtet," *Philologica Pragensia* 5 (1962): 6–19.

Theme (topic)[3]: the younger son

Rheme (comment): set off for a distant country

Another Prague School linguist from whose work I benefited was Jan Firbas. He was concentrating at the time on what he called "Functional Sentence Perspective" and was proposing a number of functional reasons for changes in the order of constituents in a sentence[4]—observations that I would build on when studying constituent order in New Testament Greek.

After I completed my MA, our family returned to South America and, in 1974, I held a workshop in Panama, during which the participants first studied discourse features of the local languages and then applied their results to the translation of New Testament passages into those languages. When we came to this second part, we discovered to our horror that, whereas we had gained a reasonable understanding of a number of discourse features of the local languages, no one seemed to have studied the corresponding features in New Testament Greek. This eventually led to me returning to University of Reading to undertake doctoral studies on the Greek of Acts, majoring on the factors that influenced constituent order and on distinguishing the functions of the different particles and conjunctions used in that book (see further below).

I completed my doctorate in 1980 but have continued to refine my approach to discourse analysis as I encounter relevant insights from other linguists. The following are five of these insights.

Dryer's Language Types

When linguists started to divide languages into types, they initially classified them as SVO (subject-verb-object), VSO (verb-subject-object), and so on. So you will find New Testament Greek listed as a VSO language.[5] A breakthrough occurred when Matthew Dryer proposed that languages should be classified on the basis of two variables: whether or not the object follows the verb (verb-object [VO] versus object-verb [OV]) and whether or not the subject

3. In Beneš's approach, the theme (topic) is usually the subject, and the rest of the sentence is the rheme (the constituent about which a comment is made).

4. Jan Firbas, "On Defining the Theme in Functional Sentence Analysis," *Travaux de Cercle Linguistique de Prague* 1 (1966): 267–80.

5. See, e.g., Georg Benedikt Winer, *A Treatise on the Grammar of New Testament Greek*, trans. W. F. Moulton, 3rd ed. (Edinburgh: T&T Clark, 1882), 684–702. For a critique of this claim, see Stanley E. Porter, *Idioms of the Greek New Testament*, 2nd ed. (Sheffield: Sheffield Academic, 1994), 292–97.

commonly follows the verb (verb-subject [VS] versus subject-verb [SV]).[6] This led to New Testament Greek being classified as a VS/VO language.[7] A number of discourse features tend to correlate with Dryer's variables.

Dik's Constituent Order Template for Verb-Subject Languages

Simon Dik's template was originally proposed for Hungarian, but it is equally applicable to ancient Hebrew and New Testament Greek. The template is P1 P2 V X, where position P1 can be occupied by one or more points of departure (Dik calls them "TOPIC constituents"), position P2 can be occupied by a FOCUS[8] constituent (to give it contrastive or emphatic prominence), V is the verb or verb phrase, and X refers to any post-verbal constituents.[9]

First Thessalonians 5:7a (below) illustrates the P1 and P2 positions. The sentence concerns "those who sleep" (theme/topic), which is in P1. The rheme/comment about the theme is "sleep at night," and the focus is νυκτός, "at night," which is in P2.

Sentence: οἱ γὰρ καθεύδοντες νυκτὸς καθεύδουσιν.

Translation: "For those who sleep at night sleep."[10]

P1: οἱ γὰρ καθεύδοντες

P2: νυκτὸς

V: καθεύδουσιν

Relevance Theory Claims about Marked Forms and Added Implicatures

In his article on the English progressive (be + V-ing), Vladimir Zegarač argues for the need to distinguish between the "meaning" of the construction

6. Matthew S. Dryer, "On the Six-Way Word Order Typology," *Studies in Language* 21, no. 2 (1997): 69–103.

7. "I consider a language to be of the VS type if it is common in narratives for NP [noun phrase] subject-topics to follow the verb." Stephen H. Levinsohn, "Self-Instruction Materials on Narrative Discourse Analysis," §0.3, SIL, https://www.sil.org/resources/archives/68643.

8. The focus is "the information in the sentence that is assumed by the speaker not to be shared by him and the hearer." R. S. Jackendoff, *Semantic Interpretation in Generative Grammar* (Cambridge, MA: MIT Press, 1972), 230.

9. Simon C. Dik, *The Theory of Functional Grammar, Part 1: The Structure of the Clause* (Dordrecht: Foris, 1989), 363. Dik's template has P0 instead of P2. For a more comprehensive discussion of constituent order in NT Greek, see Stephen H. Levinsohn, "Constituent Order and 'Emphasis' in the Greek New Testament" (paper presented at a lunchtime seminar, Tyndale House, Cambridge, UK, January 2014), https://www.sil.org/resources/archives/68433.

10. Translations into English are based on the NRSV, adapted as appropriate to more closely reflect the Greek text.

and the different "overtones" that arise when the construction is used in certain contexts, such as "mild reproof," "insincerity," or "temporariness."[11]

Zegarač also distinguishes between contexts in which the tense-form is the default or "more relevant" way of portraying an event and "marked" usages of the form.[12] If one tense-form is the most relevant way of portraying an event, but an author chooses to use a different form instead, then "he must have intended to convey special contextual effects."[13] By choosing the more marked form, "the communicator makes the utterance more costly to process, . . . [and] this would entail that she intended to convey additional implicatures to compensate for the increase in processing effort."[14] What is crucial to this relevance theory approach to default and marked forms (and one that distinguishes it from those of both Stanley Porter and Robert Longacre) is that the effect of using a marked form varies with the context.

So, as I argued in an article on aspect and prominence in the Synoptic accounts of Jesus's entry into Jerusalem,

> Distinguishing between the "meaning" of a tense-form such as the imperfect, which remains basically unchanged, and the "overtones" associated with it, which vary with the context, results in an approach to prominence that is intuitively more satisfying than one in which a fixed degree of prominence is assigned to each tense-form. It is helpful, too, to distinguish between occasions when the tense-form is the most relevant way of portraying an event and those in which it is not, as this explains why the same form sometimes seems to be a foregrounding device while, in other passages, it [is] not.[15]

The Relevance Theory Approach to Particles and Conjunctions

Most New Testament grammarians describe Greek connectives in terms of the different "senses" in which they are employed.[16] However, my experience as a discourse linguist in Latin America made me realize that for native speakers of a language, each conjunction imposes a specific *constraint* on the

11. V. Zegarač, "Relevance Theory and the Meaning of the English Progressive," *University College London Working Papers in Linguistics* 1 (1989): 20, 22.

12. Zegarač, "Relevance Theory," 29.

13. Ernest-August Gutt, *Translation and Relevance: Cognition and Context* (Oxford: Blackwell, 1991), 103.

14. Gutt, *Translation and Relevance*, 41. See also Dan Sperber and Deirdre Wilson, *Relevance: Communication and Cognition*, 2nd ed. (Oxford: Blackwell, 1995), 220.

15. Stephen H. Levinsohn, "Aspect and Prominence in the Synoptic Accounts of Jesus' Entry into Jerusalem," *Filología Neotestamentaria* 23 (2010): 170.

16. See, e.g., Porter, *Idioms of the Greek New Testament*, 205–17.

way the sentence concerned is to be processed with reference to its context.[17] This position is formalized in a book by Anne Reboul and Jacques Moeschler,[18] in which they view each conjunction as a linguistic marker that "(a) links a linguistic or discourse unit of any size to its context; (b) gives instructions as to how to relate this unit to its context; (c) constrains conclusions to be drawn on the basis of this discourse connection that might not have been drawn had it been absent."[19] This definition means, for example, that if γάρ is read in Galatians 1:11, then the way that verse 11 is to be related to its context is different from the way that it is to be related to its context if the variant δέ is read. I return to this point below.

The third part of the definition ("constrains conclusions to be drawn on the basis of this discourse connection that might not have been drawn had it been absent") also leads to rejection of assertions such as "οὖν is used in an adversative sense."[20] Instead, when inferential οὖν is used in an adversative context, it indicates that the following sentence "constrains what follows to be interpreted as a distinct point that advances an argument in an inferential way."[21]

The Perfect in Context

I have to confess that I was unaware of recent work on the pragmatics of the English perfect until I attended a conference in 2016 on the perfect in Indo-European languages.[22] There, I learned of Astuko Nishiyama and Jean-Pierre Koenig's analysis of a corpus of English texts, which contained six hundred instances of the perfect.[23] No less than 583 of these instances involved the elaboration of an existing topic by referring to a past state of affairs that is of current relevance to that topic. Newspapers, for example, often introduce

17. See Stephen H. Levinsohn, *Discourse Features of New Testament Greek: A Coursebook on the Information Structure of New Testament Greek*, 2nd ed. (Dallas: SIL International, 2000), 69.

18. Anne Reboul and Jacques Moeschler, *Pragmatique du discours: De l'interprétation de l'énoncé à l'interprétation du discours* (Paris: Armand Colin, 1998), 77.

19. This is my translation of Reboul and Moeschler: see Stephen H. Levinsohn, "'Therefore' or 'Wherefore': What's the Difference?," in *Reflections on Lexicography: Explorations in Ancient Syriac, Hebrew, and Greek Sources*, ed. Richard A. Taylor and Craig E. Morrison, Perspectives on Linguistics and Ancient Languages 4 (Piscataway, NJ: Gorgias, 2014), 326.

20. See, e.g., H. E. Dana and Julius R. Mantey, *A Manual Grammar of the Greek New Testament* (Toronto: Macmillan, 1955), 257–58.

21. Levinsohn, "'Therefore' or 'Wherefore,'" 327.

22. For papers from that conference, see Robert Crellin and Thomas Jügel, eds., *Perfects in Indo-European Languages and Beyond*, Current Issues in Linguistic Theory (Philadelphia: Benjamins, forthcoming October 2020).

23. Astuko Nishiyama and Jean-Pierre Koenig, "The Perfect in Context: A Corpus Study," *University of Pennsylvania Working Papers in Linguistics* 12, no. 1 (2006): 265–78.

a topic in an article title and then in the tag line, they elaborate on it in the perfect tense, as in this example:

Spending on deaf slashed in past four years
Funding of specialist equipment for people in Wales with hearing loss has
  been slashed over the past four years because of budget cuts.[24]

At first sight, the Greek perfect appears to function in a similar way to its counterpart in English—namely, to elaborate on an existing topic by referring to a past state of affairs that is of current relevance to that topic. In Hebrews 1:5c (citing Ps. 2:7 LXX), for instance, "I today have begotten [γεγέννηκά] you" elaborates on "You are my Son" (Heb. 1:5b). However, if translations into English are compared with the Greek text, it quickly becomes apparent that English often uses a present perfect when the Greek has an aorist. For example, a perfect is typically used in English in the second part of the opening sentence of Hebrews ("Long ago God spoke to our ancestors in many and various ways by the prophets, but in these last days he *has spoken* to us by a Son"; Heb. 1:1–2a), since the second clause elaborates on the topic of God speaking that was introduced in the first clause, and the event concerned took place in the past but has current relevance to that topic. Nevertheless, the Greek verb (ἐλάλησεν) is in the aorist ("spoke").

This discrepancy results at least in part from the fact that English is a tense-prominent language, whereas New Testament Greek is an aspect-prominent language.[25] The following paragraph summarizes my conclusions about the pragmatic effects of translating Greek aorists in Hebrews with the present perfect:

Because NT Greek is an aspect-prominent language and uses the aorist (perfective)
verb form for present events as well as those that took place in the past, there is less

24. "Spending on Deaf Slashed in Past Four Years," inews.co.uk, February 20, 2017. In the other seventeen instances, speakers used "a perfect at the beginning of a conversation to set up a topic" (Nishiyama and Koenig, "Perfect in Context," 271). See Stephen H. Levinsohn, "The Perfect in Context in Texts in English, Sistani Balochi, and New Testament Greek," in Crellin and Jügel, *Perfects in Indo-European Languages and Beyond*, §1, for further discussion of pragmatic uses of the perfect in English.

25. Darbhe N. Shankara Bhat, *The Prominence of Tense, Aspect and Mood* (Philadelphia: Benjamins, 1999). Perfect in a tense-prominent language involves a "temporal view: past event with current (present) relevance." In an aspect-prominent language, it involves an "aspectual view: completed (perfective) event with continuing (imperfective) relevance" (170). Bhat continues, "My claim that the concept of 'perfect' is being viewed by languages from the point of view of their prominent category is supported by the various constraints shown by these languages on the occurrence of their respective perfect forms. These constraints appear to depend upon the most prominent category" (175).

need to actualise past events than in a tense-prominent language. This explains why English sometimes translates Greek aorists with present perfects. Rather than the perfect indicative being employed every time reference is made to a past event that elaborates on an existing topic, Greek tends to limit its use to restatements of past events or speeches, often with the implication that exposition of the topic is now completed. When aorist-perfect alternation occurs and readers/hearers might have expected the aorist to be used, the so-called aoristic perfect is a marked form with added implicatures. When found at or towards the end of a passage, assertions in the perfect often clinch the argument or are of a climactic nature. When used at or near the beginning of a narrative passage, in contrast, the perfect is more of a backgrounding device, pointing forward to and highlighting what follows.[26]

The conclusion I draw from the preceding five instances in which the insights of other linguists influenced my thinking is that New Testament Greek discourse studies can benefit greatly from advances made by linguists who are looking at discourse features in other languages (and especially if the language concerned is also aspect-prominent).

As I move into the second part of this chapter, I would like to point out that I approach the discourse features of the Greek New Testament from a *functional* perspective—namely, one that attempts "to discover and describe what linguistic structures are used for: the functions they serve, the factors that condition their use."[27] One basic principle of a functional approach is that *choice implies meaning*.[28] So, when an author has the option of expressing himself or herself in more than one way, the ways differ in significance; there are reasons for the variations. For example, there is often a choice as to which particle or conjunction is the most appropriate way to link two sentences (I have already mentioned Gal. 1:11, where the preferred reading in NA[28] is γάρ, but δέ is a variant). Choosing a particular connective instead of another is not just a question of style; rather, there is a functional reason for choosing each one.

■ Methodology

The following is a series of steps that an analyst might follow when considering the discourse structure of the Greek text of a New Testament book. I illustrate each of these steps from Galatians.[29]

26. Levinsohn, "Perfect in Context," §4.
27. Levinsohn, *Discourse Features*, vii.
28. Here "meaning" is used loosely to denote any semantic or pragmatic distinction. Levinsohn, *Discourse Features*, viii.
29. The following sections are based on Stephen H. Levinsohn, "Galatians," in *Discourse Analysis of the New Testament*, ed. Todd Scacewater (Dallas: Fontes Press, forthcoming), §2.

Determine the Nature of the Discourse

The text of Galatians is a letter with the apostle Paul as the stated author (1:1) and the churches of Galatia as the stated recipients (1:2). Hans Dieter Betz argues that Galatians is "an example of the 'apologetic letter' genre,"[30] constructed according to contemporary rhetorical principles with seven main elements:

1. Epistolary prescript (1:1–5)
2. Exordium (1:6–11)
3. Narratio (1:12–2:14)
4. Propositio (2:15–21)
5. Probatio (3:1–4:31)
6. Paraenesis (5:1–6:10)
7. Epistolary postscript or conclusio (6:11–18)[31]

F. F. Bruce, however, notes that, although "Betz's analysis corresponds well enough to the development of Paul's argument, . . . one may wonder . . . if in the excitement and urgency of the crisis with which he was suddenly confronted Paul would have been consciously careful to construct his letter according to the canons of the rhetorical schools."[32]

Richard Longenecker goes further and feels that "what Betz has done, in effect, has been to push a good thesis too hard and too far."[33] In particular, according to Christopher Vaz's summary of Longenecker's position, Betz "has ignored the influence of epistolary conventions, Old Testament rhetoric and Paul's own Pharisaic background."[34] Instead, Longenecker concludes, "In his Galatian letter (as elsewhere in his writings), Paul seems to have availed himself almost unconsciously of the rhetorical forms at hand, fitting them into his inherited epistolary structures and filling them out with such Jewish theological motifs and exegetical methods as would be particularly significant in countering what the Judaizers were telling his converts."[35]

---

30. Hans Dieter Betz, "The Literary Composition and Function of Paul's Letter to the Galatians," *New Testament Studies* 21 (1974–75): 354.
31. Betz, "Literary Composition," 355–74.
32. F. F. Bruce, *The Epistle to the Galatians: A Commentary on the Greek Text* (Exeter: Paternoster, 1982), 58.
33. Richard N. Longenecker, *Galatians*, WBC (Dallas: Word, 1990), cxi.
34. Christopher Augustin Vaz, "Functional Equivalent Translation of New Testament Hortatory Discourse into Hill Madia" (PhD diss., Fuller Theological Seminary, 2011), 57.
35. Longenecker, *Galatians*, cxix.

Determine the Broad Genre of the Letter

The broad genre of the letter is hortatory, since its concern is to change the behavior of the recipients.[36] Walter Hansen describes it more specifically as having "the 'rebuke-request' form," since "letters of rebuke also contained requests to set things right."[37] It follows that we can expect the rebukes and exhortations of Galatians to constitute the theme line of the letter, where the theme line "presents the backbone of the discourse—whether this be . . . the main points of an argument or the main commands of an exhortation—while the supportive material provides all that is necessary as a background for understanding the story, procedure, or argument as a whole."[38]

Determine the Major Division of the Discourse

It is helpful to determine where there is a general consensus as to the major divisions of the text and where there are disagreements among exegetes. This is done by consulting a representative set of commentaries and versions, since the divisions they propose will usually reflect where they perceive a change of theme. John Beekman and John Callow write, "The basic criterion [for delineating a unit] is that a section or a paragraph deals with one theme. If the theme changes, then a new unit has started. . . . What gives a section or paragraph its overall coherence as a semantic unit is the fact that one subject matter is being dealt with."[39] Robert Stutzman's *Exegetical Summary of Galatians* summarizes the divisions proposed in twenty-one commentaries and reference books and in eleven translations into English.[40]

One of the reasons I look at how exegetes have divided the text of a New Testament book is that I do not expect discourse analysts to come up with radically new ideas as to the structure of the book. Rather, discourse analysis provides a tool for evaluating existing proposals and for favoring some of them over against others.

36. "The central purpose of the letter is to arrest the progress of the judaising propaganda . . . which the Galatians were on the very point of accepting, and to win them back to faith in Jesus Christ apart from works of law." Ernest De Witt Burton, *A Critical and Exegetical Commentary on the Epistle to the Galatians* (Edinburgh: T&T Clark, 1921), lv.

37. G. Walter Hansen, *Galatians* (Leicester: Inter-Varsity, 1994), 22.

38. Mary Breeze, "Hortatory Discourse in Ephesians," *Journal of Translation and Textlinguistics* 5, no. 4 (1992): 314.

39. John Beekman and John C. Callow, *Translating the Word of God* (Grand Rapids: Zondervan, 1974), 279.

40. Robert Stutzman, *An Exegetical Summary of Galatians*, 2nd ed. (Dallas: SIL International, 2008), 7.

Find Surface Features That Support Different Boundaries

Surface features that can be cited as supporting evidence for the different boundaries that have been proposed on thematic grounds include the following:[41]

- A *fronted constituent* in P1 (see the discussion of Dik's constituent order template, above) that presents a new theme or situation.[42] See, for example, the fronting of τὸ εὐαγγέλιον τὸ εὐαγγελισθὲν ὑπ᾽ ἐμοῦ ("the gospel that was proclaimed by me"; 1:11),[43] as well as the change of situation described at the beginning of 6:1 in the conditional clause ἐὰν καὶ προλημφθῇ ἄνθρωπος ἔν τινι παραπτώματι ("if anyone is detected in a transgression").
- A *closure* such as ἀμήν ("Amen!"; 1:5).
- A *chiastic* structure such as that found in 3:2–14. "Chiastic structures indicate that the material concerned forms a self-contained unit . . . , which should be treated as a block over against that which precedes and follows."[44]
- An *inclusio* structure involves "the bracketing of a pericope by making a statement at the beginning of the section, an approximation of which is repeated at the conclusion of the section."[45] See, for example, the repetition of τῷ σπέρματι αὐτοῦ ("to his offspring") in 3:16 as τοῦ Ἀβραὰμ σπέρμα ("Abraham's offspring") in 3:29.
- A *summarizing expression*. "Summarising expressions unite together the information to which they allude and thereby imply that the preceding material is to be treated as a block, over against what is to follow."[46] In 4:31, διό, ἀδελφοί, οὐκ ἐσμὲν παιδίσκης τέκνα ἀλλὰ τῆς ἐλευθέρας ("So then, brothers, we are children, not of the slave but of the free woman") is a summarizing expression and conclusion that, according to Betz, "is not only the résumé of the meaning of the allegory 4:21–31, but of the entire *probatio* section."[47]

---

41. See Levinsohn, *Discourse Features*, 279–82.

42. Stephen H. Levinsohn, "Self-Instruction Materials on Non-Narrative Discourse Analysis," §8.2, SIL, 2015, https://www.sil.org/resources/archives/68640.

43. Unless otherwise indicated, references are to Galatians.

44. Levinsohn, *Discourse Features*, 279. Vaz discusses various proposals as to the entire epistle being constructed chiastically (Vaz, "Functional Equivalent Translation," 63–68) but concludes that *"Paul may not have deliberately chosen a chiastic structure"* (68, emphasis original).

45. George H. Guthrie, *The Structure of Hebrews: A Text-Linguistic Analysis* (Grand Rapids: Baker, 1998), 14.

46. Levinsohn, "Self-Instruction Materials on Non-Narrative Discourse Analysis," §8.4.

47. Betz, "Literary Composition," 374.

- A *rhetorical question* that introduces a theme, such as τίς ὑμᾶς ἐβάσκανεν ("Who has bewitched you?"; 3:1).

- An *apparently redundant reference* to an entity, such as ἐγὼ Παῦλος ("I, Paul"; 5:2).

- A *vocative* such as ἀδελφοί ("brothers"; 1:11) and Ὦ ἀνόητοι Γαλάται ("You foolish Galatians!"; 3:1).

- An *orienter verb* that introduces a new theme, such as Θαυμάζω ("I am astonished"; 1:6) and Γνωρίζω . . . ὑμῖν ("I want you to know"; 1:11).[48]

- A shift of two or more of the following *verbal features*: tense-aspect, mood, and person. For example, the final verb of 6:10 (ἐργαζώμεθα, "let us work") is a first-person plural present subjunctive, whereas the initial verb of 6:11 (Ἴδετε, "See . . . !") is a second-person plural aorist imperative.

- *Back-reference*, which "involves reference to the preceding paragraph or paragraphs or to a point or points within preceding paragraphs. Back-reference often occurs at the beginning of a new paragraph."[49] Such references are particularly significant when they reintroduce a concept or entity that has not featured in the immediate context. For example, the last reference to "you" (the Galatians) before 3:1 is in 1:13.

- *Hook words*, which, according to George Guthrie, are "a rhetorical device used in the ancient world to tie two sections of material together. A word was positioned at the end of one section and at the beginning of the next to effect a transition between the two."[50] See, for example, the positioning of κληρονόμοι, "heirs," at the end of 3:29, in anticipation of ὁ κληρονόμος, "the heir," becoming thematic in 4:1.

Although the surface features listed above may be cited as supporting evidence for a boundary proposed because of a perceived change of theme, there may be other reasons for them to be used. For example, vocatives are used not only at the beginning of a new section but also as a means of highlighting an important assertion, as in 4:19 (τέκνα μου, οὓς πάλιν ὠδίνω μέχρις οὗ μορφωθῇ Χριστὸς ἐν ὑμῖν, "My little children, for whom I am again in the pain of childbirth until Christ is formed in you").

48. Levinsohn, "Self-Instruction Materials on Non-Narrative Discourse Analysis," §8.10.
49. Linda Lloyd Neeley, "A Discourse Analysis of Hebrews," *OPTAT* 3–4 (1987): 19.
50. Guthrie, *Structure of Hebrews*, 12.

Consider the Implications of Each Inter-sentential Conjunction

As I suggested earlier, each inter-sentential[51] conjunction conveys a particular constraint on interpretation, so the presence of a conjunction at a proposed boundary will indicate how what follows is to be related to the context. The following are the constraints associated with some of the inter-sentential conjunctions found in Galatians (the + indicates that the conjunction is marked for the feature):

- ἀλλά: +Countering. It "instructs the recipient to process a corrective relation holding between two pieces of information."[52]
- γάρ: +Strengthening. It "constrains the reader to interpret the material it introduces as *strengthening* an assertion or assumption that has been presented in or implied by the immediate context."[53]
- δέ: +Distinctive. It "constrains what follows to be interpreted as a distinct point that advances Paul's argument."[54]
- ἔπειτα: "next." It marks "chronological sequence."[55]
- καί: +Associative/Additive. It "constrains the material it introduces to be processed as being added to and associated with previous material."[56]
- οὖν: +Inferential +Distinctive. It "constrains what follows to be interpreted as a distinct point that advances an argument in an inferential way."[57]
- διό: +Inferential +Continuative. "It contrasts with οὖν in that it does not move the argument on to a new point."[58]
- ὥστε: +Inferential +Result. It "constrains what follows to be interpreted as the 'result—actual, natural, conceived, intended' of what has previously been stated."[59]

51. I define a sentence as "a single independent clause, together with those clauses that are subordinated to it." Levinsohn, *Discourse Features*, 295.

52. Christopher James Fresch, "Discourse Markers in the Septuagint and Early Koine Greek with Special Reference to the Twelve" (PhD diss., University of Cambridge, 2015), 151.

53. Levinsohn, *Discourse Features*, 69.

54. Stephen H. Levinsohn, "A Holistic Approach to the Argument Structure of Romans 6" (paper presented at the International Conference of the Society of Biblical Literature, London, UK, July 2011), https://www.sil.org/resources/archives/68394, 4.

55. Longenecker, *Galatians*, 27.

56. Levinsohn, *Discourse Features*, 124.

57. Levinsohn, "'Therefore' or 'Wherefore,'" 327.

58. Levinsohn, "'Therefore' or 'Wherefore,'" 329.

59. Levinsohn, "'Therefore' or 'Wherefore,'" 334, citing Porter, *Idioms of the Greek New Testament*, 234.

Later sections discuss how the presence of some of these conjunctions impacts both the macrostructure of the letter and the flow of the argument within pericopes.

Look for Prominence-Giving Devices at Various Levels

Prominence-giving devices include the following:

- The repetition of clauses or sentences:

   ἀλλὰ καὶ <u>ἐὰν</u> ἡμεῖς ἢ ἄγγελος ἐξ οὐρανοῦ *εὐαγγελίζηται* [ὑμῖν] <u>παρ᾽</u> <u>ὃ</u> εὐηγγελισάμεθα ὑμῖν, **ἀνάθεμα ἔστω.** ὡς προειρήκαμεν καὶ ἄρτι πάλιν λέγω, <u>εἴ</u> τις ὑμᾶς *εὐαγγελίζεται* <u>παρ᾽ ὃ</u> παρελάβετε, **ἀνάθεμα ἔστω.**

   "But even <u>if</u> we or an angel from heaven *should proclaim* to you a̱.g̱o̱s̱p̱e̱ḻ.c̱o̱ṉṯṟa̱ṟy̱.ṯo̱.w̱ẖa̱ṯ we proclaimed to you, **let that one be accursed!** As we have said before, so now I repeat, <u>if</u> anyone *proclaims* to you a̱.g̱o̱s̱p̱e̱ḻ.c̱o̱ṉṯṟa̱ṟy̱.ṯo̱.w̱ẖa̱ṯ you received, **let that one be accursed!**" (1:8–9)

- The presence of particles such as ἴδε ("Behold," "Listen!"):

   Ἴδε ἐγὼ Παῦλος λέγω ὑμῖν ὅτι ἐὰν περιτέμνησθε, Χριστὸς ὑμᾶς οὐδὲν ὠφελήσει.

   "**Listen!** I, Paul, am telling you that if you let yourselves be circumcised, Christ will be of no benefit to you." (5:2)

- The use of cataphoric demonstratives and orienters such as τοῦτο ("this") and λέγω ("I say"):

   τοῦτο δὲ λέγω

   "My point is this . . ." (3:17)

- "Devices whose rhetorical effect is to slow down the story [argument] and create the expectation that the climax is about to be presented"[60] (see discussion of 1:11–12 below).

Within clauses, prominence-giving devices include the following:

- The omission of the article with reference to cognitively identifiable entities[61] (ἐγὼ γὰρ διὰ νόμου νόμῳ ἀπέθανον, ἵνα **θεῷ** ζήσω, "For through

---

60. Robert A. Dooley and Stephen H. Levinsohn, *Analyzing Discourse: A Manual of Basic Concepts* (Dallas: SIL International, 2001), 105.
61. Levinsohn, *Discourse Features*, 162–64.

the law I died to the law, so that I might live **to God**"; 2:19), where "θεῷ is contrasted with νόμῳ, and is focal and central to the argument."[62] Omission of the article gives prominence to the contrasted elements.

- The preposing to P2 of focal constituents (see the discussion of 2:19 above).

- Split focal constituents[63] (Ἴδετε **πηλίκοις** ὑμῖν **γράμμασιν** ἔγραψα τῇ ἐμῇ χειρί, "See **how large** [are the] **letters** I make when I am writing in my own hand!"; 6:11), where "it is the *size* of the letters that is in focus, rather than the phrase πηλίκοις γράμμασιν as a whole."[64]

- The violation of the "Principle of Natural Information Flow,"[65] by placing less-established information before more-established information (**κατὰ πρόσωπον** αὐτῷ ἀντέστην, "I opposed him **to his face**"; 2:11), where the focal constituent in P2 (κατὰ πρόσωπον), which is nonestablished information, is followed immediately by the pronoun αὐτῷ, whose referent is established.

■ Macrostructure of a Letter

My next step, when analyzing a text of the letter genre, is to separate off the "Epistolary Framework"[66]—"material that provides a framework for the message without being part of the message itself"[67]—from the main body of the letter. I then concentrate on the body of the letter and determine where the major divisions occur.

The Epistolary Framework

According to Mary Breeze, the framework for a letter comprises the following:

- the *introduction*, which "relates the author to the recipients and gives a greeting";
- the *closure*, which "consists of personal notes and a benediction."[68]

62. Levinsohn, *Discourse Features*, 163.
63. Levinsohn, *Discourse Features*, 57–60.
64. Levinsohn, *Discourse Features*, 58.
65. Levinsohn, "Self-Instruction Materials on Non-Narrative Discourse Analysis," 54–56.
66. Betz, "Literary Composition," 356.
67. Breeze, "Hortatory Discourse in Ephesians," 314.
68. Breeze, "Hortatory Discourse in Ephesians," 314.

In the case of Galatians, 1:1–5 constitutes the introduction or "Prescript,"[69] while 6:18 provides the closure (the concluding benediction), leaving 1:6–6:17 as the main body of the letter.[70] As I note elsewhere, "Asyndeton is typically found at the following transitions:

- from the opening salutation to the body of each letter . . .
- from the body of a letter to its closure . . .
- from one major or minor topic to another."[71]

Major Divisions

The major divisions in the body of the letter will occur where there is a major change of theme (see above). Since commentators often disagree as to where the major changes of theme are found, however, we can evaluate each proposal by looking for surface features that might support or weaken it. In my experience, a proposal is well supported if I can find three or more surface features that support it and none that weaken it.

I noted above that Betz considered Galatians to be an "apologetic letter" with seven main elements, including (2) exordium (1:6–11); (3) narratio (1:12–2:14); (4) propositio (2:15–21); and (5) probatio (3:1–4:31).[72] So this section evaluates the evidence for a boundary between each of the elements—namely, at 1:12; 2:15; and 3:1. It also examines the evidence for a boundary at 1:11.

3:1. I start with 3:1, since most commentators recognize a major division at this point.[73] The following surface features can be cited as supporting evidence for a division at 3:1:

- Asyndeton, which is consistent with the shift from one major topic to another
- The initial vocative Ὦ ἀνόητοι Γαλάται ("You foolish Galatians!")
- The rhetorical question τίς ὑμᾶς ἐβάσκανεν ("Who has bewitched you?")
- The shift from first person in 2:18–21 to second person in 3:1, which is of particular significance, given that the last reference to the Galatians as recipients of the letter was in 1:13 (Ἠκούσατε, "You heard")

69. Betz, "Literary Composition," 356.
70. Because the contents of 6:11–17 (part of the "Postscript" [Betz, "Literary Composition," 356]) include a summary of the main points of the letter, I treat it as part of the body of the letter.
71. Levinsohn, *Discourse Features*, 119.
72. Betz, "Literary Composition," 355–74.
73. Contrast F. F. Bruce, who places a major division between 2:14 and 2:15. Bruce, *Galatians*, viii.

- Calling the Galatians foolish, which can be taken as an allusion (a weak back-reference) to 1:6[74]

1:12. Whereas no overt connective is found at 3:1, γάρ is used at 1:12, which indicates that what follows strengthens the material presented in the immediate context. The sentence does begin with a fronted constituent in P1 (ἐγώ), but, as I noted above, the fronting in the previous verse of τὸ εὐαγγέλιον τὸ εὐαγγελισθὲν ὑπ' ἐμοῦ ("the gospel that was proclaimed by me"; 1:11) has already presented the theme for the section. Even Betz observes, "In v 12, the simple denial of v 11 is made more explicit."[75] So the commentators are surely right not to recognize a major division between 1:11 and 1:12.

2:15. The following surface features can be cited as supporting evidence for a division at 2:15:

- Asyndeton, which is consistent with the shift from one major topic to another
- The fronted independent pronoun in P1 (Ἡμεῖς), which signals a change of topic from σύ ("you"; i.e., Peter) to "we Jews who know that we are justified by faith [alone]"[76]

Whereas there is some supporting evidence for a division at 2:15, the next question to consider is whether the division is within the letter as a whole, as Betz's analysis would seem to imply, or whether it is a division within Paul's reported speech to Peter. We cannot know with certainty how many of these verses are a continuation of his speech.[77] Because the "we" of 2:15 does not include Gentile Christians, though, the Gentile recipients of the letter would

---

74. See John Stott, *The Message of Galatians*, The Bible Speaks Today (Leicester: Inter-Varsity, 1968), 69.

75. Betz, "Literary Composition," 363.

76. Todd Scacewater, "Galatians 2:11–21 and the Interpretive Context of 'Works of the Law,'" *JETS* 56, no. 2 (2013): 318. Comments such as "'We' is emphatic—'we' as distinct from 'them' (the Gentiles)" (Bruce, *Galatians*, 137) are misleading, as it is not the pronoun itself but the rest of 2:15 (φύσει Ἰουδαῖοι καὶ οὐκ ἐξ ἐθνῶν ἁμαρτωλοί, "Jews by birth and not Gentile sinners") that indicates that the referents of "we" are Jewish Christians. For discussion of the need to distinguish two types of "emphasis" (topical [in P1] versus focal [in P2]), see Stephen H. Levinsohn, "The Relevance of Greek Discourse Studies to Exegesis," *Journal of Translation* 2, no. 2 (2006): §3.1.

77. "Structurally speaking, these verses are a continuation of Paul's address to Peter which began with v. 14b" (Ronald Y. K. Fung, *The Epistle to the Galatians*, NICNT [Grand Rapids: Eerdmans, 1988], 112). "It is difficult to decide at what point Paul's quotation of his rebuke to Peter comes to an end and passes to his general exposition of the principle at stake. He probably summarizes his rebuke to Peter and then develops its implications, thus passing smoothly from the personal occasion to the universal principle." Bruce, *Galatians*, 136.

have assumed that Paul was still addressing Peter, together with the other Jewish Christians who were present at the time. It is noteworthy, too, that Paul switches from first-person plural to singular at the point at which γάρ introduces information that supports his earlier assertions. So it would not be unreasonable to suppose that 2:14–17 constitutes Paul's speech,[78] with 2:18–21 providing support for the Galatians' benefit, whether or not the words were spoken to Peter.

I conclude, then, that Betz's divisions at 1:12 and 2:15 are not at the same level as the one at 3:1.

1:11. Many versions and commentaries make a division between 1:10 and 1:11,[79] so I now examine evidence for a division, together with the effect of reading γάρ (NA[28]) versus the variant δέ as the connective that links 1:11 to its context.

If we follow NA[28] in reading γάρ at 1:11, then four successive verses begin with γάρ (1:10–13), and its presence indicates that what follows strengthens the material presented in the immediate context. Thus, William Hendriksen writes about the γάρ in 1:11: "In connection with the present context 'for' must mean something like 'In justification of the facts which I have stated, namely, that my gospel is of divine origin and is the only true gospel, so that anyone who distorts it is accursed, note the following corroborative facts selected from the story of my life.'"[80]

So the presence of γάρ in these verses indicates that the "solemn curse"[81] of 1:8, which is repeated in 1:9 to give it prominence,[82] is strengthened by 1:10. In turn, 1:11 strengthens 1:10, 1:12 strengthens 1:11, and 1:13–2:14 (or 2:21 [see above]) strengthens 1:12. The following flowchart (fig. 5.1) seeks to capture the constituent parts of the argument:

Figure 5.1
Flowchart of Galatians 1:6–2:14, reading γάρ at 1:11

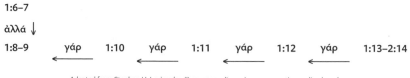

Adapted from Stephen H. Levinsohn, "Los rasgos discursivos comparativos aplicados a la traducción de Gálatas," SIL, 2007, https://www.sil.org/resources/archives/68387, 21.

78. Contra Scacewater, "Galatians 2:11–21," 317–18.

79. See, e.g., Bruce, *Galatians*, 57.

80. William Hendriksen, *A Commentary on Galatians* (London: Banner of Truth Trust, 1968), 47.

81. Stott, *Message of Galatians*, 24.

82. The introduction to 1:9 (ὡς προειρήκαμεν, καὶ ἄρτι πάλιν λέγω, "As we have said before, and now I repeat") is a slowing-down device that gives additional prominence to this curse.

This means that the autobiographical section that begins at 1:13 and continues until at least 2:14 is intended to strengthen the affirmations that "the gospel that was proclaimed by me is not of human origin; for I did not receive it from a human source, nor was I taught it, but I received it through a revelation of Jesus Christ" (1:11–12).

Whereas 1:11 should not be taken as the beginning of a macro-unit, the following surface features can be cited as supporting evidence for a second-level division at 1:11:

- The orienter Γνωρίζω ὑμῖν ("I want you to know")
- The vocative ἀδελφοί ("brothers")
- The fronting of τὸ εὐαγγέλιον τὸ εὐαγγελισθὲν ὑπ' ἐμοῦ ("the gospel that was proclaimed by me")

Although the preferred reading in NA[28] at 1:11 is γάρ, Longenecker[83] is among a number of scholars who favor reading δέ as the connective that introduces what follows. Since δέ constrains what follows to be interpreted as a distinct point that advances the argument, it can be cited as further supporting evidence for a second-level division at 1:11.

Figure 5.2 illustrates the effect on the development of the argument for reading δέ at 1:11:[84]

Figure 5.2
Flowchart of Galatians 1:6–2:14, reading δέ at 1:11

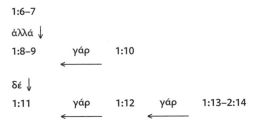

Adapted from Levinsohn, "Los rasgos discursivos," 21.

83. Longenecker, *Galatians*, 22.

84. Some commentators and versions place the second-place division before 1:10 instead of 1:11 (e.g., Herman N. Ridderbos, *The Epistle of Paul to the Churches of Galatia*, NICNT [Grand Rapids: Eerdmans, 1953], 53). Surface features that might support a division at 1:10 include the rhetorical questions and the repetition in initial position of the adverb Ἄρτι ("Now"). However, the presence of γάρ implies that the rhetorical questions do not in fact introduce a new theme but are used simply to respond to "the allegation of Paul's detractors . . . that he was 'curry-ing favor with men' by relaxing the terms of the gospel" (Fung, *Epistle to the Galatians*, 48). Donald Guthrie makes a similar point and also writes, "The 'now' in this statement reinforces the 'now' in verse 9." Donald Guthrie, *Galatians*, NCBC (Grand Rapids: Eerdmans, 1981), 65.

As for the unity of theme in 1:6–2:21, the autobiographical material of 1:13–2:10 supports the declarations of 1:11–12,[85] while the account of this confrontation with Peter (2:11–14) supports the condemnation of those who proclaim "a gospel contrary to what you received" (1:9), as well as showing that Paul was seeking not "human approval" but "God's approval" (1:10).

As noted earlier, we cannot know with certainty how much of 2:15–21 is a continuation of Paul's speech to Peter. What is certain is that these verses contribute to the rejection of those who "proclaim to you a gospel contrary to what we proclaimed to you" (1:8), "for if justification comes through the law, then Christ died for nothing" (2:21).

I conclude that Leon Morris is right to treat 1:6–2:21 as a single thematic unit ("The gospel"),[86] with a secondary division at 1:11.[87]

■ The Internal Structure of a Macro-Unit

Having evaluated the different proposals as to how the body of the letter or other text is to be divided into macro-units on the basis of a major change of theme, and having looked at the surface features that would tend to confirm or negate each one, we then move on to the internal structure of each macro-unit, to determine how the argument of the unit is developed and which parts of the unit have been given prominence. To illustrate this procedure, I now look at the internal structure of the first part of macro-section 1:6–2:21.

We have just seen that, within the macro-section 1:6–2:21, there is a second-level division at 1:11. In turn, 1:11–12 presents an expository thesis ("the gospel that was proclaimed by me is not of human origin; for I did not receive it from a human source, nor was I taught it, but [ἀλλά] through a revelation of Jesus Christ"), which is strengthened by the autobiographical section that begins at 1:13 and continues until at least 2:14.

When, as in 1:11–12, a positive assertion is preceded by two or more negative statements, this may be viewed as a slowing-down device that gives prominence to the positive assertion (in this instance, δι' ἀποκαλύψεως Ἰησοῦ Χριστοῦ, "through a revelation of Jesus Christ").[88] In 1:13–14 "the apostle describes his pre-conversion state 'in Judaism.'"[89] The imperfect tense (im-

---

85. "Throughout it all, Paul is emphasizing the point that the gospel he preached was of divine origin." Leon Morris, *Galatians: Paul's Charter of Christian Freedom* (Leicester: Inter-Varsity, 1996), 47–48.

86. Morris, *Galatians*, 30.

87. See also Burton, *Critical and Exegetical Commentary*, lxxii.

88. See also 1:16–17; 5:6; 6:15.

89. Stott, *Message of Galatians*, 31.

perfective aspect) of ἐδίωκον ("I was persecuting") and προέκοπτον ("I was advancing") both "indicates a continuing activity"[90] and is consistent with these activities being of a background nature in relation to his subsequent experiences.

As noted above, in 1:15 δέ introduces "a distinct point that advances Paul's argument"[91]—namely, what he did after Jesus Christ first revealed himself to him (1:15–17). This unit, as well as the three introduced with ἔπειτα ("next") and a time expression (1:18–20, 21–24; 2:1–10), all show that "I did not receive [the gospel that was proclaimed by me] from a human source, nor was I taught it" (1:12).

Four sentences make up 1:15–17, and the connectives used to link them are all associative or additive. The unit begins with a complex adverbial clause of time that includes a lengthy description of God's work in Paul: ὅτε δὲ εὐδόκησεν [ὁ θεὸς] ὁ ἀφορίσας με ἐκ κοιλίας μητρός μου καὶ καλέσας διὰ τῆς χάριτος αὐτοῦ ἀποκαλύψαι τὸν υἱὸν αὐτοῦ ἐν ἐμοί, ἵνα εὐαγγελίζωμαι αὐτὸν ἐν τοῖς ἔθνεσιν ("But when God, who had set me apart before I was born and called me through his grace, was pleased to reveal his Son to me, so that I might proclaim him among the Gentiles"). This clause provides the point of departure for the nuclear part of the sentence, but its sheer length acts as a slowing-down device that gives prominence to what follows. As in 1:11–12, the placement of two negative statements (εὐθέως οὐ προσανεθέμην σαρκὶ καὶ αἵματι οὐδὲ ἀνῆλθον εἰς Ἱεροσόλυμα πρὸς τοὺς πρὸ ἐμοῦ ἀποστόλους, "I did not confer with any human being, nor did I go up to Jerusalem to those who were already apostles before me"; 1:16–17) before the positive assertions may again be viewed as a slowing-down device that gives prominence to those positive assertions: ἀλλὰ ἀπῆλθον εἰς Ἀραβίαν καὶ πάλιν ὑπέστρεψα εἰς Δαμασκόν ("but I went away at once into Arabia, and again I returned to Damascus"; 1:17).

Finally, 2:11–14 is introduced with a time expression and δέ, as it advances Paul's argument against the Judaizing teachers who were proclaiming to the Galatians "a gospel contrary to what you received" (1:9). Figure 5.3 on page 124 shows how the overall argumentation of 1:11–2:14 is developed and which elements have been given prominence.

■ Conclusion

This chapter has argued, in the first instance, for the importance of being aware of advances in discourse analysis in the wider linguistic scene, as we

90. Morris, *Galatians*, 52.
91. Levinsohn, *Holistic Approach*, 4.

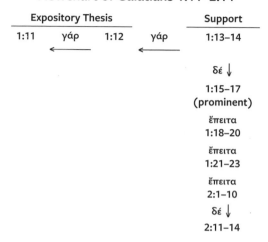

Figure 5.3
Flowchart of Galatians 1:11–2:14

Expository Thesis					Support
1:11	γάρ	1:12	γάρ		1:13–14
	⟵		⟵		
					δέ ↓
					1:15–17
					(prominent)
					ἔπειτα
					1:18–20
					ἔπειτα
					1:21–23
					ἔπειτα
					2:1–10
					δέ ↓
					2:11–14

Adapted from Levinsohn, "Los rasgos discursivos," 22.

should expect proposals about discourse features of New Testament Greek
to make sense in other languages, especially those in which aspect rather than
tense is prominent. It has then outlined a series of steps that a Bible scholar
might follow when considering the discourse structure of the Greek text of a
New Testament book. Divisions of the text into smaller units will be based
on perceived changes of theme, but surface features of the text can help the
analyst evaluate the relative merits of conflicting proposals as to how the text
should be divided. Greek has a rich collection of inter-sentential particles and
conjunctions, each of which indicates a specific way of relating what follows
to the context, so flowcharts can be produced that show how the argument
of a passage is developed and supported.

6

Interpreting Constituent Order in Koine Greek

STEVEN E. RUNGE

T he highly inflected case system of Greek offers far greater latitude in how clause elements are ordered compared to English. However, under-standing the motivations behind this variation has proven difficult: "It may be argued that if attempts to establish general rules have ended in doubt and confusion, that is the fault not of the enquirers after the truth but of the truth itself, Greek word order being 'free,' 'arbitrary' or 'indeterminate.' I do not sug-gest that such a view is unscholarly or disreputable. It speaks, after all, with the voice of experience and can draw upon a superabundance of evidence."[1] Kenneth Dover's words still ring true for many today, sixty years after they were written. While there is widespread agreement that the variation in order is meaningful, few confidently claim to understand the nuances motivating it.

All languages have some means for writers to structure discourse, prioritize information, and organize it based on their communication goals. English relies heavily upon intonation to accomplish these tasks; Koine Greek utilizes its flex-ibility in ordering clause elements.[2] The purpose of this chapter is to provide an overview of the advances in Greek linguistics that offer insight for exegetes

---

1. Kenneth James Dover, *Greek Word Order* (Cambridge: Cambridge University Press, 1960).
2. Steven E. Runge, *Discourse Grammar of the Greek New Testament: A Practical Introduc-tion for Teaching and Exegesis* (Peabody, MA: Hendrickson, 2010), 181.

desiring to better understand the ordering of Greek clauses. More properly, we will speak of "constituent order" instead of word order, since phrases and clauses are what is moved rather than just select words.[3] We will begin with a brief overview of different approaches that have been used to address this conundrum, followed by foundational linguistic concepts that can offer English speakers a framework to better understand this mismatch between the languages. This framework is then applied to selections from John's Gospel to illustrate the principles in action and the insights they can offer for exegesis.

■ Approaches to the Problem

The traditional grammarians were well aware of the problems encountered when trying to describe what motivated the New Testament writers to change the ordering of clause constituents in a given context. Pragmatic motivations were ascribed for breaking with what scholars felt was the "normal" order; only, nailing down normal proved difficult. Consider these quotes from A. T. Robertson on the matter: "The predicate very commonly comes first . . . simply because the predicate is most frequently the main point in the clause."[4] Then, after criticizing Friedrich Blass for overstating his claim about verb-subject-object (VSO) ordering, Robertson concludes that there is no "unalterable rule in the Greek sentence save that of spontaneity."[5]

Robertson and the other grammarians postulated two basic motivations for changes in constituent order: contrast and emphasis. Contrast was associated with fronted elements that signaled a switch of time, place, participant, or topic, typically a subject or prepositional phrase of some kind.[6] Claims of emphasis stemmed from the fronting of predicate elements like objects and adverbs.[7] Consider the following statements:

- Friedrich Blass: "A prior position gives emphasis, a position at the end of the sentence does so only indirectly, where the word is torn from its natural context and made independent."[8]

3. See David Crystal, *A Dictionary of Linguistics and Phonetics*, 3rd ed. (Oxford: Blackwell, 1991), 75–76.
4. A. T. Robertson, *A Grammar of the Greek New Testament in the Light of Historical Research*, 4th ed. (Nashville: Broadman, 1923), 417.
5. Robertson, *Grammar of the Greek New Testament*, 417.
6. Robertson, *Grammar of the Greek New Testament*, 417–18.
7. Stanley E. Porter, *Idioms of the Greek New Testament*, 2nd ed. (Sheffield: Sheffield Academic, 1994), 295–96; Friedrich Blass, *Grammar of New Testament Greek*, trans. Henry St. John Thackeray (London: Macmillan, 1898), 288.
8. Blass, *Grammar of New Testament Greek*, 288.

- Stanley E. Porter: "The subject is placed in initial position apparently to mark this emphasis or shift from the outset of the clause, minimizing any potential ambiguity."[9]
- A. T. Robertson: "Indeed the Greek only expressed the personal subject as a rule where clearness, emphasis or contrast demanded it."[10]

Such observations tended to be intuitive, based on the scholar's internalized pragmatic sensibilities gleaned over decades of wide reading. Hence, not every fronted subject signaled contrast, nor did every fronted adverb signal emphasis; the grammarians knew it when they encountered it, even if they were at a loss to adequately describe the principles governing the phenomenon. Commentators have typically followed this binary nomenclature in their analysis of specific passages, though with varying precision and accuracy. This approach has left students and others who lack the same internalized sense of the grammar without much to guide their own analysis.

In an effort to find a more rigorous basis for differentiating motivated departures from "normal" constituent order, Dover and Porter sought in their works to chart a new path by incorporating statistical data into their analysis. Dover's 1960 publication focused on Classical Greek, whereas Porter's work (and that of those he trained) focused on Koine Greek. Dover's objective was to test the various rationales that had been claimed for varying constituent order by generalizing these into basic rules and testing these on random selections from representative classical texts. Once he had established "'normal' and 'abnormal' orders," he then attempted "to discover conditions which were present in all the abnormal instances but absent from all the normal."[11] To illustrate this fallacy he offered the example of subject (S) / predicate (P) ordering versus PS. If SP is predominately observed with statements and PS is the normal order for questions, "we should content ourselves with the pair of discoveries that (a) statement determines the order SP, (b) interrogation determines order PS."[12] Thus global statements about the significance of one order versus another in main clauses with finite verbs could be quite misleading. His point was that beneficial insight would come only from drilling down into the data, not just relying upon higher-level patterns.

Dover demonstrates a keen awareness of the limitations of statistical data for making judgments about normal versus abnormal order. He notes, "It is easy, but wrong, to equate 'statistically normal' with 'natural' and 'statistically

---

9. Porter, *Idioms of the Greek New Testament*, 296.
10. Robertson, *Grammar of the Greek New Testament*, 391.
11. Dover, *Greek Word Order*, 4–5.
12. Dover, *Greek Word Order*, 5.

abnormal' with 'distorted,' 'inverted,' etc."[13] Furthermore, he notes that certain word classes are much more likely to occur at the beginning of a clause than others, leading him to classify these as "preferential words." These include interrogatives, negatives, relative pronouns, and sequential adverbials like πρῶτον or ἔπειτα.[14] In other words, not all subjects or adverbs are created equal; statistics require nuanced understanding so that they are not misleading. Simply drawing conclusions on the basis of higher-level grouping of the data is thus fraught with peril.

Despite the disadvantages he faced in terms of the 1960 state of the art, Dover's claims anticipate the cognitive-functional approach described below in significant ways. In his chapter on logical determinants, he highlights the critical importance of context, particularly in regard to the status of the information communicated in the utterance. He correlates changes in Greek word order to "modification of the tone and volume of the voice, so that two utterances which are identical in writing may be revealed in speech as standing in quite different logical relations to their contexts."[15] He illustrates this with the simple expression "Dogs bite." Although "dogs" is the grammatical subject and "bite" the grammatical predicate, changing the context naturally changes what each contributes to the context. "If the context of this utterance is a discussion of the habits of dogs, syntactical and logical subject coincide. . . . If, on the other hand, the context is a discussion of creatures which bite, the logical classification of the elements of the utterance is the reverse of the syntactical; 'bite' becomes the logical subject, and 'dogs' the logical predicate."[16] The key to understanding this difference, according to Dover, is understanding that "'dogs bite' is an answer to an implicit question; in the first context, 'what do dogs do?,' and in the second, 'which animals bite?'"[17] Much more could be said here, but the key point is that although statistics are typically helpful for identifying general patterns, they are insufficient in themselves for understanding the writer's motivation for variations in constituent order. The information status of each constituent in a given context is determinative for differentiating emphasis from contrast.

The early work of Porter also relies upon statistical analysis, offering data to help us better understand why differences in genre (e.g., narrative, hortatory, expositional, etc.) naturally lead to differences in constituent order patterns. After noting the fact that many Greek clauses lack any explicit

13. Dover, *Greek Word Order*, 5.
14. Dover, *Greek Word Order*, 20–22.
15. Dover, *Greek Word Order*, 32.
16. Dover, *Greek Word Order*, 34.
17. Dover, *Greek Word Order*, 35.

subject due to the morphological information encoded in Greek finite verbs, he states, "In independent and dependent clauses (so far the results do not warrant differentiating structural patterns of these clauses), the two most frequent patterns (in no designated order) are simply predicate and predicate-complement structures. These are followed (again in no designated order) by complement-predicate and subject-predicate structures. In other words, the most common patterns are when a verb or a verb and its object (with their accompanying modifiers) are used."[18] Thus, the most common order would be verb-object in contexts where the subject has been omitted, likely based on the fact that it is already established from the preceding context. The next most common order is for either the subject or object to precede the verb, which has long been understood to be pragmatically motivated, as noted above.

Regarding placement of the subject at the beginning of a clause, it "gives new or emphatic information and the predicate elucidates it"; however, "when the subject is placed in the second or third position in the clause (i.e., after the predicate and/or complement), its markedness or emphasis apparently decreases. . . . Moving the subject to a subsidiary position, however, does not necessarily elevate another element in the clause to a position of prominence."[19] His claims are consistent with those of earlier grammarians regarding the association of initial positioning in the clause with prominence, whereas the order verb-subject-object is more neutral and lacks pragmatic implicatures. Porter continues, "The expressed subject is often used as a form of topic marker or shifter (in a 'topic and comment sequence'), and is appropriately placed first to signal this semantic function. What this means is that when the subject is expressed it is often used either to draw attention to the subject of discussion or to mark a shift in the topic, perhaps signalling that a new person or event is the center of focus."[20]

In sum, Porter's observations mesh well with the findings of typologists and linguists regarding the most neutral or "default" ordering of clause constituents in Koine Greek. In subsequent writings, Porter has posited an inverse correlation between statistical frequency and prominence but achieves mixed results.[21] As will be shown in the next section, Dover's emphasis on context

18. Porter, *Idioms of the Greek New Testament*, 292.
19. Porter, *Idioms of the Greek New Testament*, 296.
20. Porter, *Idioms of the Greek New Testament*, 295–96.
21. See especially Stanley E. Porter, "Prominence: An Overview," in *The Linguist as Pedagogue*, ed. Stanley E. Porter and Matthew Brook O'Donnell (Sheffield: Sheffield Phoenix, 2009), 45–74. See Ivan Shing Chung Kwong, *The Word Order of the Gospel of Luke: Its Foregrounded Messages* (London: T&T Clark, 2005) and accompanying critique: Steven E. Runge, "Review of Ivan Shing Chung Kwong, *The Word Order of the Gospel of Luke: Its Foregrounded Messages*," *Review of Biblical Literature* 4 (2008): 1–8. See also Martin Haspelmath, "Against Markedness

offers an important caveat to statistical analysis that has been confirmed by multiple linguistic approaches.[22] These principles, described in the next section, offer exegetes a more fruitful and reliable account for the variation in constituent order we find in Greek. Importantly, they are consistent with principles describing other highly inflected, verb-prominent languages and with the intuition-based observations made by traditional Greek grammarians.

■ Foundational Principles

Stephen Levinsohn's contribution to this volume provides an overview of foundational principles that undergird the approach described here.[23] Recall that Michael Halliday's preliminary division of clauses into *theme* (what the clause is about) and *rheme* (the comment made about the theme) was improved upon by Eduard Beneš with the notion of a point of departure to account for clause-initial constituents besides subjects, such as adverbial modifiers.[24] Beneš's development allowed theme and rheme to be applied to languages like ancient Greek that manifested far more flexibility in ordering compared to English. Recall also Simon Dik's Functional Grammar template for verb-prominent languages, which provided a typologically informed linguistic framework that has proven invaluable for analyzing constituent order in ancient Greek, as demonstrated by Levinsohn's description and my application to the analysis of the entire Greek New Testament.[25]

and What to Replace It With," *Journal of Linguistics* 42, no. 1 (2006): 25–70; Edna Andrews, *Markedness Theory: The Union of Asymmetry and Semiosis in Language* (Durham, NC: Duke University Press, 1990), 136–39.

22. Christopher S. Butler, "Focusing on Focus: A Comparison of Functional Grammar, Role and Reference Grammar and Systemic Functional Grammar," *Language Sciences* 27, no. 6 (2005): 585–618, https://doi.org/10.1016/j.langsci.2005.07.004.

23. For examples of typologically informed, cognitive-functional approaches to information structure, see Stephen H. Levinsohn, *Discourse Features of New Testament Greek: A Coursebook on the Information Structure of New Testament Greek*, 2nd ed. (Dallas: SIL International, 2000); Nicholas A. Bailey, "Thetic Constructions in Koine Greek" (PhD diss., Vrije Universiteit, Amsterdam, 2009), https://research.vu.nl/ws/portalfiles/portal/42185508/complete+dissertation.pdf; Rutger J. Allan, "Clause Intertwining and Word Order in Ancient Greek," *Journal of Greek Linguistics* 12, no. 1 (2012): 5–28, https://doi.org/10.1163/156658412X649733; Rutger J. Allan, "Changing the Topic: Topic Position in Ancient Greek Word Order," *Mnemosyne* 67, no. 2 (2014): 181–213. For a recent generative theoretical approach, see Allison Kirk, "Word Order and Information Structure in New Testament Greek" (PhD diss., Netherlands Graduate School of Linguistics, 2012).

24. Eduard Beneš, "Die Verbstellung im Deutschen, von der Mitteilungsperspektive her betrachtet," *Philologica Pragensia* 5 (1962): 6–19, as translated in Paul L. Garvin, "Czechoslovakia," in *Current Trends in Linguistics*, vol. 1, ed. Thomas A. Sebeok (The Hague: Mouton, 1963), 508.

25. See Simon C. Dik, *Functional Grammar* (Dordrecht: Foris, 1981); Levinsohn, *Discourse Features*, 38; Runge, *Discourse Grammar*, 179–314; Steven E. Runge, *Lexham Discourse Greek New Testament*, Lexham Bible Reference Series (Bellingham, WA: Logos Bible Software, 2008).

Dik's template features two preverbal slots, P1 and P2, with the former including Beneš's "point of departure" information. P2 represents rheme information that has been moved to the preverbal slot in order to add prominence to it. Subsequent work on these issues from the perspective of cognitive linguistics has clarified the notions of theme and rheme.[26] Theme, variously referred to as "topic," "ground," "given," "presupposed," or "established information," serves as the basis for a proposition. This established or accessible information is based on the preceding discourse, one's knowledge of the world, or general human experience. This means that the simple mention of something as mundane as a restaurant or a football game inevitably activates a host of associated entities in our minds.[27] For example, once "a restaurant" is mentioned, I can begin making definite reference to "the waiter," "the menu," and so on. So too with football, as in reference to "the ball," "the goal line," or "the opposing coach," even if no other context is known. The rheme, variously referred to as "comment," "figure," "newly asserted," or "focus," is best understood as the difference between what is already presupposed and what is newly asserted.[28]

Recall also the natural tendency across languages to move from what is most known to what is least known, referred to by Levinsohn as "Natural Information Flow" (NIF). This is manifested in the practice in English of beginning a story by predicating the existence of some situation and then gradually building upon that basic idea. The italicized information in the example below identifies what is newly asserted, whereas the rest is established either from one's knowledge of the world or from the preceding discourse.

Once upon a time *there was a prince.*

The prince *lived in a castle.*

The castle *had a large moat around it.*

In the moat *there lived an old and wily fish.*

26. Avery Andrews, "The Major Functions of the Noun Phrase," in *Language Typology and Syntactic Description*, vol. 1, ed. Timothy Shopen (Cambridge: Cambridge University Press, 1985), 77–79.

27. Linguists have referred to such complex activation of information as "scripts," "frames," or "scenarios." See Robert A. Dooley and Stephen H. Levinsohn, *Analyzing Discourse: A Manual of Basic Concepts* (Dallas: SIL International, 2001), 25–26.

28. Rheme is more commonly referred to as "focus." For a more thorough introduction, see Knud Lambrecht, *Information Structure and Sentence Form: Topic, Focus, and the Mental Representations of Discourse Referents* (Cambridge: Cambridge University Press, 1996), 213.

Note how NIF leads to the newly asserted information of one clause becoming the topic of the next. The point here is that as soon as information is introduced, it becomes the topical framework for the newly asserted information that follows.

One final concept to introduce is that of mental representations. When we read or listen to a discourse, we are not storing the words but rather building a mental representation of what they communicate. The writer's or speaker's decisions about how to phrase things influence how we process and store this information. Robert Dooley and Stephen Levinsohn state, "The organization that hearers associate with a discourse is . . . a reflection of how the content comes together and is stored in the mind."[29] The information-structuring devices used in the discourse guide our construction of the intended mental representation of the discourse. Thus, we can think of grammatical, syntactic, and pragmatic information as the writer's instructions shaping how we process and store the information.

■ Application

Violating Natural Information Flow

The significance of Dik's Functional Grammar model stems from its ability to explain both pragmatically neutral and pragmatically marked constructions. As noted by Levinsohn, traditional grammarians have rightly understood Greek's most neutral constituent order to be VO or VS, which is consistent with claims of linguistic typologists and the observations of Porter and others.[30] However, when there is a pragmatic motivation for doing so, writers can place constituents before the verb to *mark* or signal the presence of some linguistic feature that use of the default order would not have signaled. That feature may or may not be present in the default order; linguists refer to this as "unmarked," based on the ambiguity. Departure from the expected norm evokes the additional implicature that something more is happening.

Let's take a look at examples illustrating these principles, beginning with some exhibiting default order. Figure 6.1 summarizes Levisohn's four "default ordering principles," which can at times clash with one another just like text-critical principles. His principles are as follows:[31]

---

29. Dooley and Levinsohn, *Analyzing Discourse: A Manual of Basic Concepts*, 10.
30. For a more detailed discussion, see Steven E. Runge, "Is There a Default Word Order in NT Greek?" (paper presented at the Annual Meeting of the Evangelical Theological Society, Philadelphia, 2006).
31. Levinsohn, *Discourse Features*, 29–32.

- Principle 1 predicts the placement of pronominal constituents immediately after the verb by default.
- Principle 2 predicts core arguments (i.e., subjects and objects) before peripheral elements (e.g., prepositional phrases).
- Principle 3 predicts propositional topics, like subjects, precede the non-verbal constituents of the predicate, such as objects and prepositional phrases.
- Principle 4: If Principles 1–3 "do not determine the relative order of constituents, place the more focal [i.e., newest and most salient] constituent after the less focal one."

Language is messy due to the creative nature of communication. However, figure 6.1 offers a heuristic summary as an introduction. The parentheses around pronoun and subject indicate their expected position when present; acknowledging that they are omitted in some cases.[32]

Figure 6.1
Expected Order for Finite Verbal Clauses

Verb—(Pronoun/Subject)—Object—Indirect Object

Simon C. Dik, *The Theory of Functional Grammar, Part 1: The Structure of the Clause* (Dordrecht: Foris, 1981), 363.

John 15:15 and 13:22 illustrate the positioning of the pronoun and subject immediately following the verb, as indicated in bold in example 1.

EXAMPLE 1

John 15:15: οὐκέτι λέγω **ὑμᾶς** δούλους, ὅτι ὁ δοῦλος οὐκ οἶδεν τί ποιεῖ αὐτοῦ ὁ κύριος.[33]
No longer do I call **you** slaves, because the slave does not know what his master is doing.

John 13:22: ἔβλεπον **εἰς ἀλλήλους οἱ μαθηταὶ** ἀπορούμενοι περὶ τίνος λέγει.
The disciples began looking **at one another**, uncertain about whom he was speaking.

32. By "pronoun" I mean any independent pronominal form regardless of case, hence a nominative subject, an accusative object or dative independent object, or the object of a prepositional phrase.
33. All Greek texts are quoted from Michael W. Holmes, ed., *The Greek New Testament: SBL Edition* (Bellingham, WA: Logos Bible Software, 2010). English translations are from W. Hall Harris III et al., eds., *The Lexham English Bible* (Bellingham, WA: Logos Bible Software, 2012).

Note that a pronoun typically follows the verb regardless of whether that pronoun is a direct object or simply a possessive. Since pronouns are by definition highly established information, it makes sense that they come so early in the clause, based on the principle of NIF.[34] The same principle holds true for John 13:22, where the pronoun occurs in a prepositional phrase—typically found at the end of the clause—followed by the subject. When default ordering is encountered, there is nothing special to be gleaned or claimed; the writer has not chosen to signal the presence of some pragmatic feature using constituent order.

Contrast this default ordering with pragmatically motivated departures from this norm, as described in figure 6.2. As noted above and in Levinsohn's chapter 5, the positions P1 and P2 represent the pragmatic fronting of theme and rheme, respectively, for the purpose of adding prominence.

Figure 6.2
Violating Natural Information Flow

(P1)—(P2)—(Pronoun)—Verb—X

Dik, *Theory of Functional Grammar*, 363.

The information provided in P1 serves as a frame of reference for what follows. It often signals a switch of some kind, a change in time, place, participants, or topic. Although such changes represent a discontinuity of some kind, this P1 information also provides a cohesive link between the units by signaling the primary basis for relating what follows to what precedes.[35] Thus, P1 information plays a critical role not only in signaling transitions in the discourse but also in connecting these parts together into a unified whole.

The information in position P2 is rhematic or part of what is newly asserted in the clause. Since the purpose of the utterance is to convey new information, the rheme is by definition the most important part. Fronting what was already the most important adds prominence to it, resulting in what grammarians have traditionally called "emphasis" (though this term has acquired a much broader and less helpful meaning). Fronting this new information signals that it is especially important, particularly in contexts where some kind of correction is involved.

34. Friedrich Blass makes the insightful observation that unemphatic pronouns "have a tendency to be placed in immediate connection with the verb." Blass, *Grammar of New Testament Greek*, 287.

35. Levinsohn refers to P1 as a "point of departure." For more, see Levinsohn, *Discourse Features*, 8.

The variations in John 15:5–6 illustrate the fronting of theme and rheme. P1 is underlined and P2 is bolded in all of the following examples.

EXAMPLE 2: JOHN 15:5–6

⁵ἐγώ εἰμι ἡ ἄμπελος, <u>ὑμεῖς</u> τὰ κλήματα. <u>ὁ μένων ἐν ἐμοὶ κἀγὼ ἐν αὐτῷ</u> οὗτος φέρει καρπὸν πολύν, ὅτι <u>χωρὶς ἐμοῦ</u> οὐ δύνασθε ποιεῖν οὐδέν.
⁶<u>ἐὰν μή τις μένῃ ἐν ἐμοί</u>, ἐβλήθη ἔξω ὡς τὸ κλῆμα καὶ ἐξηράνθη καὶ συνάγουσιν αὐτὰ καὶ **εἰς τὸ πῦρ** βάλλουσιν καὶ καίεται.

⁵"I am the vine; <u>you</u> are the branches. <u>The one who remains in me and I in him</u>—this one bears much fruit, <u>for apart from me</u> you are not able to do anything.
⁶<u>If anyone does not remain in me</u>, he is thrown out as a branch, and dries up, and they gather them and throw them **into the fire**, and they are burned.

The personal pronouns ἐγώ and ὑμεῖς in verse 5 signal the rapid switch from one subject referent to another, helping readers track the change. The expression ὁ μένων ἐν ἐμοὶ κἀγὼ ἐν αὐτῷ activates a complex referent, making it easier for the hearer to activate this person in their mental representation.[36] The οὗτος that follows refers back to this now activated referent, summarizing it before moving on to the comment about such a person. The prepositional phrase χωρὶς ἐμοῦ offers the same kind of orienting for the main clause, making clear that the P1 information restricts the proposition that follows.

The conditional clause that begins verse 6 instructs the reader that what follows must be processed in light of this. The balance of the verse is neutrally ordered until we reach the penultimate clause. There the prepositional phrase εἰς τὸ πῦρ, the landing place of the thrown branches, is fronted. Based on the fact that this information is newly asserted, the fronting of it is construed as P2 rather than P1. With its rigid clause-ordering principles, the English counterpart to fronting is signaled by intonational stress. Thus, reading this verse in translation, "into the fire" naturally receives the primary stress of the clause.

Another clustering of representative examples is found later in the same chapter. As you read, consider the framing role that the conditions and subjects in P1 serve to frame or signal switches within the discourse. The P2 elements, indicated by bold text, fill in the blanks between what is presupposed and what is being asserted.

36. Linguists call this a "left dislocation" due to it being formally detached from the main clause, whereas grammarians have called it a *casus pendens* or "hanging nominative." For more, see Runge, *Discourse Grammar*, 287–313.

EXAMPLE 3: JOHN 15:18–19

¹⁸Εἰ ὁ κόσμος ὑμᾶς μισεῖ, γινώσκετε ὅτι ἐμὲ πρῶτον ὑμῶν μεμίσηκεν.

¹⁹εἰ ἐκ τοῦ κόσμου ἦτε, ὁ κόσμος ἂν τὸ ἴδιον ἐφίλει ὅτι δὲ ἐκ τοῦ κόσμου οὐκ ἐστέ, ἀλλ᾽ ἐγὼ ἐξελεξάμην ὑμᾶς ἐκ τοῦ κόσμου, διὰ τοῦτο μισεῖ ὑμᾶς ὁ κόσμος.

¹⁸If the world hates you, you know that it has hated **me before** it hated you.

¹⁹If you were of the world, the world would love **its own**. But because you are not of the world, but I chose you out of the world, **for this reason** the world hates you.

In verse 18, the fact that the disciples are hated suggests that someone else might be hated as well. The fronting of ἐμὲ πρῶτον (P2) underscores the fact that what they experience is a natural consequence of the hatred first expressed toward Jesus. The new condition in verse 19a shifts from the world's response to the disciples to the origin of that response. They know they are no longer of the world because otherwise the world would have loved them. The ὅτι clause that begins verse 19b signals a shift from the preceding condition as the point of departure to a reason. Note that this reason is part of the rheme; that is, it is newly asserted. However, it is too long and complex for P2. The workaround for such situations is to activate the information first, and then reiterate it using a demonstrative pronoun in P2 to emphasize it. Verse 18 addresses whether or not the world hates them, but not the reason for the hatred. Verse 19a eliminates the possibility that the hatred stems from membership in the world. Rather, it is the fact that they are not of the world that has caused the hatred rather than something else.

To summarize, most clauses are a combination of theme and rheme, presupposed and newly asserted information. Unless there are pragmatic motivations to do otherwise, the most neutral order for Koine Greek finite verbal clauses is the verb followed by pronouns (of any grammatical case) and subject if present, followed finally by direct and indirect objects. Figure 6.1 above summarizes Levinsohn's four default ordering principles.[37] The phenomenon of NIF undergirds all of them. If the verb represents the starting point of NIF, pronouns and the subject are typically the most presupposed information in non-interrogative sentences. Required verbal arguments come next, followed finally by the non-required adverbial information, typically conveyed in prepositional phrases. However, if one or more of these elements convey newly asserted information, NIF can motivate writers to shift it to the end of the clause.

---

37. Those wanting further description are directed to Levinsohn, *Discourse Features*, 29–32.

When NIF is violated, as summarized in figure 6.2, the same underlying principles are still in play. Presupposed information that is fronted (P1) still precedes newly asserted information (P2), as expected. In other words, instead of the verb signaling the beginning of the information flow, the P2 element may fulfill this role. The option of placing highly presupposed pronominal information immediately after P2 information might be motivated by one or more factors. First, it might be attributable simply to NIF itself, following the perceived need to begin with P2. Second, when only one element has been fronted, it can be unclear whether the author intends it to be P1 or P2. Placing a pronoun or subject immediately after the fronted element effectively disambiguates that it must be P2.

Yet another possible motivation is sharpening the perceived newness of the P2 information by contrasting the newest, most salient information with the most established and least salient. Placement of these established clause constituents after P2 flaunts the violation, making it stand out all the more. While the analyst cannot definitively ascertain why the established information was moved, these principles can still help us better appreciate the motivations behind the ordering we find in the New Testament. Let's apply these principles to John 14:9.

> **EXAMPLE 4: JOHN 14:9**
>
> λέγει αὐτῷ ὁ Ἰησοῦς· **Τοσούτῳ χρόνῳ** μεθ᾽ ὑμῶν εἰμι καὶ οὐκ ἔγνωκάς με, Φίλιππε; <u>ὁ ἑωρακὼς ἐμὲ</u> ἑώρακεν τὸν πατέρα· **πῶς** σὺ λέγεις, Δεῖξον ἡμῖν τὸν πατέρα;
>
> Jesus said to him, "Am I with you **so long a time** and you have not known me, Philip? <u>The one who has seen me</u> has seen the Father! **How** can you say, 'Show us the Father?'"

In the first clause of his response to Philip, Jesus underscores the length of time he's been with the disciples to highlight the expectation that Philip ought not to have needed to ask. The preverbal placement of μεθ᾽ ὑμῶν may well just be NIF, especially since copular verbs like εἰμί typically are found in the final position of the clause. Alternatively, a case could be made for a pragmatic motivation, in that we would naturally apply extra intonational stress in English to such a statement. On this view, the movement of the pronominal prepositional phrase flaunts the violation, adding extra prominence to the P2 constituent. Much more work is needed to better understand such nuanced implications for specific authors, but these principles hold great promise for future research.

Ordering of Dependent Adverbial Clauses

One of the most beneficial and possibly most overlooked aspects of constituent order analysis concerns the relationship of dependent adverbial clauses to the main clause on which they depend, especially participles. The fact that adverbial participial clauses are regularly translated into English as finite verbs makes it all the harder to appreciate the exegetical implications of the writer's grammatical choices. First and foremost, recognize that the information conveyed in the dependent participial clause could just as easily have been conveyed using a finite verb in most cases. This observation is attested by grammarians using such labels as "independent participle" to describe those situations where the connection to a main clause is difficult to find.[38] That may well be, and a participle may not be a translation possibility in English. Nevertheless, here are some considerations to bear in mind.

First, the choice to use a dependent participial clause represents the choice *not* to use an independent finite verb of some kind. Hence, there are exegetical implications for passages like Ephesians 5:18–21. Had the writer chosen to use a series of imperatival forms instead of participles, each of the verbal clauses would have stood on a coequal grammatical footing with πληροῦσθε rather than being dependent upon it. The participial clauses are italicized:

[18]And do not be drunk with wine (in which is dissipation),
but be filled by the Spirit,
   [19]*speaking to one another in psalms and hymns and spiritual songs,*
   singing and singing praise in your heart to the Lord,
   [20]*giving thanks always for all things in the name of our Lord Jesus*
   Christ to the God and Father,
   [21]*being subject to one another out of reverence for Christ.*

In other words, selection of a dependent participial clause represents the writer's choice to create a single complex clause instead of a series of independent clauses.

Second, the decision to use dependent verbal forms requires that the writer select one of them as the main clause on which the others depend. Such a decision could have been avoided had they all been finite verbal clauses, giving each the same grammatical significance.[39] The need to select a main clause impacts

---

38. Robertson, *Grammar of the Greek New Testament*, 1132–33.
39. Other factors would then be taken into account to determine the relative salience of each verb (e.g., semantic, rhetorical, logical, etc.), but the point here is to note the consequence of choosing finite versus nonfinite verb forms.

the clause's perceived salience vis-à-vis the dependent ones. Consequently, we could liken selection of a main clause to anointing it as the most important part of the clause, with the other elements supporting it.

Third, promotion of one member to main-clause status has natural exegetical consequences for the others. The dependent clauses are effectively backgrounded compared to the main clause. This is not to say that the dependent elements have been demoted; such a claim is unwarranted even if theoretically possible. Rather, selection of the main clause naturally leads to the lessening of the perceived salience of the others by comparison. Had the writer intended that readers understand them as equally salient to the main clause, this could have been unambiguously signaled by using an independent verb form instead. Consider these implications for the following example. The participial clauses are italicized, while P1 elements are underlined and P2 elements are bold as above.

EXAMPLE 5: JOHN 13:1

<u>Πρὸ δὲ τῆς ἑορτῆς τοῦ πάσχα</u> *εἰδὼς ὁ Ἰησοῦς*
    ὅτι ἦλθεν αὐτοῦ ἡ ὥρα ἵνα μεταβῇ ἐκ τοῦ κόσμου τούτου πρὸς τὸν πατέρα,
ἀγαπήσας τοὺς ἰδίους τοὺς ἐν τῷ κόσμῳ
εἰς τέλος ἠγάπησεν αὐτούς.

Now <u>before the feast of Passover</u>, *Jesus, knowing*
    that his hour had come that he would depart from this world to the Father,
and having loved his own in the world,
loved them **to the end**.

The first participial clause (εἰδὼς ὁ Ἰησοῦς) conveys circumstantial information that sets the scene for the main clause. The second participial clause (ἀγαπήσας τοὺς ἰδίους τοὺς ἐν τῷ κόσμῳ) shares the same verbal lemma as the main clause (i.e., ἠγάπησεν), resulting in significant overlap between the two. Use of a participle for this initial statement lends extra prominence to the restatement in the main clause. This is especially true since the only newly asserted information in the main clause is the duration of his love. Contrast this one statement about loving them to the end with the hypothetical alternative—three statements that all feature indicative verbs ("Before the feast of the Passover, Jesus knew that . . . he loved his own in the world, he loved them to the end"). This theoretical alternative still builds to a climax, heightened by the amount of semantic overlap between the second and third clauses. However, the backgrounding of the first two clauses via the selection of participles results in the spotlight unambiguously resting upon the one main clause of the sentence.

There is another important consideration regarding dependent adverbial clauses besides the choice to create a single, complex clause rather than a series of independent clauses: the positioning of the adverbial clause before or after the main clause. Holger Diessel's analysis of adverbial modifiers across languages has found that in verb-object (VO) languages like Greek, English, and most European languages, adverbial modifiers are regularly found both before and after the main clause.[40] This contrasts with object-verb (OV) languages like Turkish or Korean, where these adverbials always precede the main clause.[41] This distribution of adverbials is not random.

Clause-initial adverbials tend to contain information that is pragmatically presupposed or readily accessible and thus easily understood by the reader, typically conditional or temporal information. It serves as thematic grounding for the main clause that follows and tends to have a wider semantic scope compared to adverbial information that typically follows the main clause. Consider the clause-initial elements in example 6. Dependent adverbial information is italicized as above and serves the clause-initial framing function of P1 material.

EXAMPLE 6: JOHN 13:2–4

²καὶ δείπνου γινομένου,
τοῦ διαβόλου ἤδη βεβληκότος εἰς τὴν καρδίαν
    ἵνα παραδοῖ αὐτὸν Ἰούδας Σίμωνος Ἰσκαριώτου,
³εἰδὼς
    ὅτι πάντα ἔδωκεν αὐτῷ ὁ πατὴρ εἰς τὰς χεῖρας,
    καὶ ὅτι ἀπὸ θεοῦ ἐξῆλθεν καὶ πρὸς τὸν θεὸν ὑπάγει,
⁴ἐγείρεται ἐκ τοῦ δείπνου
καὶ τίθησιν τὰ ἱμάτια
καὶ λαβὼν λέντιον διέζωσεν ἑαυτόν.

²*And as a dinner was taking place,*
when the devil had already put into the heart of Judas son of Simon Iscariot
    that he should betray him,

40. Holger Diessel, "The Ordering Distribution of Main and Adverbial Clauses: A Typological Study," *Language* 77, no. 3 (2001): 433–55.
41. For a helpful introduction to the differences between OV and VO languages, see Stephen H. Levinsohn, "Introduction to Features of OV Languages" (paper presented at the Translation Consultants' Seminar, Horsleys Green, UK, 2008).

³[*knowing*]

> *that the Father had given him all things into his hands,*
> *and that he had come forth from God and was going away to God,*
⁴he got up from the dinner
and took off his outer clothing,
and *taking a towel,* tied it around himself.

Most of the adverbial clauses are participles that establish a situational frame of reference for what follows. The semantic scope of the content conveyed is fairly broad. The result is one complex clause in verses 2–4a rather than a series of independent clauses.

Contrast this with clause-final adverbials, which typically convey newly asserted information and elaborate on what precedes. Consequently, the semantic scope of this information tends to be much narrower based on the tight connection to the main verb. Common clause-final adverbials include reason, result, purpose, and causal adverbials along with adverbial participles that expand upon the main action, illustrated by John 6:19.

EXAMPLE 7: JOHN 6:19

ἐληλακότες οὖν ὡς σταδίους εἴκοσι πέντε ἢ τριάκοντα θεωροῦσιν τὸν Ἰησοῦν
περιπατοῦντα ἐπὶ τῆς θαλάσσης καὶ ἐγγὺς τοῦ πλοίου γινόμενον,
καὶ ἐφοβήθησαν.

Then when they had rowed about twenty-five or thirty stadia, they saw
    Jesus *walking on the sea and coming near the boat,*
and they were afraid.

Contrast the connection of the adverbials that precede the main clause with those that follow. The rowing bears little connection to seeing Jesus, whereas his walking on the water and drawing near spell out in greater detail what exactly the disciples saw. Figure 6.3 summarizes Diessel's findings as a continuum, with the elements at either end of the spectrum more regularly occurring in that position, whereas those toward the middle are found in both positions, though favoring one.

Because temporal and causal adverbials are regularly used to convey both presupposed and newly asserted information, they are found both before and after the main clause. There are important pragmatic implications when something like a conditional, which is expected to be clause initial, occurs at

Figure 6.3
Adverbial Modifiers and Typological Ordering

conditional	temporal	causal	result/purpose

preposed   postposed

Diessel, "Ordering Distribution of Main and Adverbial Clauses," 446.

the end of the clause, as in example 8. Contrast the framing function it plays before the main clause with the effect it achieves at the end of the clause.

EXAMPLE 8

If you answer my question, I'll buy you a steak dinner.

I'll buy you a steak dinner *if you answer my question.*

John 15:14: ὑμεῖς φίλοι μού ἐστε ἐὰν ποιῆτε ἃ ἐγὼ ἐντέλλομαι ὑμῖν.

You are my friends *if you do what I command you.*

Placing the condition at the end of the clause adds the pragmatic effect of surprise, as though what had been understood as an unconditional statement is now unexpectedly limited by this new information. Based on the fact that the condition affects the truthfulness of the main clause, it makes sense that the condition typically occurs at the beginning to alert the reader that the main clause is contingent upon the fulfillment of the condition. Clause-final placement can thus have the effect of a "gotcha," where the reader expected the main proposition to be true, only to find out afterward that there was a catch.

Recognizing the writer's choice to cluster adverbial clauses around a single main clause, regardless of how this complex clause might need to be translated, is a simple yet highly significant exegetical payoff of attending to the Greek text. Relative clauses are another strategy commonly used to link significant amounts of modifying information to a main clause using dependent relationships. This is particularly the case where that dependent information could be understood as highly salient and representing a new tack in the discourse. The so-called Christ hymn in Philippians 2:6–11 exemplifies this in that the significance of the Christology it contains can overshadow the fact that it serves as a practical illustration of what like-mindedness looks like. The commands of verses 2 and 5 represent the main idea for this section of the discourse. The dependent section introduced by the relative clause in verse 6 actually has two parts: Christ setting aside what was his in obedience to the Father (vv. 6–8) and the Father's response of giving Jesus the name above every name and having every knee bow to him instead of the Father (vv. 9–11). Notwithstanding the significant theological implications of Paul's statement, Paul's primary purpose in the context is providing his readers a compelling call to action. Just as Christ willingly and humbly set aside his interests for the sake of the Father's, so too should the Philippians. Clarifying the theological implications of the Father's actions is beyond the scope of both this passage and this chapter. In exegeting this passage we must not let a preoccupation with Christology obscure Paul's intent to foster obedience to his commands in verses 2 and 5. Much more could be said here, but the important takeaway is to engage Greek on its own terms rather than through the lens of English or theological persuasion. If a dependent relation is present that is awkward in translation, we must be sure to attend to the exegetical implications regardless of how we might end up translating it. If we are truly concerned with identifying authorial intent as much as possible, respecting grammatical choices like dependency relationships is a simple yet important way of doing so.

■ Conclusion

Analysis of constituent order is one of a growing number of tasks that a cognitive-functional approach to linguistics can offer exegetes to obtain greater clarity and precision when studying the Greek text. As Levinsohn and Porter have made clear in their contributions to this volume, linguistics is a field that is constantly growing and adapting to insights gleaned from different subdisciplines. Each linguistic theory that Porter catalogs was developed in response to some aspect of language that the originators of the theory felt had been inadequately addressed up to that point. However, as the field continues to grow and expand, approaches like Systemic Functional Linguistics, Functional Grammar, Role and Reference Grammar, and relevance theory face a two-part challenge: continuing to pursue the questions for which they were spawned, while also incorporating new insights from other approaches. To do the former without attention to the latter will render that approach irrelevant to those outside that specific theoretical community.

The typical response to this challenge, especially for those using a functional approach, is to adapt and integrate these new insights within one's own theoretical framework rather than reinventing the wheel. This is precisely what we have seen happen with the analysis of information structure based on the groundbreaking work of Knud Lambrecht from within construction grammar.[42] Christopher Butler, a leading authority on functional-linguistic approaches, provides a very useful comparison of how different approaches have responded to and incorporated Lambrecht's insights.[43]

Some within New Testament studies have denigrated such incorporation of insights from different, compatible theoretical frameworks, demonstrating a lack of awareness of how necessary and pervasive such adoption is within the broader field of linguistics proper.[44] The personal narrative of Levinsohn's chapter in particular illustrates how innovations that I now take for granted required him to significantly revise his ideas.[45]

First, language is messy, and our understanding about it is constantly developing. Demands for theoretical purity within biblical studies will relegate linguistics to the ivory tower of theoretical contemplation instead of the messy trenches of practical application. The complexities of language, coupled with our constantly evolving understanding of how it works, means that methodologies and theories need to keep pace.

Second, analysis of constituent order is impossible apart from careful attention to the discourse context. The complexity of cognitive activation, as illustrated by the restaurant and football examples above, demonstrates that determining what qualifies as "presupposed" or "known" for a first-century Palestinian Greek speaker is incredibly complex. Analysis of information structure presupposes that the exegete is steeped enough in historical and cultural background information so as to recognize when referents have been pragmatically activated in association with some related concept, increasing the importance of attention to such information. The focus is on how and when their encyclopedic knowledge of the world, and that of Second Temple Judaism, is activated in the reader's mental representation.[46] What was newly asserted in one clause becomes presupposed in the next. However, if something in the context activates an entity without any specific reference, then such information is better understood as presupposed. For example, in John 18:28 there are two references to Caiaphas bringing Jesus εἰς τὸ πραιτώριον ("to the governor's headquarters"). Then, in verse 29, since the Jews were

---

42. Lambrecht, *Information Structure and Sentence Form.*

43. Butler, "Focusing on Focus," 585–618.

44. See, e.g., Constantine R. Campbell, *Advances in the Study of Greek: New Insights for Reading the New Testament* (Grand Rapids: Zondervan, 2015), 176, 190.

45. Contrast Levinsohn's claims regarding constituent order from 1987 versus those in 2000, following Lambrecht's treatise. See Stephen H. Levinsohn, *Textual Connections in Acts* (Atlanta: Scholars Press, 1987), 1–81; Levinsohn, *Discourse Features,* 7–68.

46. For a recent example addressing this divide, see Michael S. Heiser, *Reversing Hermon: Enoch, the Watchers, and the Forgotten Mission of Jesus Christ* (Crane, MO: Defender Publishing, 2017).

unwilling to enter the building because doing so would make them unclean, ὁ Πιλᾶτος comes out to them. Typically, a referent's proper name is anarthrous at first reference, yet here the first reference to Pilate in the book is articular.[47] This suggests that mention of the praetorium was sufficient to activate other entities associated with it—namely, the home's principal occupant.

Analysis of constituent order has developed a solid foundation of research within New Testament studies, yet much remains to be done. A point of departure is only one of several ways to signal a discontinuity in the context. Connectives like δέ can also serve to segment a discourse, often operating alongside pragmatically ordered constituents.[48] We also need to better understand differences in authorial style—for example, John's use of constituent order versus that found in Matthew or Luke. Finally, verbless clauses and noun phrases also follow similar principles of pragmatic ordering, but more research is needed to elegantly delineate them.

47. Levinsohn, *Discourse Features*, 152–53.
48. Levinsohn, *Discourse Features*, 113–18.

7

Living Language Approaches

T. MICHAEL W. HALCOMB

In his *Confessions*, Augustine describes how he acquired Latin but strug-
gled with and even came to despise Greek. He asks, "Why, then, did I
despise the Greek works which, as a youngster, I studied? Even now my
exploring is left unsatisfied."[1] Referring to Greek as a "foreign language," he
says, "Certainly, the difficulty, the difficulty of entirely learning the foreign
language, as it were, sprinkles bitterness into all the sweetness of the Greek
fable stories."[2] Later, he contrasts language acquisition in Latin and Greek.
He says, "I, of course, did not know Latin when I was an infant; nevertheless,
it is worth noticing that I learned without pain and torture. For, between
my charming nurses and laughing jokers and happy playmates, I learned
truly, without the urge to endure punishment. When my heart urged me
to give birth to its own desires, which would not have even been the case
unless I had learned other words, not from those teaching (grammar) but

---

I would like to thank David Black and Benjamin Merkle for the invitation to participate in
this project.

1. Augustine, *Confessions* 1.13.20 (translation mine). The Latin text reads, *Quid autem
erat causae, cur Graecas litteras oderam, quibus puerulus imbuebar? Ne nunc quidem mihi
satis exploratum est.*
2. Augustine, *Confessions* 1.14.23 (translation mine). The Latin text reads, *Videlicet difficultas, difficultas omnino ediscendae linguae peregrinae, quasi felle aspergebat omnes suavitates
graecas fabularum narrationum.*

from those speaking, I also brought forth (in speech) everything I desired in their hearing."[3]

Theodore Haarhoff asked about this in 1920: "What, then, exactly was wrong with the teaching of the second language?" He concluded: "Partly, it undoubtedly was (as has been indicated) that stupid concentration on the dry bones of grammar which persists up to the present day in the teaching of a strange language. . . . But there was a deeper cause. Augustine gets to the root of the matter when he says that it was *unnaturalness*."[4] For him, attempting to learn a language via grammar and rules is unnatural. Listening, speaking, joking, and so forth make learning a language natural.

The word "natural" has become something of a synonym for "living." And it is the matter of "living languages" or "living language approaches" that I have been tasked with addressing. I think it helpful to begin by clarifying the moniker "living language." Historical precedent is important, for it provides us with context; so, I begin there. The first description of a language as "living" appeared in 1540 CE. Alessandro Citolini, in his *Lettera in difesa della lingua volgare*, contrasted *la latina è morta* (dead Latin) with *la volgare è viva Italia* (the living Italian vernacular).[5]

It is significant to the discussion that, at that time, debates were in full swing between two schools of thought: the classicists and the vernacularists. In their European context, many vernacular (or what we might call "modern spoken") languages were garnering interest and vitiating the use of Greek and Latin. Resistant, the classicists were attempting to advance the argument that Latin should retain its place of prestige not merely as an academic but also as an international language. Yet the vernacularists challenged these views. One way to make their point was to distinguish between changing (i.e., a productive image presaging linguistic notions of "generative") and stagnant languages. Italian was thus viewed "as a new creation by a process of *generatio* out of the corruption of Latin." As a result, the "*generatio* theory" led to the idea of "Latin as dead and the newly generated Italian as living."[6] Interestingly,

---

3. Augustine, *Confessions* 1.14.23 (translation mine). The Latin text reads, *Nam et Latina aliquando infans utique nulla noveram, et tamen advertendo didici sine ullo metu atque cruciatu, inter etiam blandimenta nutricum et ioca adridentium et laetitias adludentium, didici vero illa sine poenali onere urgentium. Cum me urgeret cor meum ad parienda concepta sua, et qua non esset nisi aliqua verba didicissem non a docentibus sed a loquentibus, in quorum et ego auribus parturiebam quidquid sentiebam.*
4. Theodore Haarhoff, *Schools of Gaul: A Study of Pagan and Christian Education in the Last Century of the Western Empire* (Oxford: Oxford University Press, 1920), 226–27.
5. On this I am indebted to R. Glynn Faithfull, "The Concept of 'Living Language' in Cinquecento Vernacular Philology," *Modern Language Review* 48, no. 3 (1953): 278–92.
6. Faithfull, "Concept of 'Living Language,'" 286.

mercury, also known as "quicksilver" because of its silver color, was understood at the time as mobile, changing, or "living" and, as such, was contrasted with stagnant or "dead" water.[7] This, not the human body, became a guiding metaphor of the times for dead and living language.

In 1693, John Locke wrote, "The Latin tongue would be easily taught the same way if [a student's] tutor, being constantly with him, would talk nothing else to him, and make him answer still in the same language. But because French is a *living* language, and to be used more in speaking, that should be first learn'd."[8] Thomas Paine's dictum around that same time was that "a youth will learn more of a *living* language in one year, than of a *dead* language in seven."[9] He also said, "It is but seldom that the teacher knows much of it himself. The difficulty of learning the *dead* languages does not arise from any superior abstruseness in the languages themselves, but in their *being dead*."[10]

One of the first dictionary definitions of "dead language" is from Noah Webster in 1831: "a language which is no longer spoken or in common use by people, and known only in writers; as the Hebrew, Greek, and Latin."[11] Interestingly, Webster doesn't give a definition for "living language," but he does use the phrase four times throughout his dictionary.[12] We see that "dead" was associated with being written only, not spoken, and not productive or growing. "Living" (productive, changing, and growing) was understood as both written and spoken. It was only in the eighteenth century that the biological understanding of dead/living languages came into view. Research shows that in 1800 CE there were 144 uses of "dead language" while there were 78 for "living language." Two hundred years later there were 2,342 for "dead language" and 991 for "living language." For the most part, since 1800 CE there has been a consistent uptick in using these terms.[13]

---

7. In the work of Francesco Filelfo, the notion of "mother tongue" (*Litteralis limatior est fortasse et proprius magis quam maternus*) appears. See Mirko Tavoni, *Latino, grammatica, volgare: Storia di una questione umanistica*, Medioevo e umanesimo 53 (Padova: Antenore, 1984), 275. See also Josef Eskhult, "Vulgar Latin as an Emergent Concept in the Italian Renaissance (1435–1601): Its Ancient and Medieval Prehistory and Its Emergence and Development in Renaissance Linguistic Thought," *Journal of Latin Linguistics* 17, no. 2 (2018): 209. Faithfull ("Concept of 'Living Language,'" 291) alludes to this.

8. John Locke, *Some Thoughts concerning Education* (London: Paternoster-row, 1693), 192.

9. Thomas Paine, *The Age of Reason: Being an Investigation of True and of Fabulous Theology* (Philadelphia: James Carey, 1797), 33.

10. Paine, *Age of Reason*, 33.

11. Noah Webster, *A Dictionary of the English Language* (New York: E. H. Barker, 1831), 210.

12. Webster, *Dictionary of the English Language*, ii, iii, xxv, 11.

13. Interestingly, there have been several decades when attestation of the terminology has dropped. For example, in 1920–40 the use of both terms declined. The same goes for 1970–80. I would be remiss not to mention the fact that I used Mark Davies's helpful tool, BYU Corpora,

In the 1900s, James Hill said, "The method of teaching *living* foreign languages in the United States has been stubbornly and radically wrong. . . . The
ear and the vocal organs are the means nature provides for language study.
Americans have endeavored in vain to acquire *living* languages by the eye and
from books. A book never taught anyone to speak any language, even his
native tongue. *Living* languages must be learned from the lips of those who
speak them with spontaneous ease."[14] Hill's sentiment is a bit too simplistic.
As Wilfried Decoo says, "A simplified historical outlook tends to categorize
just a few noteworthy methods that are used to characterize whole periods.
Moreover, these methods are sometimes reduced to their bare bones without
considering their own development and complexity."[15]

This, I think, is the case with where things stand today among Bible scholars
and ancient language pedagogy. Operating in all-or-nothing and either-or bi-
naries, one teaches with either a grammar-translation or a spoken approach—
there's nothing in between. The conversational approach is often viewed as less
historically mature, while the grammar-translation approach is often viewed
as outdated. Both sides are wrong. This is too simplistic of an outlook on a
complex matter. Decoo speaks more correctly of a third approach, which he
calls the "didactic approach." He uses "didactic" in its "positive educational
sense: learner-focused, geared to efficiency, simplification, and facilitation
. . . also its strong attention to content systematization. These distinctions
. . . do not imply a strict separation between them: many methods mingle all
three, and the balance and sequence of approaches are very much part of the
systematization they pursue."[16]

When we look back to the past, we discover that this was the case from
the beginning of language teaching and learning. As W. F. Mackey has noted,
however, "Much of the field of language method has become a matter of
opinion rather than of fact. It is not surprising that feelings run high in these

---

to run these tests. Also, it is interesting to hypothesize what might have led to the decline of
usage during these time spans. Might, for instance, World War I and the Great Depression, as
well as later the Vietnam War, have played a role in affecting publication in general? It is also
curious that "dead language" always appears more than "living language." Again, might the
wars and suffering have had a part in this? Or might it be attributed to the notion that since the
study of "dead languages" and "living language" approaches comprised two different fields of
study, terminology was used separately? These are questions worth considering, but pursuing
them is outside the scope of the present study.

14. James J. Hill, "The Proper Education of the People Is the Duty of the Economist," *Public
Policy: A Journal for the Correct Understanding of Public Questions and the Development of
Good Citizenship* 6, no. 7 (February 15, 1902): 100.

15. Wilfried Decoo, *Systemization in Foreign Language Teaching: Monitoring Content Progression* (New York: Routledge, 2011), 42.

16. Decoo, *Systemization in Foreign Language Teaching*, 42–43.

matters, and that the very word 'method' means so little and so much."[17] Indeed, the reason for this "lies in the state and organization of our knowledge of language and language learning. It lies in willful ignorance of what has been done and said and thought in the past."[18]

When one surveys language teaching and learning from a variety of ancient cultures, the varied picture that emerges from the evidence is one of an ancient multisensory or multimodal pedagogical approach in which the teachers employed speaking, reading, writing, copying, composing, translating, and grammatical analysis.[19] The master modeled these things, and the students imitated. Importantly, language education, although perhaps limited in resources, seemed rather well rounded in each of those cultures and learning contexts. Moreover, curriculum existed in varying ways, and teachers were directly involved. Not insignificantly, elements of the Greco-Roman progymnasmata were nearly always present, even before the Greco-Roman era. Finally, the role of the teacher cannot be overlooked. Regardless of the scenario—a father teaching at home, teachers teaching in place of fathers, or like situations—the teacher-student dynamic was ever-present in the process of language acquisition.

■ From Renaissance to Reform

I now want to draw attention to a couple of key voices on the topic of language teaching-learning in the time span from the Renaissance (1300–1600) up to the era of Reform (1882–1900s). Part of my aim is to reiterate that there were educators who employed holistic approaches that included, at once, the skills of reading, writing, speaking, grammar study, and translation. Additionally, I want to assert, as does Anthony Pym, that even in this time period "there was basically no such thing as 'grammar translation' as single orthodoxy."[20]

Thomas Siefert, in his detailed study, finds that the label "grammar-translation" arose from within the ranks of modern teachers, those using a communicative approach to differentiate themselves and "remain 'on top' of

17. W. F. Mackey, *Language Teaching Analysis* (London: Longmans, Green & Co., 1969), 139.

18. Mackey, *Language Teaching Analysis*, 139.

19. In a fuller version of this chapter, which due to its length and scope could not be included here but may be published elsewhere in the future, I examine language teaching and learning in Sumerian, Akkadian, Hebrew, Greek, and Latin. I also survey data up through the Renaissance.

20. Anthony Pym, "Rebranding Translation" (paper presented at the Languages & Cultures Network for Australian Universities Conference, Adelaide, Australia, November 27–29, 2017), 4, http://usuaris.tinet.cat/apym/on-line/training/2018_Rebranding_translation_revised_web.pdf.

the competition from the past, . . . giving CLT [Communicative Language Teaching] power while actually robbing the GTM [Grammar Translation Method] of its more complex and not so easily summarized history."[21] This is similar to Glenn Levine's assessment that "even the eclectic approaches that come under the heading of CLT . . . are not 'natural,' but derive from the particular historical trends and trajectories in language education of the last few hundred years, and perhaps from popular, intuitive beliefs, or beliefs based on anecdotal evidence (which themselves have historical roots that one could trace)."[22] This is substantiated, at least partially, by the fact that in the era of Reform and beyond, various fields of psychology, especially behaviorism, have heavily influenced language pedagogy.

Near the end of the Renaissance, renowned author and educator Roger Ascham rose to prominence. His book for schoolmasters, aptly titled *The Scholemaster*, was billed by Ascham himself on the cover page as a perfect way to teach, understand, write, and speak Latin.[23] Because working with the language is a text-based endeavor, Ascham always requires the presence of a master teacher, even with a single student—something typical of sixteenth-century education.

Pym notes that, during this period, grammar teaching, translation, speaking, and writing were all used. He says, "There are actually very few textbooks that do not allow space for spoken exchange, in addition to or alongside the written exercises. . . . The learner was incited to discover grammar through contact with the language, with translation exercises being used to introduce points of comparative grammar. . . . The pedagogical progression in translation activities meant moving from simple to hard, with various checks on acquisition along the way."[24]

Another one of the Renaissance's notable educators was Jan Amos Komenský or, in Latin, Comenius. In his work, communicative, or usage-based, pedagogy was often combined with grammar-based materials.[25] In his *Opera*

21. Thomas R. Siefert, "Translation in Foreign Language Pedagogy: The Rise and Fall of the Grammar Translation Method" (PhD diss., Harvard University, 2013), 30.

22. Glenn S. Levine, *Code Choice in the Language Classroom* (Tonawanda, NY: Multilingual Matters, 2011), 17.

23. Roger Ascham, *The Scholemaster: Book I*, ed. J. T. Margoschis (1520; repr., London: Higginbotham, 1877). For the view that Ascham's translation practice, often dubbed "double translation," is erroneously derived from a mistranslation of Pliny the Younger, see William E. Miller, "Double Translation in English Humanistic Education," *Studies in the Renaissance* 10 (1963): 163–74.

24. Pym, "Rebranding Translation," 4.

25. Margaret Thomas, *Universal Grammar in Second Language Acquisition: A History* (New York: Routledge, 2004), 95.

didactica omnia or, as it has come to be known, *The Great Didactic*, he provides twenty-six guiding principles for language teachers. He asserts, near the beginning, that teaching the second language must be done with age- or cognition-level appropriate materials, and as far as is possible, every foreign word must be linked to a concrete object. Using his approach, he contends that "Latin can be learned in two years, Greek in one year, and Hebrew in six months."[26]

For Comenius, part of the philosophy is that "all languages are easier to learn by practice than from rules." His contention is that "hearing, reading, re-reading, copying, imitating with hand and tongue, and doing all these as frequently as is possible" will yield the greatest successes in the least amount of time. At the same time, he says, "Rules assist and strengthen the knowledge derived from practice." For him, the rules, whether encountered explicitly or implicitly, follow from language use rather than precede it.[27]

Previously, I noted the presence of progymnasmatic elements in language pedagogy. The progymnasmata of antiquity were well known and "available to schoolmasters and school boys in European grammar schools throughout the sixteenth and seventeenth centuries in Latin translations."[28] As to what this looked like, David Clark says,

> One thing, common to all textbooks of progymnasmata, accounts for their success and hence their continued use at least through the seventeenth century. They all give patterns for the boys to follow. They present a graded series of exercises in writing and speaking themes which proceed from the easy to the more difficult; they build each exercise on what the boys have learned from previous exercises; they repeat something from the previous exercises, yet each exercise adds something new. The schoolmasters who taught the classes and wrote, translated or adapted the textbooks never took anything for granted except a teacher with a group of boys assembled for the purpose of learning to compose themes.[29]

It was in the sixteenth century, however, that grammars for foreign languages began to emerge. The typical textbook would have within it "a short preface; a grammar section; idiomatic phrases; dialogues; and personal and commercial letters. Texts might also contain a word-list, proverbs, some texts

26. John A. Comenius, *The Great Didactic*, ed. M. W. Keatinge (London: Adam and Charles Black, 1896), 357.

27. Comenius, *Great Didactic*, 358.

28. David L. Clark, "The Rise and Fall of Progymnasmata in Sixteenth and Seventeenth Century Grammar Schools," *Speech Monographs* 19, no. 4 (1952): 261–63.

29. Clark, "Rise and Fall of Progymnasmata," 260.

for reading, and other practice material."[30] As Nicola McLelland notes, "By the early nineteenth century, then, the idea of learning foreign languages from a grammar with accompanying graded exercises, including translation into and out of the language, was established. It was this that grew into what was later disparagingly called 'the' grammar-translation method." Regardless of its detractors, says McLelland, "its intentions were laudable: to provide both a grammatical foundation *and* appropriate, targeted exercises to allow learners to practise applying the rules as they learnt them, step by step."[31]

It seems that for me, and for McLelland too, distinguishing between grammar, translation, grammar-translation, and communication within the language teaching-learning process isn't so easy to do. The actual history is, as she says, "less simplified" than the lay view that "in the (imprecisely defined) Old Days, language teaching was all about grammar and translation, but nowadays, things are 'better,' and people learn to speak the language." What is closer to reality is the fact that "grammar and translation did not dominate all language teaching until the twentieth century, nor was it a new idea to pay attention to the spoken language."[32] At nearly every stage from Sumerian on, excepting later educators who made it a point to draw lines in the sand, these approaches coexisted and were used to suit the purposes of educators and students.

■ Era of Reform

The period of time when lines began to be distinctly drawn in the sand, although not by all, was the period of Reform (ca. 1882–1902). It should be stated here that, at this time, education had moved predominantly to a school model, and although tutors were still used, the one-on-one master-apprentice model ultimately became less prominent. Influences on education, such as the Industrial Revolution, were certainly part of the reason for this change. Also, near the end of the seventeenth century and up through the nineteenth,

---

30. Nicola McLelland, *Teaching and Learning Foreign Languages: A History of Language Education, Assessment and Policy in Britain* (London: Routledge, 2017), 94. Given the research dealing with pre-Renaissance-era language teaching-learning in this chapter, I do question how on-point the following remark by McLelland about the cited portion of her work is: "The history that follows deals with methods of teaching European languages in Europe and, occasionally, with Europeans learning non-European languages in other parts of the world. That is the history about which most is known. The history of language learning by speakers of non-European languages is little researched, and so too is the history of how non-European languages were learned" (85).

31. McLelland, *Teaching and Learning*, 99.

32. McLelland, *Teaching and Learning*, 85.

attention was shifting away from rhetorical education in general, and as a result, the progymnasmata also "fell into a sharp decline."[33] Thus, the teaching-learning enterprise began to look quite different than it had in the past.

With regard to language teaching and learning, the influences of the science of psychology were gaining interest and, on occasion, drawing insights from behaviorism, which paid great attention to habit formation as well as the developmental stages of people in general and children in particular. In 1853, some thirty years before the Reform Movement is said to have officially started, Claude Marcel published a work titled *Language as a Means of Mental Culture and International Communication*. Marcel, a prominent figure of the Reform Movement, promoted the idea that, prior to learning any of the classical languages, one must first learn modern languages. Indeed, the entire enterprise of learning the classical languages is that it will serve to benefit the students' abilities in their native tongue. Marcel says of the classical languages, "They should be studied, not for their own sake; not as an end, but as a means; and, under a rational system, they may be most useful auxiliaries to mental discipline and improvement in the native tongue, without interfering with the other departments of education."[34]

Marcel contends that the amount of time spent teaching the languages in classical schools is disturbing. Indeed, "He who spends six years in teaching what can be learned in three, robs his pupil of so much previous time."[35] Mackey argues that, for Marcel, the focus was on teaching language "first through comprehension of texts, through abundant listening, then through the reading of simple and familiar material, followed later by speaking and writing."[36] Grammar would be learned inductively along the way and then, at a later stage, could be reviewed deductively if desired.[37] What is perhaps most significant about Marcel's approach is that it was text oriented. This meant that, for learners, the entryway into the foreign language was through reading. This he called a "rational method," which later became known as

---

33. Sean Patrick O'Rourke, "Progymnasmata," in *Encyclopedia of Rhetoric and Composition: From Ancient Times to the Information Age*, ed. Theresa Enos (London: Routledge, 1996), 563.

34. Claude Marcel, *Language as a Means of Mental Culture and International Communication; or, The Manual of the Teacher and the Learner of Languages*, vol. 1 (London: Chapman & Hall, 1853), 150.

35. Marcel, *Language as a Means of Mental Culture*, 151.

36. Mackey, *Language Teaching Analysis*, 139.

37. On this, see too Lambert Sauveur, *Introduction to the Teaching of Living Languages* (New York: Holt, 1883). Sauveur advocated the view that grammar was learned inductively and that teaching it deductively was not only a distraction but also a joke. Thus when asked what grammar book to use after learning to speak the language, he quipped that his response was "I do not recommend to you any" (36).

the "reading-first method."[38] The "four branches" of his approach were (1) to understand the spoken language, (2) to speak, (3) to understand the written language, and (4) to write.[39]

Another figure, François Gouin, just prior to the rise of the Reform Movement, composed a book in 1880 titled *The Art of Teaching and Studying Language*.[40] Gouin's retelling of his frequent attempts to learn a foreign language are, although depressing, likely familiar to many students of ancient languages. He asks, "Are ten years of one's life under ten teachers absolutely necessary to learn Latin?" The resounding answer is, of course, no! He says, "Whether it be acknowledged or not, there is for each language a definite foundation, a first footing, upon which is based all its ulterior developments, literary or otherwise. This foundation is no more dead in Latin than in German. To teach it, it is necessary to speak Latin as one would speak German."[41] Having essentially thrown his arms up in defeat after attempting numerous learning techniques, including exerting the energy to memorize a foreign dictionary and failing, he had a eureka moment that led him to what became known as his "series approach."

For Gouin, every event happened within a series, which invites the repetitive use of nouns and other terms, while also introducing new verbs and vocabulary. For example, scene one would repeat lots of nouns but offer new verb forms: "The maid **takes** hold of the pail by the handle, the maid **lifts** up the pail, the maid **goes** across the kitchen, the maid **opens** the door," and so on.[42] Gouin's approach was widely adopted and became popular in schools. It, of course, had its critics, even from within the Reform Movement. Henry Sweet, for instance, another prominent voice in this era who is certainly worth reading, remarked that "the 'series method' may in itself be a sound principle, but it is too limited in its application to form even the basis of a fully developed method."[43]

As Sweet saw it, "In its present form the Gouin method is incapable of teaching the pupil to say, 'I think so,' or 'I would rather not do it,' or, indeed, to express anything that falls under the categories of emotion or intellect."[44]

38. A. P. R. Howatt and H. G. Widdowson, *A History of English Language Teaching*, 2nd ed., OAL (Oxford: Oxford University Press, 2004), 171.

39. Howatt and Widdowson, *History of English Language Teaching*, 2nd ed., 323.

40. François Gouin, *The Art of Teaching and Studying Languages*, trans. H. Swan and V. Bétis (London: George Philip & Son, 1892). The French version was published in 1880.

41. Gouin, *Art of Teaching and Studying Languages*, 367.

42. Gouin, *Art of Teaching and Studying Languages*, 97–103.

43. Henry Sweet, *The Practical Study of Languages: A Guide for Teachers and Learners* (London: J. M. Dent & Co., 1899), 3.

44. Sweet, *Practical Study of Languages*, 178.

Moreover, he concluded that "some of the series, such as that which gives a detailed description of opening and shutting a door, . . . are as uninteresting as they are useless."[45] Regarding grammar, Gouin desired that it be learned both implicitly and explicitly. Thus, Gouin says, "In itself the grammatical teaching is necessary; but such as is given in the schools of today has proved useless, nay, even harmful for the acquisition and the practice of languages. Conclusion: we must not abolish the teaching of grammar; we must reform it."[46]

The final individual to bring into view here is Wilhelm Viëtor.[47] Often described as the catalyst for the Reform Movement, Viëtor penned an anonymous pamphlet in 1882 titled *Language Teaching Must Start Afresh!*[48] In it, he rails against overburdening students with homework and unnecessary academic exercises. These he views as damaging and harmful. He says that when a student begins with grammatical rules, "nothing that language teaching has to offer later on, reading in particular, can undo or make up for the damage that has already been done. . . . It is very unclear what purpose reading the text is supposed to fulfill in foreign language teaching, except, in my view, to exemplify the grammatical rules yet again."[49] The assertion that a teacher who begins with grammar rules will void any desire a student initially had to read the text is quite striking.

---

45. Sweet, *Practical Study of Languages*, 114.

46. Gouin, *Art of Teaching and Studying Languages*, 211. Of Gouin's approach we read elsewhere, "Several methodological weaknesses tend to jeopardize the effectiveness of Gouin's approach. His opposition to phonetics, reading and written exercises, and his recommendation of a large vocabulary not graded by difficulty or frequency, are both weaknesses in the light of modern applied linguistics. Furthermore, unlike Comenius, Pestalozzi and more modern teachers, Gouin distrusted realia and pictorial representation and placed his faith instead in a vague intuitive awareness. Finally, the exaggerated analysis of speech and behavior into 'micro-segments' and the excessive use of translation (especially in the early stages) endanger the positive effects of Gouin's main procedures." Renzo Titone, "History: The Nineteenth Century," in *Routledge Encyclopedia of Language Teaching and Learning*, ed. Michael Byram (London: Routledge, 2000), 268.

47. Like Gouin, Wilhelm Viëtor drew on the work of Samuel Brassai, whose work did not reach the level of popularity that either of theirs did. Admittedly, Brassai's works have been difficult to track down, but for a few helpful descriptions of him and his work, see Levente T. Szabó, "À la recherche . . . de l'editeur perdu. Sámuel Brassai and the First International Journal of Comparative Literary Studies," in *Storia, identità e canoni letterari*, ed. I. Both, A. Saraçgil, and A. Tarantino, SDR 152 (Florence: Firenze University Press, 2013), 177–88; and János Balázs, "The Basic Principles of Modern Sentence Theory in the Works of a Transylvanian Polymath in the 19th Century," in *Prehistory, History and Historiography of Language, Speech, and Linguistic Theory*, ed. Bela Bogyanyi, CILT 64 (Cambridge: Cambridge University Press, 1992), 64–72.

48. Wilhelm Viëtor, *Der Sprachunterricht muss umkehren! Ein Beitrag zur Überbürdungsfrage* (Heilbronn: Henninger, 1882). Here, however, I am citing the English translation by Anthony P. R. Howatt, *History of English Language Teaching* (Oxford: Oxford University Press, 1984), 344–63.

49. Viëtor, in Howatt, *History of English Language Teaching*, 357.

Not surprisingly, like Marcel, Viëtor asserts that, in order to learn a "dead language," it is first beneficial "to think in other languages than our own and know what language really is; in other words, we must have a sound acquaintance with living tongues."[50] This preparatory stage not only sets the students up to succeed but also sets the teachers up to succeed. He says, "If we can bring our pupils to think and express themselves in the foreign language in addition to their mother tongue, we shall have accomplished what we set out to do." The teacher shall "never lose sight of the two basic aims: comprehension and text reproduction."[51]

For Viëtor, as I have intimated already, grammar "grows naturally out of reading the texts themselves." Teachers should, at "regular intervals," make it a point to "revise the texts with a specific grammar point in mind, and present the results of this study systematically alongside earlier work so that the grammar builds up over the course of time. Also, it goes without saying that the foreign language should always be spoken in class." This also goes for teaching the classical languages. Viëtor, in something of a prophetic statement concerning teaching biblical languages today, perceptively concluded, "The more reluctant the classical language teaching profession is to follow this precept, the more doubtful their claim to a place in the schools at all."[52]

From the above overview, which is purposefully and necessarily abbreviated, there are several items worth noting. First, the role of text in the language teaching-learning process is significant. While it may have a different place within some of the methods, it's always present. Moreover, it is always used in engagement with speaking. Alongside reading and speaking come activities such as writing, using gestures, and looking at pictures. Orderliness and sequentiality are important as well. Another item we pick up in this era is an emphasis on the role of culture in language learning. Finally, we see that grammar is not viewed as the enemy per se, but its appearance at the appropriate stage in the process must be considered. If it is introduced too soon or out of order, it can be damaging. On this topic, too, grammar should be taught and learned inductively first and, as such, precede any deductive explanations. When seen in this view, understanding grammar, even deductive grammar, as the enemy is simply problematic and an unfair reading of the data. A well-rounded, holistic approach makes use of listening, reading, writing, speaking, grammar study, and translating.

---

50. Viëtor, in Howatt, *History of English Language Teaching*, 358.
51. Viëtor, in Howatt, *History of English Language Teaching*, 361.
52. Viëtor, in Howatt, *History of English Language Teaching*, 361.

■ The Modern World

On the heels of the Reform Movement came the modern world with new scientific approaches. I begin with Walter Ripmann, a noted voice among the reformers and beyond. He was deeply interested in language, attested by both his job within the educational system and his publications on teaching languages like Latin, English, French, German, and Italian. In his book *Hints on Teaching French*, he mentions the aims of his pedagogy: "Our pupils' object in learning a modern language is, in the first place, that they may understand, speak, and write it."[53] A large part of his practice focused on associating images with objects, especially early on, to aid in language acquisition.[54] He was also keen on aligning content with age development.[55]

As McLelland notes, "For Ripman, the spoken language was a means to a higher end."[56] At the fore of the *New First German Book*, he wrote a word to learners: "What I want you to learn first is to think in this foreign language, until it almost ceases to be foreign. Do not be afraid to speak in class; for the more you do so, the sooner you will be able to read."[57] Thus, Ripmann views speaking as a type of cognitive stepping stone toward the end goal of reading. Or, as McLelland puts it, "Giving space to the spoken language did not mean conversation was the sole goal—it was a stage on the way to be able to read, first simple passages, but ultimately literature."[58] In some cases, although certainly not all, this became known as the Direct Method and was known, in large part, for discouraging learners from using the mother tongue, engaging in translation, and being concerned with formal grammatical rules and terminology.[59]

Ripmann's model was text centered, which meant placing a high premium on reading. He also promoted speaking as a means to an end, not an end in

53. Walter Ripman, *Hints on Teaching French: With a Running Commentary to Dent's First and Second French Books* (New York: Dutton & Co., 1913), 2.

54. Ripman, *Hints on Teaching French*, 5–8.

55. Walter Ripman, *A First English Book for Boys and Girls Whose Mother-Tongue Is Not English*, 9th ed. (New York: Dutton & Co., 1936), v–vi. Note that his surname is spelled two ways in his publications: *Ripman* and *Ripmann*. Each is used here in accordance with how it was published.

56. McLelland, *Teaching and Learning*, 106.

57. Walter Ripman, S. Alge, and S. Hamburger, *Dent's New First German Book* (New York: Dutton & Co., 1917), vi.

58. McLelland, *Teaching and Learning*, 106.

59. McLelland, *Teaching and Learning*, 106. Ripmann, Alge, and Hamburger, when writing about teaching German, permit using English in the class sparingly: "When it will contribute to both accuracy of thought and economy of time, English should be used." Walter Ripmann, S. Alge, and S. Hamburger, *Newson's First German Book*, ed. W. Ripmann and W. H. Buell, NMLB (New York: Newson & Company, 1901), vi.

and of itself. Listening was also an important factor, but again, he was not concerned with translation or formal grammar training. Notably, Ripmann was one of the first to begin drawing lines in the sand on this matter. As the twentieth century progressed, this became more and more of a trend and, in the end, often led to educators choosing one side and disparaging the other. It was out of this, however, that additional methods arose.

That brings us to the Natural Method, also known as the Nature Method. Here meaning is derived inferentially, and there is no use for the first language, translation, or, at least early on, metalanguage or grammatical terminology. This is not to say that there is no place for grammar at all; rather, it is used in later stages and often referenced for corrective purposes. In the Natural Method, the preferred learning order is listening, speaking, graded reading, writing, and grammar.[60] This was popularized by Marcel, who placed great emphasis on being able to think in the language.

Caleb Gattegno, too, desired that students be able to think in the language, but as the progenitor of the Silent Way methodology, his route of getting students there was different. For Gattegno, it was important that a teacher "remain almost silent, giving the students the time and space necessary to practise the language . . . and placing the onus for learning squarely on their shoulders."[61] They gained awareness of the language through their mistakes, corrected by the teacher mostly and mainly through silence and gestures. The learner's exploration of the language through use is, in the Silent Way, a trait common to a number of methods of the day, albeit in a rather different way.

Suggestopedia, which was developed by a Bulgarian psychologist (Georgi Lozanov) and used in the public school system there for some time, was influenced by the Direct Method. Here the unconscious was tapped by way of "certain yogic techniques of physical and mental relaxation."[62] In addition to yogic techniques, the use of music, relaxation, memorization, speaking, games, storytelling, sketches, plays, reading, grammar, and translation is employed within this method. The emphasis on embodiment and interaction, engaging the senses, relief from foreign-language anxiety, and the use of basically all means available are elements that rose to prominence through the nineteenth and twentieth centuries.

One insight that came to prominence during this time, noted especially by Valerian Postovsky, was that comprehending a foreign language is easier

60. Mackey, *Language Teaching Analysis*, 152.
61. Roslyn Young, "The Silent Way," in Byram, *Routledge Encyclopedia of Language Teaching and Learning*, 547.
62. Meng-Ching Ho, "Suggestopedia," in Byram, *Routledge Encyclopedia of Language Teaching and Learning*, 587.

than producing it. This means attempts at speaking and composing should be delayed until listening and comprehending have been practiced. As David Crystal says, "A basic receptive competence is established, and this is used as a foundation for work involving retrieval skills."[63] This was known as the Delayed Oral Practice Method or Comprehension Approach. Thinking in the target language is inherent to most methods in this era.

Another method that focused on listening was the Audio-Lingual Method, also known as the Aural-Oral Method. This was used in the 1930s and '40s among soldiers fighting in World War II who traveled to foreign lands and needed to acquire basic conversational skills in a short amount of time. High-frequency vocabulary and phrases were used from the start, along with the repetition of common structures. Listening and speaking were foundational for fluency. Reading, writing, and grammatical study came later, but the latter received very little attention.[64]

One of the most popular methods, heralded especially by James Asher, was the Total Physical Response and Storytelling Method. Like the Audio-Lingual Method, much of the focus was on "the importance of aural comprehension" in "the early months of learning."[65] As Crystal notes, "The name derives from the emphasis on the actions that learners make when given simple commands. More advanced language is introduced by building up chains of actions, using either spoken or written commands."[66] Asher and other advocates purposefully frontload listening. Asher says, "The first element is that listening skill is far in advance of speaking. . . . Listening precedes speaking. It may be that listening comprehension maps the blueprint for the future acquisition of speaking."[67]

Quite different from this is the Grammar Translation Method (known early on as the Prussian Method). Here, the goal is a "meticulous analysis of the written language, in which translation exercises, reading comprehension, and the written imitation of texts play a primary role."[68] In most grammar-translation classrooms there is usually no listening, speaking, or storytelling in the target language. While comprehension is a component, the additional or foreign language is always filtered through the first language. While Jack Richards and Theodore Rodgers assert, "It is a method for which there is no

---

63. David Crystal, *The Cambridge Encyclopedia of Language* (Cambridge: Cambridge University Press, 1987), 375.

64. Crystal, *Cambridge Encyclopedia of Language*, 374.

65. Crystal, *Cambridge Encyclopedia of Language*, 375.

66. Crystal, *Cambridge Encyclopedia of Language*, 375.

67. James J. Asher, *Learning Another Language through Actions*, 7th ed. (Los Gatos, CA: Sky Oaks, 2012), 23.

68. Crystal, *Cambridge Encyclopedia of Language*, 374.

theory,"[69] it continues to be used because it does not require an educator to be a fluent speaker, and both classroom and curriculum variables are easy to control.

Pym advocates a method he calls Communicative Translation. For him, translation "is always a communicative activity."[70] He asserts that the distinction between spoken translation (interpreting) and written translation (translation) is not useful; learners should be speaking and writing all the way through; since speaking is the primary situation, all written translation should begin from spoken translation; and success is judged by way of communication, not just equivalence. This pedagogy uses both spoken and written modes.

This brings us to the Eclectic (or Active) Method, which might be viewed as something of a compromise method—that is, a compromise between the Direct Method and something akin to the Grammar Translation Method. It is one of the most popular methods at the moment because it seeks to balance the workload between teacher and student. Language skills "are introduced in the following order: speaking, writing, understanding and reading."[71] Activities can "include oral practice, reading aloud, and questions and answers" along with "translation, . . . some deductive grammar, and some audio visual aids."[72] John Archibald states, "Recent trends in second language pedagogy have tended to downplay the idea that a single method of instruction will work for all people. . . . Currently, teachers tend to adopt an eclectic approach to second language instruction. What this means is that a variety of methods and approaches are utilized."[73] Moreover, as Richards and Rodgers note, "Changes in language teaching methods throughout history have reflected recognition of changes in the kind of proficiency learners need, such as a move toward oral proficiency rather than reading comprehension as the goal of language study."[74] Thus, the "kind of proficiency" desired and needed by the student goes a long way in shaping the teaching approach. Teachers of ancient languages must ask what kind of proficiency is desired and needed. I resist a pat answer on this because educational circumstances are fluid and ever changing. Even for those who might advocate this position, there must

69. Jack C. Richards and Theodore S. Rodgers, *Approaches and Methods in Language Teaching* (Cambridge: Cambridge University Press, 1986), 7.

70. Pym, "Rebranding Translation," 9.

71. Mackey, *Language Teaching Analysis*, 154.

72. Mackey, *Language Teaching Analysis*, 154.

73. John Archibald, "Second Language Acquisition," in *Contemporary Linguistics: An Introduction*, 4th ed., ed. W. O'Grady, J. Archibald, M. Aronoff, and J. Rees-Miller (Boston: Bedford-St. Martins, 2001), 481.

74. Richards and Rodgers, *Approaches and Methods*, 3.

be some recognition that teachers will necessarily have to make their own adaptations. Thus, openness to variability and a posture of humility might go a long way.

I now want to mention one more figure: Hans Ørberg. I mention Ørberg because his work could be something of a guiding light for those of us who teach biblical languages and create and use biblical language resources. Ørberg's method, based on Arthur Jensen's,[75] is at home within the Natural Method, but because of certain nuances it is known as the Contextual Induction Method. This underlies the "Lingua Latina" series, which also has audio readings by Ørberg himself.

Ørberg asserts that his approach rationally accelerates the learning process without compromising the natural stages of learning. The aim "is to make every sentence presented to the students immediately intelligible *per se*, or *self-explanatory*, by grading and organizing the introduction of vocabulary and grammar." What this means is that the need for students "to translate or explain grammatical points in the students' own language"[76] is largely eradicated. For the most part, Ørberg succeeds. I must say, however, that in my own use of his works in the classroom, as the language proceeds to get tougher, there are occasions when the vocabulary and syntax require explanation in English. This, however, does not necessarily detract from the work.

Ørberg notes that "words and grammatical forms only make sense *in context* and therefore should be learned in context." In his work he discusses "a variety of contexts or situations in which the words and structures that are to be learned make sense in such a way that the meaning and function of all new words and grammatical forms appear unambiguously from the context in which they occur, or, if necessary, from illustrations or marginal notes using vocabulary already learned."[77] Thus, repetition is a major facet of the series. The strategy is that "in every chapter the new words introduced be in proportion no greater than one to every 25–30 words already learned."[78] Christopher Brown and Luigi Miraglia suggest, "With this lexical foundation, the student will be able to read most works of Latin literature with relative ease."[79] Indeed, one of the best results of using Ørberg's works with students is that little effort or time must be exerted in the process.

75. Arthur M. Jensen, *English by the Nature Method* (Switzerland: The Nature Method Institute, 1956).

76. Hans H. Ørberg, "Lingua Latina per se Illustrata: Lecture Given by Hans H. Ørberg on Various Occasions," *ARTL Weblog*, document last accessed at https://tinyurl.com/t97u6kp.

77. Ørberg, "Lingua Latina per se Illustrata."

78. Christopher G. Brown and Luigi Miraglia, *Latine Doceo: A Companion for Instructors* (Bemidji, MN: Focus, 2004), 6.

79. Brown and Miraglia, *Latine Doceo*, 6.

At this point, I want to highlight one more item. McLelland has aptly noted, "Hand in hand with the view formulated in the 1960s that the goal of language teaching was communication, came the tendency to conceptualize communication as consisting of skills." This, of course, "is anything but new." Indeed, Quintilian saw teaching as requiring "the interrelation of four activities: reading, writing, speaking, and listening. No one was more important than the others."[80] Indeed, these four skills have played a major role in shaping language teaching-learning across time.

Crystal says, "In the long search for the best way of teaching a foreign language, hundreds of different approaches, or methods, have been devised. . . . Ambitious claims are often made for a new teaching method, but none has yet shown to be intrinsically superior."[81] For language teachers, this has caused a present-day shift where "the contemporary attitude is flexible and utilitarian: it is recognized that there are several ways of reaching the goal of FL (Foreign Language) competence, and that teachers need to be aware of a range of methods, in order to find the one most appropriate to the learner's needs and circumstances, and to the objectives of the course."[82]

■ Concluding Remarks

When I was a student, I often questioned the payoff of learning Greek. At times, it seemed aloof and out there—something reserved for the intellectually and/or spiritually elite. As a Greek educator, I have suspicions that some quite like and prefer it that way. I have, with much regret, seen too many colleagues post on social media examples of how they have scared or terrified their Greek students with quizzes, tests, homework, and so on. At one point, I even began creating an archive of such examples. It got so depressing that I stopped.

When I was a student, Greek mostly seemed irrelevant, except to those teaching it and writing grammar books. It was a recurring question: What use was there for Greek? The inquiry concerning Greek's relevance is, I think, one that educators must take seriously. From a fiduciary or economic standpoint, academic institutions are certainly listening. As we all know, enrollment in biblical language courses is, across the board, in decline. While there may be a few institutions that occasionally buck this trend, it is the norm. So, rather than rushing to defend the value of the existence of language courses, maybe those of us who are educators could take a cue from those handling

---

80. McLelland, *Teaching and Learning*, 119.
81. Crystal, *Cambridge Encyclopedia of Language*, 274.
82. Crystal, *Cambridge Encyclopedia of Language*, 274.

the administrative duties at our schools and stop, listen, and make some reconsiderations.

We need not be like the Stoic philosophers whose view Cicero summarizes in his *Pro Murena* (61): "The philosopher surmises nothing, repents of nothing, is never wrong, and never changes his opinion." We need not be described with a similar epithet: "The Koine Greek teacher surmises nothing, repents of nothing, is never wrong, and never changes his opinion." We are all apologists for our pet views. We are keen to defend what we've built a career researching and publishing on. Some of us have chosen the linguistic hills we are willing to die on, that we are willing to stake our names on. We deliver our conference papers with vigor and marshal troops in the form of graduate and postgraduate students to carry on our views. Repent? Be wrong? Change an opinion? Despite the fact that we all likely value the scientific method, sometimes our blind spot with regard to it is not in the research itself but in our own disposition.

We must listen. As teachers, our constituents are speaking, with their mouths, their money, and their feet. If students refuse to enroll in Institution A because they feel they are wasting money on irrelevant language courses, the school loses money. Institution B recognizes this and, in order to stay in business, removes the language requirement and brings those students in. Institution A finally takes notice and begins reconsidering, eventually following suit. The constituents have taken control of the market and shaped it to their liking, leaving us dead on our ink-covered hills, bodies draped in flags that read "Perfect Tense," "Pronunciation," "Pedagogy," and the like.

I'm not, of course, of the mindset or saying that digging our heels in and engaging in challenging research is not a worthy endeavor—it is. I am, however, attempting to draw our attention to the fact that we, the educators, are part of what is contributing to making ourselves irrelevant. This is a hard truth, but the numbers do tell an important story, and they don't lie.

Let us consider, then, the data from the Modern Language Association with regard to both ancient Greek and Biblical Hebrew.[83] For Biblical Hebrew, the statistics from 2002–16 should give us pause. In 2002, there were 14,183 students enrolled in these courses. Four years later, in 2006, that number had dropped slightly to 14,137. Three years after that, 13,764. In 2013, the number had reached 12,596. And in 2016, the number was 9,587. Thus, in the fourteen-year span from 2002 to 2016, enrollment in Biblical Hebrew saw a

83. Dennis Looney and Natalia Lusin, "Enrollments in Languages Other Than English in United States Institutions of Higher Education, Summer 2016 and Fall 2016: Preliminary Report," Modern Language Association, February 2018, https://www.mla.org/content/down load/83540/2197676/2016-Enrollments-Short-Report.pdf.

national decrease to the tune of 4,596 students. This is a 32 percent decrease, and the trend shows no signs of waning.

Let's turn to ancient Greek. In 2006, there were 22,842 students enrolled in Greek nationwide. In 2009, it dropped to 21,515. That dropped quite a bit in 2013, to 16,961. In 2016, the number was at 13,264. This is an end-result decrease of nearly 10,000 students (or 9,578 to be exact), which is right at 42 percent. Beyond the fact that this is a greater drop than with Hebrew, what else is significant is that it has happened over a shorter period of time. Whereas a 32 percent decrease in enrollment occurred across fifteen years for Hebrew, a 42 percent decrease took place with Greek in just over a decade. Again, the trend shows no signs of waning.

Across the board, enrollment in ancient-languages classes is fast declining. There is no one reason for this. We can likely attribute some of it to the internet and online educational trends. We can also attribute some of it to students not wanting to take it and institutions bending to that demand. We can likely attribute some of it, too, to what may be a cultural trend of a lack of interest in Christianity. There may be other factors as well. I think we are kidding ourselves, however, if we don't also consider that, in general, we educators may be part of the problem. Or, let me rephrase that: as educators, our pedagogy may be part of the problem.

These days, for me, pedagogy seems to be one of my hills. My motivation is, I believe, well placed: I want students, for instance, to enroll in Greek classes, embrace the language, study it, and use it. Perhaps we're too far in and the trend cannot be turned around; yet, I am of the mindset that if we do not try, we've failed our field, our students, and ourselves as educators. I do think the trend can be reversed; I think Greek enrollment can take an upward swing and be revitalized. I also think that pedagogy may well be the place to start. Current Western culture, in the wake of postmodernism's emphasis on experience, seems to be enjoying a renaissance of sorts with regard to dynamics between the body and experience. Could it be the case that considering a more embodied and holistic approach would bode well for our cause of teaching ancient and biblical languages?

A more holistic and embodied approach *is* needed. This would be text-based, driven by contextual induction, eclectic in methodology, open to Focus on Form technique, and guided by curricular principles of the progymnasmata. Here, all activities—whether imitation, listening, reading, writing, speaking, grammar study, or translation—orbit around and derive from text. Teaching should be conducted by a master teacher and, as far as is possible, be gradually sequential. Moreover, grammar should be acquired largely in an inductive way in the early stages; moreover, this means leading with listening, speaking, responding, and reading first. Any deductive grammar teaching should, as far as is possible, also be conducted in the target language and be presented subsequent to inductive grammar learning. Also, historical context should be used to introduce the language; that is, contextual induction should be given merit. This type of presentation should be done in ways that are engaging and relevant.

To accomplish this, we will all have to work hard and be willing to take risks. We will also have to (a) require that future generations of biblical language teachers earn degrees in linguistics, perhaps with a focus on language acquisition, and (b) push to have linguistics courses as part of college, Bible college, university, and seminary curricula. I've repeatedly heard it said that the field of biblical studies is consistently a decade or two behind advances in the sciences, including linguistics and language teaching and learning. This may only be anecdotal, but it's likely not far from being true; in fact, it may even be worse. To remedy that with regard to advances in the biblical languages, future generations must be formally trained in linguistics. We need look no further than the plethora of regurgitated Greek grammars on our hands, sorely lacking in any formal linguistic expertise, to prove this. We can and must do better.

In the words of A. P. R. Howatt and H. G. Widdowson, when it comes to writing a history of some subject, "it is always tempting to prick the balloon of contemporary self-satisfaction by demonstrating that what has been taken as evidence of progress in our time has, in fact, 'all been done before.'"[84] I have succumbed to that temptation here but, I believe, for a good and just cause: to remind us that, as Bible scholars and teachers of ancient languages, we have a rich history. In choosing to embrace that past, we also choose not to embrace the divisive tale, commonly spun, that is built on anachronism and framed by a lust for relevance. In that vein, at the very least, I hope that advocates of various methods can entertain the notion that those with a different pedagogy are not enemies but colleagues, are not naive but using the means available to them, and are not outdated or outmoded but developing in their own thought, praxis, and pedagogy.

---

84. Howatt and Widdowson, *History of English Language Teaching*, 2nd ed., 170–71.

8

The Role of Pronunciation
in New Testament Greek Studies

RANDALL BUTH

From one perspective, the topic of Greek pronunciation is uncompli-
cated. Common wisdom says that pronunciation is irrelevant for those
who want to *read* the Greek New Testament, so for some, this chapter
might be seen as ἀδιάφορα (*adiaphora*, i.e., not essential).

In fact, pronunciation has a very important effect on our whole field, albeit
indirect. In order to properly address the question of pronunciation, we must
first discuss the role of speech itself in the field of New Testament studies and
language pedagogy in general. *Speech is vital* for the field of New Testament
studies if the field is to mature. Most scholars assume the opposite of this
simple truth, so we need to address this issue before proceeding.

■ Speech Is Vital for Reading

Where does twenty years of studying Greek, especially New Testament Greek,
put someone? Students often assume that when they finish a PhD they will be
"thinking in Greek." At the end of studies they often change their tune and
say that such is not necessary for a dead language, or sometimes they may
claim that it is not even possible.

Reading requires a minimum speed if it is to be true reading and if the reader is going to have understanding when they arrive at the end of a sentence and at the end of a paragraph. This claim can be demonstrated if a sentence is read slowly, pausing for one or two seconds after every word. Try reading the next paragraph with your hands covering each word except one and then waiting two seconds before uncovering the next word, and so on to the end of the paragraph. The reader will experience some confusion, which may be explained psycholinguistically. According to a study by Catherine Walter, working memory "consists of a central executive plus slave systems. One of the slave systems is the phonological loop, a short-term memory mechanism that stores information in phonological form and automatically rehearses that information by unconscious sub-vocalisation."[1] Let me clarify a point in that paragraph: subvocalization is not consciously heard and does not refer to mumbling; it is a process internal to the brain before conscious thought.

The reason for the confusion when reading too slowly is a result of a phonological loop in the brain that operates at about two seconds.[2] After a couple of seconds the brain needs to store a summary, picture, or concept, or else the reading fails and the brain must reprocess. Furthermore, readers do not see what they read; they hear it.[3] Naturally, if the brain is overly engaged in these lower-level processes, repeating and reprocessing until finally they "get the point," the brain does not have full resources available for thinking and higher-level processing of understanding the reading. If a reader wants to interpret and engage the thought of a written communication, they need to develop an ability to process the language at the speed of speech. This is what happens with fluent readers of a foreign language.

The application of this psycholinguistic process mentioned above has a direct implication for teaching the reading of Greek. Walter's psycholinguistic testing has statistically significant correlations for reading in a second language. In her words: "What does this [research] imply? First of all, it means that for progress in reading, classroom time will be better spent in increasing

---

1. Catherine Walter, "Phonology in Second Language Reading: Not an Optional Extra," *TESOL Quarterly* 42, no. 3 (2008): 457.

2. "The phonological loop holds about 2 seconds of speech, which listeners record automatically when they hear speech." Walter, "Phonology in Second Language Reading," 457.

3. "The phonological loop comes into play in a somewhat counterintuitive way in the reading of alphabetic languages. Strange as it may seem, L1 readers of languages with alphabetic writing systems store the most recently read material (about as much as the reader can say in 2 seconds) in their phonological loop rather than in their visuospatial sketchpad. L1 readers of these languages do not mentally see what they have just read: They hear it" (Walter, "Phonology in Second Language Reading," 458). L1 refers to a person's first language or mother tongue.

proficiency and exposure to the spoken language generally than in attempting to teach comprehension skills."[4]

Diane August and Timothy Shanahan provide another study testifying to the need for oral proficiency in order to produce enhanced reading skills: "An important finding that emerges from the research is that word-level skills in literacy—such as decoding, word recognition and spelling—are often taught well enough to allow language-minority students to attain levels of performance equal to those of native English speakers."[5] Let me apply this finding to New Testament Greek studies: this is good news. There is every expectation that we can train our students to achieve parsing skills equal to those of native Greek speakers, whether ancient or modern.

But we must return to August and Shanahan's study: "However, this is *not* the case for text-level skills—reading comprehension and writing. . . . The research suggests that the reason for the disparity between word- and text-level skills among language-minority students is *oral English proficiency*. . . . It is not enough to teach language-minority students reading skills alone. Extensive *oral* English development *must* be incorporated into *successful literacy instruction*."[6] Let me apply this point to New Testament Greek studies: this is not so good news, or rather, it is a call to radical changes in our pedagogy. Reading comprehension directly relates to what is termed "exegesis" in biblical studies. If we want to increase exegetical comprehension skills in Greek, we need to provide extensive oral Greek development.

We should also carefully refine our ideas about reading itself. What we commonly call "reading" a source text probably does not qualify as reading, at least not as described and studied by research. Researchers on reading define true reading as something that happens unconsciously when a literate person encounters a written text in a language that they know. In terms of speed, this reading takes place at least at the rate of speech and generally faster, closer to two hundred words per minute and faster. This is a direct result of the phonological loop within the brain. Such reading skills are desirable for high-level text comprehension, and we can see that psycholinguistic research indicates that we need high *oral* skills if we want to develop such reading skills and to internalize the language.

---

4. Walter, "Phonology in Second Language Reading," 470.
5. Diane August and Timothy Shanahan, "Executive Summary," in *Developing Literacy in Second Language Users: Report of the National Literacy Panel on Language-Minority Children and Youth*, ed. Diane August and Timothy Shanahan (Mahwah, NJ: Lawrence Erlbaum Associates, 2006), 4.
6. August and Shanahan, "Executive Summary," 4 (emphasis added).

The next question becomes, How can we possibly achieve or make progress toward such goals? Helpful guidance comes from the American Council for the Teaching of Foreign Languages (ACTFL):

> *Research indicates* that *effective* language instruction must provide significant levels of meaningful communication* and interactive feedback in the target language in order for students to develop language and cultural proficiency. The pivotal role of target-language interaction in language learning is emphasized in the *K-16 Standards for Foreign Language Learning in the 21st Century. ACTFL therefore recommends that language educators and their students use the target language as exclusively as possible (90% plus) at all levels of instruction during instructional time and, when feasible, beyond the classroom.* In classrooms that feature maximum target-language use, instructors use a variety of strategies to facilitate comprehension and support meaning making.[7]

We may make the following observations based on this recommendation:

1. The best practices recommendation in a classroom is use of the target language 90 percent of the time or more, which essentially can be termed an "immersion" approach.
2. This is a conclusion by an organization of language-pedagogy professionals, based on research, and is not an individual's hypothesis.
3. Classical languages are recognized to have different emphases and will target written goals and, presumably, primarily use written assessment. However, they still need to run a classroom 90 percent of the time, and to do that efficiently and effectively, there is no escape from rapid, extensive language use in aural-oral interaction.
4. The ACTFL recommendation meshes seamlessly with research that spoken language is necessary for improving reading.

With this introduction and background, we can return to the question of Koine Greek pronunciation—ἡ κοινὴ προφορά. Is the question important? Absolutely! What psycholinguistics and studies in Second Language Acquisition show is that *speech is vital* if we want to internalize the language of our interest and *to develop high-level reading skills.* Once we conclude this, then pronunciation becomes an issue, especially with multiple pronunciation systems for Greek in use around the world.

---

7. Approved by the ACTFL Board of Directors, May 22, 2010. See "Use of the Target Language in the Classroom," ACTFL, May 21, 2010, https://www.actfl.org/advocacy/position-state ments/use-the-target-language-the-classroom-old (emphasis added). The asterisk marks this footnote in the ACTFL document: "Communication for a classical language refers to an emphasis on reading ability and for American Sign Language (ASL) to signed communicative ability."

■ Principles for Choosing a Greek Pronunciation

Choosing a pronunciation system should be informed by many principles. Because some of the principles work against each other, we may expect to have to reach a reasonable compromise. Here are seven primary factors or principles for pronunciation today:

1. **Period specific:** A pronunciation system based on the Roman period in the land of Israel, 63 BCE to 325 CE, is a natural choice for persons wishing to learn Koine Greek.

2. **A "Chaucer principle":** A distinctly earlier pronunciation system is generally not used for a later period of a language. English speakers and English scholars do not use Chaucerian pronunciation for reading and studying Shakespeare.[8] We can call this the "Chaucer principle." Not using an earlier pronunciation for a later pronunciation mitigates against simply using a Homeric or Platonic phonology or orthography for later periods.

3. **Phonemic principle:** The pronunciation should preserve the same significant sound distinctions that were used in the Roman period. This means that the pronunciation system should be "phonemic." (This term will be explained below.)

4. **Historical:** The pronunciation system should, as far as practical, be historical—that is, it should reflect the way the language sounded in the Roman period. One would not use a sound for a phonemic unit that was not historically related to that unit. For example, one would not use [a] for [o].

5. **Adaptability to historical outcomes:** When options are available, the pronunciation should help students with adapting to other dialects of Greek, whether ancient or modern. When in doubt, decisions should fit with the known historical outcome.

6. **Practicality for speakers of widely used modern languages:** When options are available, the pronunciation should be practical for speakers of languages such as English, Spanish, French, and German.

---

8. The parallel between English and Greek is highly instructive. English pronunciation went through the Great Vowel Shift between the time of Chaucer (ca. 1343–1400) and Shakespeare (1564–1616). The social movements following the Black Death in 1347–51 may have been a major contributor to the rapid language change. Greek, too, went through a massive vowel shift after the worldwide spread of Greek language and culture following Alexander the Great (356–323 BCE). These Greek vowel shifts will be documented and discussed below.

7. **Carrying capacity:** The carrying capacity for live, new communication must be considered. This principle recommends against simply adopting modern Greek pronunciation for Koine. Modern Greek can easily be used for reading the ancient dialects, but the modern pronunciation hinders live communication using the ancient dialects by not providing enough phonemic distinctions. This lack of carrying capacity led to spelling changes in later dialects of the language such as εμείς and εσείς ("we" and "you all") because ἡμεῖς and ὑμεῖς sounded alike toward the end of the first millennium (both are pronounced *imis*).

At this point we must deal with a "straw man" about pronunciation that is often assumed in the field: "There are no MP3 recordings of NT Greek, so we can't know what it sounded like. In any case, there would have been dialectical differences from region to region and even city to city. So pronunciation can be ignored as irrelevant."

Fortunately, linguistic study allows us to reconstruct a phonemic analysis of Koine Greek. We know that travelers around the Mediterranean Sea were able to communicate in Greek, and we can reconstruct what the general sound patterns were like, even if we cannot describe the sub-phonemic differences that would have been met in any one city.

▓ Phonemes

Phonemes are sounds that in a given language distinguish one word from another. In this chapter we primarily consider vowel phonemes. For example, consider five one-syllable words that, in many English dialects, differ only in their vowel sounds: "beat" (IPA [bit]),[9] "bit" [bɪt], "bait" [beɪt], "bet" [bɛt], and "bat" [bæt].[10] Because these are five different words, we may speak of these vowel sounds as five phonemes of English. Now, English also has three words pronounced [bit]: the vegetable "beet"; a verb "to beat something, to hit it"; and a musical rhythm, as "the beat goes on." These three are homophones in English. They now have the same vowel sound—that is, have the same vowel phoneme—regardless of how they might have been pronounced or spelled in the past. The three homophones are the same phonemically,

9. IPA = International Phonetic Alphabet. The IPA, which dates back to the late nineteenth century, is a standardized listing of the sounds of spoken languages. Traditionally, brackets enclose sounds or words written using IPA.

10. In this chapter, brackets are generally used for phonetic material while slashes are used for phonemic material.

unlike the five words above, which are distinguished by their five different vowel phonemes.

Physically, these vowel phonemes are made by placing the tongue in different heights within the mouth. Many languages use fewer vowel height distinctions (i.e., fewer vowel phonemes) than English. Figure 8.1a is a left-facing mouth that shows the approximate position of tongue height for producing the vowels [i, a, u].

Figure 8.1a
Vowels Formed in Mouth by Tongue Height

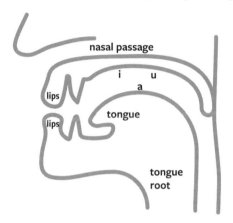

In a language with only three phonemic vowels, the tongue could go anywhere in those three areas in order to signal those phonemes. This little area is magnified in figure 8.1b.

Figure 8.1b
Magnified Area for a 3-Vowel Language

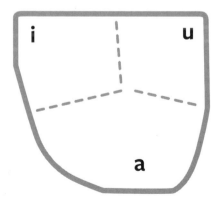

Figure 8.2

Magnified Area for 5 Vowel Areas (Plus Rounded-Lip ü, = 6 Phonemes)

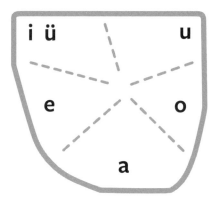

This is still a sideways look at a left-facing mouth. In addition, approximate boundary lines are drawn to show where a speaker's tongue height needs to be in order to clearly signal one vowel versus another (and therefore one word versus another). A foreigner or a speaker from a different dialect may put the tongue at a slightly different spot within the three vowel areas, but as long as they stay within the appropriate area for the appropriate vowel (and word), the sounds will be clear and meaningful. The exact borders, of course, will be different for different languages and dialects.

Items other than tongue position can affect phonemes in a language. Figure 8.2 shows five vowel areas, where an additional phoneme in one area is added by lip rounding.

In most languages the vowels on the right side, the "back" vowels, tend to use rounded lips. Thus, back-vowel areas "u" and "o" typically have lip rounding. However, vowels on the front column, the left column, typically use unrounded, flat lips. In addition, some languages, like French, German, and ancient Greek, have two high-front vowels: one with unrounded lips and one with lip rounding. Thus, two phonemic vowels used the same high front tongue area as pictured in figure 8.2, which represents some Byzantine Greek dialects.

For Koine Greek we need to move to figure 8.3a, where there are three phonemic heights with the front vowels. Overall, there are six tongue-position areas, plus an extra front vowel that uses rounded lips. For convenience, in figure 8.3b the phonemic spaces are labeled with Greek script.

Finally, in 8.4a and 8.4b we see an added feature for vowel phonemes: length. "Length" refers to the relative time involved for pronouncing the vowel.

Figure 8.3a
Magnified Area for 6 Vowel Areas
(Plus Rounded ü as 7th Phoneme)

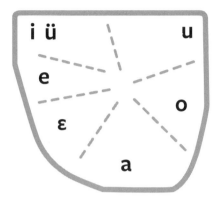

Figure 8.3b
Magnified Area for 6 Vowel Areas
(7 Phonemes, with Koine Greek Symbols)

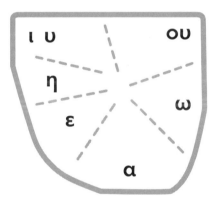

In 8.4a the number of tongue-position areas is the same as in 8.3a. However, most of the areas have a long vowel and a short vowel. The different lengths of the vowel sound can be used to distinguish different words. This is a feature of language that does not exist in English but was a part of pre-Alexandrian ancient Greek.[11] Colons are used with a vowel symbol in 8.4a

11. I have named this the Allen-Daitz system after W. Sidney Allen, who wrote a monograph arguing for this pronunciation for the fifth century BCE (*Vox Graeca: The Pronunciation of Classical Greek*, 3rd ed. [Cambridge: Cambridge University Press, 1987]), and Stephen Daitz, who published several recordings of readings in this ancient Greek system.

Figure 8.4a
Magnified Area for 6 Vowel Areas Plus Long (:) and Short Duration

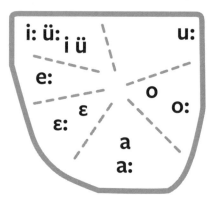

Restored Attic pronunciation, fifth-century BCE Erasmian (Allen-Daitz).

Figure 8.4b
Magnified Area for 6 Vowel Areas Plus Long and Short Duration

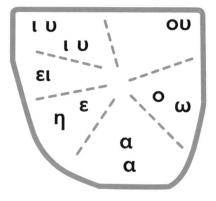

Restored Attic pronunciation in Greek symbols. The long and
short duration are partially marked in Greek script.

to mark the long phoneme, and the same vowel symbol is used without a colon to mark the short phoneme. In the areas for [ɛ], [a], and [o], the short vowels are written closer to the center and the long vowels are written farther away from the center. That reflects physical reality. Short vowels are held a relatively shorter amount of time. That means that the tongue does not have as much time to articulate the vowel, so typically in languages the shorter vowels are slightly more centralized. In this way, the position of a long vowel and a short vowel may be slightly different. Persons who use a US-seminary

Erasmian pronunciation should pay attention to the area for "o." The long vowel is slightly lower than the short vowel. This means that omega sounded closer to "aw" and omikron sounded closer to "o." The Machen-style Erasmian does exactly the opposite, asking students to pronounce omikron like "aw," as in the English words "law" and "awe." The greatest travesty, though, is with what I call the Astarte Erasmian pronunciation. Students are asked to move omikron from above omega all the way into the alpha area and to pronounce omikron as "ah," like the "a" in "Father." The words τὸν θεόν sound like τὰν θεάν, which is the Doric accusative for a female goddess. This is a point where live speakers in a language would typically start to correct a foreigner, because they have crossed phonemic boundaries and are starting to say things that they did not intend to say.

If a language system were to lose a feature like length from its phonological system, one might expect to see changes like a move from figure 8.4a to figure 8.3a. This is the change that took place in Greek after Alexander, when the Greek language spread out during the following two centuries over the whole Near East and eastern Mediterranean regions.

■ Koine Greek Vowel Phonology (First Century BCE/CE) and Its Evidence

Alexander the Great spread the Greek language from Greece to India and throughout the Middle East, and it became the premier language in the world for government and commerce. However, during the two centuries following Alexander, Greek vowels went through a relatively rapid and comprehensive phonological change. From thousands of language examples, we are able to reconstruct the phonology of Koine Greek in Egypt, in the land of Israel, around the Aegean, and in Rome. There is a broad consensus among linguists on the Koine vowels. Some representative examples are listed here, particularly from the Judean Desert Greek texts and also texts from the Roman catacombs.[12]

Vowel pair 1: Consider the following spelling in a letter from the year 100 CE: τωι οιειωι. How easy is this to read? It was and is clear for those who speak the Koine dialect. This was part of a letter from a father to his son. The standard Attic spelling would be τῷ υἱῷ ("to the son"), which is what "Normalized" in the following tables refers to.

12. Harry Joshua Leon, "The Language of the Greek Inscriptions from the Jewish Catacombs of Rome," *Transactions and Proceedings of the American Philological Association* 58 (1927): 210–33. "It is generally agreed among scholars that the remains from the Jewish catacombs belong chiefly to the second and third centuries of the Christian era" (211).

Table 8.1. Vowel Pair 1: ι for Attic ει, and ει for both short and long ι

	Attestation	Normalized	English
Ben Kosiba 1.9	ισ	εἰς	to, for (132–135 CE)
Ben Kosiba 1.7	συνεξελθιν	συνεξελθεῖν	go out with
Babatha 25.4	επιδη	ἐπειδή	since (131 CE)
Babatha 25.6	νυνει	νυνί	now (Attic short ι)
Babatha 15.8	υμειν	ὑμῖν	for you (125 CE)
Papyrus 109.2	τωι οιειωι	τῷ υἱῷ	to the son (100 CE)
Nazareth 6	επιδιξη	ἐπιδείξη	should prove
Nazareth 20	τειμαν	τιμᾶν	to honor (Attic long ι)
Babatha 20.39	ειδιαις	ἰδίαις	one's own (130 CE, short ι)

On the Jewish inscriptions in the Roman catacombs, Harry Joshua Leon writes, "ει was already confused with long ι in the third cent. BC, and with short ι in the second cent. BC. The confusion was quite general in the Roman period."[13] Leon notes fifty-five examples of κιτε and κιται for κεῖται ("here lies").[14]

Spellings of ει for ι, like Babatha 25.6; 15.8; and Papyrus 109.2, show that it is impossible to explain this phenomenon as an accidental omission of "ε" in "ει." Quite obviously, the Judean Greek dialect was using ει for the sound [i], exactly as has been known in Egypt ever since the Egyptian papyri became well known. There is no doubt on this issue among linguists who have studied the phenomenon.[15] That makes the reverse phenomenon, ι for ει (see table 8.1), naturally explicable as a dialectical sound phenomenon rather than a scribal omission. The Nazareth Inscription shows how the spelling of official Roman decrees in the eastern Mediterranean could be affected.

Vowel pair 2: The interchange of αι for ε and ε for αι, representing only one vowel sound-unit, is also widely attested by the Roman Period Koine. They are the same sound and do not differ in vowel height or vowel length[16] (IPA [ε]), as illustrated by the examples in table 8.2:

13. Leon, "Language of the Greek Inscriptions," 221.
14. Leon, "Language of the Greek Inscriptions," 222.
15. Cf. W. Sidney Allen, *Vox Graeca: The Pronunciation of Classical Greek*, 3rd ed. (Cambridge: Cambridge University Press, 1987), 170: "About the end of the 4th c. B.C. the phonetic value of ει changed from a close mid vowel [ē] to a fully close vowel [ī]." See also Geoffrey Horrocks, *Greek: A History of the Language and Its Speakers*, 2nd ed. (Chichester: Wiley-Blackwell, 2010), 160–70.
16. As mentioned previously, vowel height refers to the relative position of the tongue in the mouth when making various vowel sounds, and vowel length refers to the relative length of time the vowel sound continues. Note that vowel length is not related to the colloquial English

Table 8.2. Vowel Pair 2: αι for ε, and ε for αι

	Attestation	Normalized	English
Papyrus 99.4	ειδηται	εἰδῆτε	"you would know" (154 BCE)
Ben Kosiba line 11	ποιησηται	ποιήσητε	"you should do"
Babatha 16.16	αινγαδδων	(gen. pl.)	"En Gedi" (127 CE)
Babatha 11.1	ενγαδοισ	(dat. pl.)	"En Gedi" (124 CE)
Babatha 37.8	εταιροισ	ἑτέροις	"for others" (131 CE)
Babatha 24.18	αποδιξε	ἀποδεῖξαι	"to declare" (130 CE)

Vowel pair 3: The interchange of ω for ο and ο for ω, representing only one vowel sound-unit, is another widespread substitution in the Roman Period Koine. As with all these vowel equivalencies, there is only one vowel length. Originally omega had been longer in time, and omicron had been shorter in time. In Koine Greek they had the same time length. They also had the same vowel height (IPA [o] or [ɔ]). Note well: both ο and ω were either [o] or [ɔ] in any dialect, but without distinction. The use of one or the other made no difference in meaning (see table 8.3).

Table 8.3. Vowel Pair 3: ω for ο, and ο for ω

	Attestation	Normalized	English
Papyrus 100.2	ομνυο	ὀμνύω	"I adjure" (152 BCE)
Babatha 15.10, 11	ηγεμωνοσ	ἡγεμόνος	"of governor" (125 CE)
Babatha 20.16, 40	ανθομολογημενης	ἀνθωμολογημένης	"acknowledged"
Papyrus 109.14	αυτον	αὐτῶν	"of them" (100 CE)
Papyrus 109.15	ενπιροσ	ἐμπείρως	"skillfully"
Nazareth 10	δώλῳ	δόλῳ	"by fraud"

Vowel pair 4: The interchange of οι for υ and υ for οι, representing only one vowel sound-unit, [y], is another widespread substitution in the Roman Period Koine (+y, German ü; see table 8.4).

Table 8.4. Vowel Pair 4: οι for υ, and υ for οι

	Attestation	Normalized	English
Papyrus 103.12	επυησεν	ἐποίησεν	"did" (95 BCE)
Papyrus 109.2	τωι οιειωι	τῷ υἱῷ	"to the son" (100 CE)

term "long vowel," which many English speakers use to refer to different vowel heights. English speakers say the words "note," "not," "knot," and "naught" with different vowel heights and positions, not with different lengths.

	Attestation	Normalized	English
Papyrus 109.3	πυησασ	ποιήσας	"having done"
Papyrus 110.14	λυπον	λοιπόν	"remaining" (100 CE)
Babatha 20.30	ηνυγμενον	ἠνοιγμένον	"opened" (130 CE)

Two additional points on υ.

- The pronunciation of the spellings οι and υ had not yet merged with that of the spellings /ει, ι/ as they did with the modern, itacistic change.[17]
- Notice the extra ι in the following example, probably reflecting a rounded-front vocalic [y; German: ü] pronunciation here of υ:

    Babatha 21.17, 25: δια ενγυιου → διὰ ἐγγύου (= "by guarantor" [130 CE])

Ἰῶτα Adscript

An *iōta adscript* was written inconsistently, appearing only in some texts.[18] The fact that a grammatical iōta was often left off in writing shows that it was no longer pronounced in the first century. It was a grammatical spelling when correctly added, as in Papyrus 109.2, τωι οιειωι, above. Compare the lack of the iōta in a subjunctive, Nazareth 6, επιδιξη, above, and in a dative:

Babatha 21.24: ενι εκαστω → ἐνὶ ἑκάστῳ (= "for each one")

17. The six modern Greek vowels and diphthongs ει, η, οι, υ, ι, υι are all pronounced [i]. The process of the change is called "itacism," since the various historical vowels changed their sound into iōta.

18. There was no writing of *iōta subscript* in antiquity. This writing convention developed after 900 CE. In pre-Koine Greek there were three special diphthongs that ended in ι: ωι, ηι, ᾱϊ. They were especially common in certain grammatical contexts like in nouns in the δοτική (dat.) and in verbs in the ὑποτακτική (subj.). These were pronounced ω, η, α in Koine Greek. Compare Dionysios Thrax, *Technē* 14: περισπωμένων δὲ ῥημάτων συζυγίαι εἰσὶ τρεῖς, ὧν (α΄) ἡ μὲν πρώτη ἐκφέρεται ἐπὶ δευτέρου καὶ τρίτου προσώπου διὰ τῆς ει διφθόγγου, οἷον νοῶ νοεῖς νοεῖ· (β΄) ἡ δὲ δευτέρα διὰ τῆς αι διφθόγγου, προσγραφομένου τοῦ ι, μὴ συνεκφωνουμένου δέ, οἷον βοῶ βοαῖς βοαι. . . . "There are three conjugations of circumflexed verbs: (a) the first is carried in the second and third persons with the diphthong ει, as νοω νοεις νοει; (b) the second by the diphthong αι, written with ι but not pronounced, as βοω βοαις βοαι. . . ." Sometimes ancient Koine writers wrote the ἰῶτα on the line in order to show the historical spelling, and such an ἰῶτα is called ἰῶτα adscript. Sometimes they ignored the ἰῶτα in order to show the correct pronunciation. The ἰῶτα subscript was a compromise. It was written under the main vowel in order to show that it was not pronounced, but it was written, nevertheless, in order to help to mark the grammatical category.

The Status of η

While the decision on the above four sets of phonemic vowel sounds was easy and unambiguous because of their frequent repetition in the papyri and inscriptional evidence, for other issues a more cautious judgment and approach are necessary. The vowel η has a more stable spelling history in our early New Testament manuscripts. As we'll see, in the second century CE, η was pronounced [ē] in Judea.

In vowel pair 2, above, "En Gedi" is written both with αι and with ε, as is expected from similar spellings in the Septuagint and Josephus. Josephus writes Αιν for the first part of the name עין, and the Septuagint has Εν (1 Kings 24:1–2; 2 Chron. 20:2 [A]) and Αιν (Ezek. 47:10). But Babatha 20.4, 6, 8, 23, 25, 26, 29; 23.3, 12; 24.2; 26.3 all use η in the name "En Gedi." The scribe of documents 20–26 was especially poor in Greek and cannot be representing any kind of historical or correct spelling. It is a vulgar spelling and shows that η had not yet merged with ι in the Judean Greek dialect and maintained a separate phonemic status.

Babatha 20.8: εν ηνγαδοις (dat. pl.), "in En Gedi" (130 CE)

Babatha 26.3: ηνγαδηνη (adj., nom. f. s.), "En Gedean" (131 CE)

The scribal ην in the Judean Desert is not a conservative traditional spelling; it matches the same words with αι and ε, and it cannot already be marking the [i] sound. This means that in Judea eta (η) was still pronounced [e]. So the phonological sytem of a first-century Koine should include η as a separate phoneme in a seven-vowel system.

In contrast, the vowel η became like ι and ει around the third century CE (i.e., all pronounced [i]).[19] Francis Gignac believes that η merged with ι in sound in general in the second century CE.[20] Some might want to drop this distinct sound from a Koine inventory. Such a decision would fit with the general trend of the language and fits smoothly with modern Greek (principle 5, "adaptability to historical outcomes"). However, it would appear that most people correctly used η as a symbol for a close/mid-high [e] sound in the early

19. "Confusion between η and ι in Attic inscriptions begins around 150 A.D." (Allen, *Vox Graeca*, 74). Allen also points out (p. 75) that some areas may have preserved η into the fourth century CE. This agrees with Leslie Threatte, who comments, "There is evidence that in the speech of the educated in Constantinople the distinction of η and ι were still distinguished in the 4th c. A.D." Leslie Threatte, *The Grammar of Attic Inscriptions*, vol. 1, *Phonology* (Berlin: de Gruyter, 1980), 166.

20. Francis T. Gignac, *A Grammar of the Greek Papyri of the Roman and Byzantine Periods*, vol. 1, *Phonology* (Milan: Cisalpino-Goliardica, 1976), 242n1.

Roman period. Speakers in the first century still maintained η as a separate phoneme. That means that Luke's audiences expected to hear it and that Paul probably used it when preaching all over the Mediterranean.

Nevertheless, within a century some people were speaking this η vowel in a substandard manner, and by the end of the Roman period it disappeared from Greek speech, probably first among the uneducated and then among the upper class. Here are some examples from New Testament manuscripts that illustrate the later merging of η and ι. These are late second century or early third century CE.[21]

John 10:41 𝔓⁶⁶: εɩν (corrected to ην) → ἦν = "was" (ca. 200 CE)

John 11:44 𝔓⁶⁶, ⁷⁵: κηριαις → κειρίαις = "cloth strips" (ca. 200 CE)

2 Corinthians 12:21 𝔓⁴⁶: ταπεινωσει → ταπεινώση = "humbles" (ca. 200 CE)

These manuscripts were written at a time when εɩ sounded like ι, and they show this confusion of εɩ as ι elsewhere (e.g., 𝔓⁴⁶: Rom. 8:32, ημειν for ἡμῖν; 𝔓⁶⁶, ⁷⁵: John 3:10, γεινωσκεις for γινώσκεις), so these alternations of η and εɩ appear to indicate that η was pronounced [i].[22]

A Koine pronunciation that focuses on Judea in the first century needs to include η as a separate vowel sound. It still had popular phonemic status in the early Roman period, so the phonemic principle (principle 3) supports this inclusion of a separate sound for η. It also carries a fairly heavy functional load within the phonological system (principle 7), so this is worthwhile to keep in terms of the carrying capacity of the language.[23]

The Vowel υ Becoming a Consonant

During the Roman period, the upsilon after vowels (αυ, ευ, ηυ) began to be assimilated to φ and β—that is, to be pronounced [af, ef, if] when followed

---

21. Examples from Grace Sharon, private communication, 2008. Also 𝔓⁴⁶ Eph. 5:15: περι-πατητε → περιπατεῖτε.

22. In *The Development of Greek and the New Testament: Morphology, Syntax, Phonology, and Textual Transmission* (Grand Rapids: Baker Academic, 2006), 503–8, Chrys C. Caragounis lists 155 examples of ι instead of εɩ in 𝔓⁶⁶ of John and 139 examples of εɩ instead of ι in 𝔓⁶⁶ of John.

23. The most distinctive difference between Koine and modern Greek is η. Modern Greek speakers accept υ and οι when pronounced [y] (IPA y = German ü) because their ears interpret the sound as [i]. It lands in the correct phonemic area for their ears. However, η as [e] is rejected because they hear it as [ε] though they would expect to hear [i]. For example, for ἤδη, "already," one must say [iði], "already," and not [eðe] in order to be understood in Greece today. Students wanting to speak both modern Greek and Koine Greek will need to be careful with η.

by a voiceless consonant and pronounced [av, ev, iv] otherwise. Because "length" had dropped out of the phonological system, the second vowel was functioning as a consonant within the phonological system in that period. Throughout the Roman period, speakers were using consonantal patterns of a [w]-glide,[24] perhaps becoming an unrounded glide and finally a bilabial fricative,[25] IPA [β].[26] This Koine innovation of including the sound [β] has also been included in a Koine pronunciation as consistent with the decision on consonants below. It is certainly the outcome of the Koine process (see principle 5).

Accent and Length

The dropping of phonemic vowel length affected the accent system. In pre-Koine Classical Greek, the long vowels allowed a tonal system to function, where there was a high tone, a high-low falling tone, and a default low tone. The high-low tone was sensitive to length and was restricted to long vowels: the first half of the long vowel was high, and the second half was low. The dropping of phonemic length in the vowel system led to the simplification of the tonal system, so that only high and low tones remained. It is presumed that this change took place in the Hellenistic/Koine period. In common language we don't talk about a high-low system as tonal, but we refer to such languages as having word accents and intonation. This was the presumed state of common speech in the Koine period, and it has some profound effects and application to a sensitive reading of the Greek New Testament and oral performance of the same. We will return to this subject below.

24. For example, in our Dead Sea material, notice the extra υ (probably as consonantal [w] or even a faint bilabial) in Babatha 21.2, 22.2 ΦΛΑΥΟΥΙΟΥ for Φλαουίου ("Flavius").

25. A bilabial fricative is a consonant formed by partial air constriction through the lips brought close together but not altogether closed (e.g., the Spanish pronunciation of the second consonant in "adobe").

26. A remarkable example, though uncharacteristically early, is in a Ptolemaic papyrus with ραυδους for ράβδους ("three times"). (See Gignac, *Grammar of the Greek Papyri*, 68n1.) Another interesting, early example comes from a papyrus from 35/36 CE. The first hand wrote Πνεβτῦνι, while a second hand corrected this to Πνευτῦνι (Gignac, *Grammar of the Greek Papyri*, 70). Geoffrey Horrocks writes,

> The progressive narrowing of the articulation of the second element of the original diphthongs /au,eu/, beginning in the third century BC and leading via [aw,ew], to audible friction, i.e. [. . . aβ^{w}, . . . eβ^{w}], is first attested in the spellings a(u)ou/e(u)ou, which seem to reflect the consonantal character of the second element. By the Roman period, after the loss of simultaneous lip rounding, we seem to be dealing simply with a pronunciation [. . . /aβ, . . . /eβ], or perhaps even [af/av, ef/ev] as in modern Greek. Spellings with β . . . , become increasingly common in late Roman and early Byzantine documents. (Horrocks, *Greek*, 111)

■ Koine Greek Consonant Phonology

Greek consonants are trickier to evaluate than the vowels because they tended to remain phonemic (i.e., having a minimal sound distinction that differentiates meaning) and are often preserved with a correct spelling regardless of how they were pronounced. Thus, the correct pronunciation is actually less important for them than for the vowels. The consonants were in a state of "etic" (nonsignificant, nonmeaningful) change throughout the Roman Koine period. They preserved their independent phonemic status. Thus, π, τ, κ were distinguished from φ, θ, χ throughout the period. All six were preserved, but the aspirated stops φ, θ, χ changed to fricatives.

The ancient voiced stops β, δ, γ may have become fricatives first (IPA [β, ð, γ]) before the stops φ, θ, χ became fricatives. Already at the beginning of the Roman period β was becoming a "soft" bilabial fricative, probably like the Spanish sound of "b" in Havana/Habana (the city). The letter γ became a velar fricative, and even a palatal fricative in conjunction with front vowels. During the Roman period δ eventually became fricativized everywhere (like the English sound in "this").[27] Also, our earliest extensive New Testament papyri, 𝔓⁴⁶ (late second/early third century), already has Σιλβανοῦ at 2 Corinthians 1:19, corrected to Σιλουανοῦ. These suggest that a Koine pronunciation should either use a Spanish "v" or an English "v" or "f."

Examples of γ reflecting a fricative abound, in some cases approaching a palatal "y" sound (IPA [j]). The insertions and the substitutions with ι would not be probable without γ having become a soft fricative.[28]

ιγερου → ἱεροῦ = "of a temple, of holy" (from 5 BCE)

υγιου → υἱοῦ = "of a son" (from 16 CE)

εριευς → Ἐργεύς = "Ergeus (name)" (frequent in first century CE)

Also notice the following examples of Latin words with [v, w] transcribed in Greek with [β].[29] Historically, the Latin sound was transcribed with ου in Greek.

Σαλβίου, for the Latin [Salvius] (first century CE)

πρεβέτοις, for the Latin [privatus] (first century CE)

---

27. According to Gignac, δ first became fricativized before ι, around the first century. Interchanges between δ and ζ, as mistakes to be sure, only begin from the third century, and Gignac takes this as evidence of the complete fricativization of δ. Gignac, *Grammar of the Greek Papyri*, 75.

28. Examples are from Gignac, *Grammar of the Greek Papyri*, 70–71.

29. Examples are from Gignac, *Grammar of the Greek Papyri*, 68–70. See also note 26: Πνεβτῦνι/Πνευτῦνι.

Φλαβία, for the Latin [Flavia] (149 CE)

Φλαουβίου and Φλαυβίας, for the Latin [Flavius/-a] (120 CE)

It appears that the ancient voiced stops β, γ had already gone *soft* by the first century and should be pronounced like IPA [β, γ]. Before front vowels the /γ/ became like English "y."

On the other hand, it is impossible to know just when and where the original voiceless stops φ, θ, χ became fricatives like typical Erasmian "f," "th," "ch." Most of our colloquial papyri come from Egypt, where the local Coptic seems to have encouraged a hard [pʰ, tʰ, kʰ]. With the voiceless fricatives we have Attic inscriptions with some evidence of soft forms already in the second century CE. We might assume that the complete "soft" system (for β, φ, δ, θ, γ, χ) started in the north, as in Asia Minor. Some ancient Greek dialects were "soft," like Laconian σιος (= θεός). In any case, the Egyptian system of soft voiced consonants *v, dh, gh* (IPA [β/v, δ, γ]), and hard voiceless [pʰ, tʰ, kʰ], is a complete inversion of current Erasmian practice, where Erasmian voiced stops are "hard" *b, d, g*, and voiceless aspirated stops are fricatives *f, th, ch*. For the voiceless consonants φ, θ, χ, the typical *Erasmian* soft pronunciations of φεῖ, θῆτα, and χεῖ, common in academic circles today, were taken directly from modern Greek. Historically, these modern sounds probably entered Greek pronunciation during the Roman Imperial period. See below for a Dead Sea example where θῆτα may still have been a hard, aspirated "t" just like modern English *t*. The ancient Greek distinctions φ, θ, χ versus π, τ, κ were between hard, aspirated stop sounds like English "p," "t," "k" and between unaspirated Spanish "p," "t," "k." Notice:

Ben Kosiba 1.8: ανασθησεται → ἀναστήσεται = "he will stand up"

However, we have examples from Egyptian papyri where στ was problematic and the "t" sometimes dropped out or assimilated to "s." The spelling in Bar Kochba with *theta* may have been reflecting a similar dialectical phenomenon in the environment of "s" rather than a hard pronunciation of *theta*. The Judean evidence on *theta* is insufficient by itself, and either way it can be fit into the larger historical and dialectical picture.

If the soft pronunciation is accepted for the voiceless consonants (φ, θ, χ) as in both Erasmian and Modern, then consistency would demand that the historically earlier, and more certain, voiced fricatives (β, δ, γ) are also used. This agrees with modern Greek. Those who follow Erasmian Greek pronunciation need to consider a change.

A practical approach on these consonants (β, δ, γ, φ, θ, χ) is outlined here.

1. Recognize that whichever pronunciation we follow, we should be able to preserve its phonemic status to a high level of consistency. *Theta* will still pattern as *theta*, whether pronounced as a hard [tʰeta] or soft [θeta].

2. Accept the flow of the language and recognize that the *etic* pronunciation of the consonant system was undergoing change (already in the first century, especially in northeastern/Aegean dialects) toward a later stabilization, where they were all fricatives. Principle 5, the known outcome, would also support the soft fricative pronunciation. Depending on where someone like Luke was on this continuum, he may have sounded like lisping when speaking *f*, *th*, *ch*, in Jerusalem or Egypt, or he may have sounded "sharp" when speaking around Ephesus.

3. For consistency within the linguistic system, it would be simplest theoretically and practically to either keep all six [b, pʰ, d, tʰ, g, kʰ] "hard," or all six "soft" [β, φ, δ, θ, γ, χ]. Principle 4, the historical fit, supports a "soft" pronunciation for at least β, δ, γ, and consistency would make them all soft for an assumed "Aegean" Koine dialect.

4. Recognize that the contrast [pʰ, tʰ, kʰ] versus [p, t, k] is not phonemic in Western European languages. Principle 6, compatibility with widely known international languages, would support the soft pronunciation.

5. Thus, for phonemic Koine Greek we may accept the modern (= Erasmian) voiceless fricatives [φ, θ, χ] on historical grounds (principles 5 and 6). This was the direction in which the consonants were already in the process of moving. The voiced fricatives [β, γ, partly δ] can be accepted on historical principles already for the first century (principle 4), for both the Aegean and Egypt. In sum, the most practical and most historical mix would be to use something close to the modern Greek consonants for Koine.

■ Aspiration

During ancient times most dialects of Greek had an /h/ phoneme that would be used at the beginning of some words. Words beginning with υ always had this phoneme, as well as the demonstrative words and relative pronouns (οὗτος, ὁ, ἡ, ὅς, ὅ). However, even in some dialects in early times, like Ionic, this /h/ was not pronounced and carried a relatively light phonemic load. In the Athenian spelling reform of 403 BCE, the ancient sign for this aspiration, H, was dropped from the general writing system. Instead, they started using that old aspiration symbol for the long form of the vowel ε. This is now our η, the vowel that became pronounced [e] in Koine.[30]

Gignac lists many examples showing consonant confusion in Koine times between π, τ, κ and φ, θ, χ before words beginning with aspiration. For example, with οὐ ("not") before words that begin with vowels with rough breathing (historical /h/), one expects οὐχ, as in οὐχ ἕξ ("not six"). Before words with an initial vowel without rough breathing, however, one expects οὐκ, as in οὐκ ἐξ αὐτοῦ ("not out of it"). The lack of consistency of this phenomenon in both directions in Koine texts shows that aspiration had fallen out of common use. Gignac writes, "[These data] point to a loss of initial aspiration in the speech of many writers. Aspiration has not survived into modern Greek. It was lost during the period of the Koine."[31] Some of Gignac's examples appear in the following table.

επ οις	for: ἐφ᾽ οἷς	"on which" (46 CE)
απηλικος	for: ἀφήλικος	"of a minor" (134 CE)
καθ ετος	for: κατ᾽ ἔτος	"annually" (26 BCE)
εφιδη	for: ἐπίδη	"he might oversee" (37 CE)
εφιορκουντι	for: ἐπιορκοῦντι	"perjuring" (30 BCE)

Because aspiration was not used in a major classical dialect (Ionic), it fell out of common speech during Koine times, the sound was not part of the writing system then, and it does not appear in modern Greek.[32] It is in keeping with the Koine pronunciation of consonants to drop aspiration from the pronunciation system. This follows principle 5, and also principles 3 and 4, for the majority of Koine speakers.

▪ Long and Short Vowels

Recently there has been a proposal that long ι and short ι were perhaps still pronounced differently as late as the fourth century CE. The Tyndale House Greek New Testament researched and documented how Codex Vaticanus carefully distinguishes etymological long ι, written ει, from short ι, written ι.

---

30. Conservative spelling continued to mark aspiration in some of the ancient inscriptions by using the so-called tack eta (Ͱ), the front half of the old letter for aspiration.

31. Gignac, *Grammar of the Greek Papyri*, 137–38.

32. A century ago James Hope Moulton wrote, "De-aspiration was the prevailing tendency . . . part of the general tendency which started from the Ionic and Aeolic of Asia Minor and became universal, as Modern Greek shows." James Hope Moulton, *Prolegomena*, vol. 1 of *A Grammar of New Testament Greek*, 3rd ed. (Edinburgh: T&T Clark, 1908), 44.

This is welcome and helpful research; however, it is capable of more than one explanation. The spelling of Vaticanus may represent a scholarly Alexandrian redaction, rather than the contemporary pronunciation of Greek. In the past, Vaticanus has sometimes been suspected of being an Alexandrian redaction, and this piece of evidence would add support to that perspective. Other old manuscript witnesses to the New Testament do not show the consistency of Vaticanus. There was a writing tradition among the educated to use EI for an etymological long I and simply I for an etymological short I. Claude Brixhe writes on the Roman period: "Official documents follow Classical orthography in principle, with one exception. According to usage introduced at the beginning of the Hellenistic period, EI has virtually become the norm for ancient /ī/ (hence, e.g., ἐτείμησαν and νείκη for ἐτίμησαν and νίκη). But in other registers we can observe a multitude of exchanges between equivalent graphemes."[33] So, we cannot take the example of Vaticanus as overturning everything that we have seen evidenced around the Mediterranean from the second century BCE. The feature of length had dropped out of Koine Hellenistic Greek. Nevertheless, the observations on Vaticanus do raise questions on how information on the ancient forms of Greek were transmitted in the Roman and Byzantine periods. Furthermore, the Tyndale House editors are to be commended for putting New Testament students in closer touch with the first-century Greek New Testament. Greek readers are encouraged to correctly read ὁ δὲ Πειλᾶτος ἀπεκρίθη αὐτοῖς ("and Pilate answered them," Mark 15:9 ASV).

■ Word Accent and Pronunciation

How does all of this apply to reading and interpreting a New Testament text? Let's start with the contributions that are generated out of oral performance. Greek, including in the modern period, has preserved a sensitivity to word accent. When the word accent system is observed, the language takes on and preserves more clarity than one might assume.

Consider the accents to the following phrases: τὸν ὀφθαλμόν // τῶν ὀφθαλμῶν, "the eye" (acc. sg.) and "of the eyes" (gen. pl.). You can hear a distinction in the words on the basis of the tones: You have low tones τὸν, ὀφ-, -θαλ- and high tone -μόν versus high tone τῶν, low tone ὀφ- and -θαλ-, and high tone -μῶν, even though the first-century vowels no longer differentiated

---

33. Claude Brixhe, "Linguistic Diversity in Asia Minor during the Empire: *Koine* and Non-Greek Languages," in *A Companion to the Ancient Greek Language*, ed. Egbert J. Bakker (Malden, MA: Wiley-Blackwell, 2010), 232.

those two forms. This is to say that, phoneme by phoneme, they are identical. This happens frequently with masculine nouns. Listen to τὸν ἀδελφόν (acc. sg.) and then τῶν ἀδελφῶν (gen. pl.).

Common words like ὑμῶν ("you," gen. pl.) and αὐτόν ("he," acc. sg.) sometimes follow word order placement that appears to mimic enclitics. As such, they may have dropped their accent in normal speech. Here is an enclitic, reinforcing a marked order: ἡμεῖς δὲ τοῦ Μωϋσέως **ἐσμὲν** μαθηταί ("but we **are** disciples of Moses," John 9:28).[34] The focal τοῦ Μωϋσέως attracts ἐσμέν as an enclitic reinforcement.

Consider 1 John 2:5: ὃς δ' ἂν τηρῇ αὐτοῦ τὸν λόγον ("but whoever obeys his word"). Here αὐτοῦ is possibly attracted to the verb as an enclitic, and its accent may have dropped in actual speech. Also note 1 John 3:20: ὅτι ἐὰν καταγινώσκῃ ἡμῶν ἡ καρδία, ὅτι μείζων ἐστὶν ὁ θεὸς τῆς καρδίας **ἡμῶν** (". . . whenever our hearts condemns us; for God is greater than **our** hearts"). Perhaps ἡμῶν was treated as an accentless enclitic. More investigation is needed.

Performance and reading lead us to recognize a point of artificiality in the Greek accents currently appearing in the Greek New Testament today. They were added to New Testament texts only many centuries after they were part of the spoken language, mechanically, without regard to the pragmatic functions of topicalization and focus.

Consider John 1:1: καὶ **θεὸς** ἦν ὁ λόγος ("and the Word was **God**"). The word θεός has been fronted and reflects what is called a "focus function" in linguistics. However, the mechanical accent rules require θεός to drop its acute accent. According to the written accents, only ἦν and λό- are accented. But the most natural and predictable reading would use prosody to reinforce the focus marking on θεός. A focus reading would produce a slight pause, triggering the high tone, and we may expect that words in focus would preserve any final-syllable potential high tones. Pragmatic forces combine to produce a reading that overrides the written accent system. A sensitive reading should activate the potential high tone signaled by the grave.

Two verses later we find an interesting context where we may want to activate one of the grave accents and read with a high tone while we leave the second accent as a low tone: John 1:3–4, ὃ γέγονεν ἐν αὐτῷ ζωὴ ἦν ("What has come into being in him was life"). We may choose to read ζωή with a high tone as focus, which is marked in the word order as well. Ζωή is the new information in this context and the marked, salient information. However, in the continuation (καὶ ἡ ζωὴ ἦν τὸ φῶς τῶν ἀνθρώπων, "and the life was the light of all people"), the word ζωή is repeated information, and the best

---

34. All following Scripture translations are NRSV.

reading and interpretation appears to be as a topicalization. The salient information of the clause is τὸ φῶς τῶν ἀνθρώπων ("the light of all people"), and it comes in default word order. As the field of New Testament studies becomes sensitive to using Greek communicatively, some of these features of intonation will come more into focus.

Pronunciation also affects "traditional exegesis." A classic example is Romans 5:1: Δικαιωθέντες οὖν ἐκ πίστεως εἰρήνην ἔχομεν πρὸς τὸν θεὸν διὰ τοῦ κυρίου ἡμῶν Ἰησοῦ Χριστοῦ ("Therefore, since we are justified by faith, we have peace with God through our Lord Jesus Christ"). In the first century, εἰρήνην ἔχομεν ("we have [present ind.] peace") and εἰρήνην ἔχωμεν ("let us have [present subj.] peace") were pronounced in the same way. We must also remember that this letter was primarily communicated to the groups of believers orally. Fluent speakers had to process this without access to seeing an omicron or an omega. Now we tend to be interested in the manuscript history, which, to be sure, is evidence that we want to look at. If you look at the apparatus for NA²⁸, you'll see that these manuscripts have ἔχωμεν: ℵ* A B* C D K L 33 81 630 1175 1739* *pm* lat bo; while these manuscripts have ἔχομεν: ¹ℵ B² F G P Ψ 0220ᵛⁱᵈ 104 365 1241 1505 1506 1739ᶜ 1881 2464 *l*864 *pm* vgᵐˢˢ. However, we forget that either written record would sound the same to the audience in an oral performance. Regardless of whether the word was written with an omega or an omicron, the audience would hear and interpret the writing according to the context up to that point. This setting for the original text is why we want our exegetes today to have more fluent control of Koine Greek. What would we understand when hearing this text read out loud? Personally, I think that the indicative wins out as fitting the indicative context up through chapter 5 of Romans. We have many points of assurance. So what about the manuscripts? I am not sure that an omega or an omikron changes anything. A secretary, scribe, or copyist could have been thinking one thing and writing another. I do that all the time in English. If I mean to write "I left my book over *there*" but instead write "I left my book over *their*," it doesn't change my meaning. The context rules. Granted, that is an extreme case, because in English the context is grammatically decisive, while in Romans 5:1 both spellings are syntactically possible. What we know is that in Egypt the subjunctive spelling had widespread, but not universal, currency. Was that preserving a particular understanding or a particular written tradition? It is difficult to answer this. Let's ask the question in the most extreme form: Could Paul have meant the indicative (with omicron) and Paul's secretary wrote the subjunctive (with omega), while thinking "indicative"? And could the manuscript history continue to diverge from the beginning? I can actually read Westcott and Hort's 1881 text and the Greek Church text of 1904 as communicating the same reality, although I admit that such is probably against the intentions of Westcott and Hort.[35] These examples may raise issues on the nature of inspiration and the transmission of Scripture, but in terms of natural language they are perfectly plausible. A first-century pronunciation of Greek and a fluent control of Greek will allow today's readers to process this text and interpretation in ways that are similar to the first century. To me that is extremely valuable. Our training for the next generation needs to have this as a goal.

Fluency may contribute to understanding phrases like πίστις Χριστοῦ, "faith related to Christ." How do fluent language users process this text, where a simple genitive without an article is used? Genitives are used in communication where under-differentiation is acceptable, and the author can rely on the contextual skills of the audience. Apparently, the author felt that getting close to the abstract notion was sufficient for the meaning. It is unlikely that the author was expecting the audience to consciously specify "faith in Christ" or to differentiate "Christ's faith." I believe that is why Paul did not need to flesh out and explicitly communicate his phrase πίστις Χριστοῦ. We realize, of course, that Paul is talking about faith related to Christ, Christian faith.[36]

Finally, the most important issue with pronunciation is not the proper evaluation of the many textual issues and word choices that may have been influenced either through ambiguity or through avoiding ambiguity. The biggest and most compelling issue for Christian scholarship is to have the fluency in speech that enhances high-level textual processing and macro-comprehension in reading. That is what we demand for specialists in every other literature— Russian, German, English, and so on. That is the commitment that we owe to God as caretakers of the Bible.

35. Brooke Foss Westcott and Fenton John Anthony Hort, *The New Testament in the Original Greek* (New York: Harper & Brothers, 1881).
36. However, many languages may require a restructuring that forces some kind of unpacking of verbal nouns into a verbal clause. Consequently, clauses like "because he believes in Christ" may be acceptable options for translation but do not necessarily explain how the Greek audience cognitively processed the statement.

9

Electronic Tools and New Testament Greek

THOMAS W. HUDGINS

Technology changes fast, so fast that a chapter on electronic tools and New Testament Greek is almost futile. The good news is that Greek grammars come out about as quickly as technology changes, so there is ample opportunity for the next author to amplify what is discussed here or excise whatever becomes out of date or otherwise not useful. What follows in this discussion is not an exhaustive list of materials and resources available to students of New Testament Greek in digital format. Instead, a decision has been made to include only certain tools with some annotation. The goal of learning New Testament Greek for most is not the grammar itself but to use that knowledge in the study and interpretation of New Testament texts. This discussion is divided into four categories: (1) language acquisition, (2) textual criticism, (3) lexical analysis, and (4) syntactical analysis. Much of what is mentioned in this chapter is found somewhere on the New Testament Greek Portal.[1] The Portal is divided into fourteen categories, including Greek pedagogy and linguistics and Greek grammar and syntax. Different resources are cataloged based on where they fit into the spectrum of learning

1. See https://www.newtestamentgreekportal.blogspot.com.

and using New Testament Greek; some are for beginners, some for those further along in their studies.

■ Language Acquisition

At the very least, to use Greek with even a basic proficiency, students of the New Testament need a foundational knowledge of Greek lexemes, access to (and a willingness to consult throughout their studies) an intermediate Greek grammar, and an edition of the New Testament in Greek. The German Bible Society has made the text of the Nestle-Aland twenty-eighth edition (NA[28]) and the United Bible Societies fifth edition (UBS[5]) available online.[2] The SBL edition can be downloaded in a number of different formats on the Society of Biblical Literature webpage or accessed online at BibleGateway and Bib-lia.[3] The SBL edition is particularly helpful in that it shows where divergence exists between the texts of Westcott-Hort, Tregelles, Goodrich-Lukaszewski (i.e., the text "behind" the NIV), and Robinson-Pierpont (an edition based on Byzantine manuscripts).[4] Its apparatus, of course, does not replace the apparatus found in NA[28]. The Robinson-Pierpont 2018 edition is available online for free and features updated tags corresponding to NA[28] and the notes for Acts reflected in the *Editio Critica Maior* (ECM). And the text of *The Greek New Testament, Produced at Tyndale House, Cambridge* is available free online via Crossway's page for the English Standard Version.[5]

2. German Bible Society, "Online Bibles," https://www.academic-bible.com/en/online-bibles. Select either "Novum Testamentum Graece (NA 28)" or "Greek New Testament (UBS5)" from the navigation bar on the left side of the screen.

3. Michael W. Holmes, *The Greek New Testament: SBL Edition* (Bellingham, WA: Lexham; Atlanta: Society of Biblical Literature, 2011–13): Society of Biblical Literature, http://sblgnt.c om/download/; BibleGateway, https://www.biblegateway.com/versions/SBL-Greek-New-Test ament-SBLGNT/; Biblia, https://biblia.com/books/sblgnt. The *Lexham English Bible English-Greek Interlinear New Testament*, which utilizes the text of the SBLGNT, is available at the bottom of the SBL webpage.

4. Samuel Prideaux Tregelles, ed., *The Greek New Testament : Edited from Ancient Authori-ties, with Their Various Readings in Full, and the Latin Version of Jerome* (London: S. Bagster and Sons, 1857–79); B. F. Westcott and F. J. A. Hort, eds., *The New Testament in the Original Greek: American Edition with an Introduction by Philip Schaff* (New York: Harper & Brothers, 1881); Richard J. Goodrich and Albert L. Lukaszewski, eds., *A Reader's Greek New Testament*, 3rd ed. (Grand Rapids: Zondervan, 2015); Maurice A. Robinson and William G. Pierpont, *The New Testament in the Original Greek, Byzantine Textform* (Southborough, MA: Chilton, 2005), https://biblia.com/books/byzprsd. The 2018 digital edition, with updates by David Robert Palmer, is available at http://bibletranslation.ws/2018/07/22/robinson-pierpont-gnt-2018-update.

5. Dirk Jongkind, *The Greek New Testament, Produced at Tyndale House, Cambridge* (Wheaton: Crossway, 2018; Cambridge: Cambridge University Press, 2018), https://www.the greeknewtestament.com; https://www.esv.org/Matthew+1/. Once at the ESV page, click the

You can also reach back a few years and take advantage of high-resolution copies of some of history's most famous editions of the Greek New Testament. A copy of Erasmus's *Novum Instrumentum omne* (1516)[6] can be found on the University of Basel Library webpage.[7] And the library at Queen's College has a copy of the third edition (1522) that once belonged to the Polish reformer Jan Łaski.[8] A copy of *Novum Testamentum grece et latine*, which preceded Erasmus's Greek-Latin diglot by two years, is made available by the Complutense University's Biblioteca Histórica Marqués de Valdecilla.[9]

---

cover of the GNTTHC found in the box marked "Library," below "Original Language Tools," located on the right side of the screen. See also the page titled "Production Notes" at the Tyndale House Cambridge website: https://academic.tyndalehouse.com/thgnt/production-notes.

6. The title was changed with subsequent editions to *Novum Testamentum omne*.

7. Desiderius Erasmus, *Novum Instrumentum omne: diligenter ab Erasmo Roterodamo recognitum & emendatum, . . . una cum Annotationibus . . . Apud inclytam Germaniae Basileam* (Johannes Froben, 1516), Universitätsbibliothek Basel, BibG B 3, https://doi.org/10.3931/e-rara-2849.

8. Desiderius Erasmus, *Novum Testamentum omne: diligenter ab Erasmo Roterodamo recognitum & emendatum, . . . una cum Annotationibus . . . Apud inclytam Germaniae Basileam* (Johannes Froben, 1522), University of Cambridge, Digital Library, Queen's College C.2.9, https://cudl.lib.cam.ac.uk/view/PR-C-00002-00009/21.

9. *Novum Testamentum grece et latine in academia complutensi noviter impressum* (Arnaldi Guilielmi de Brocario, 1522), Biblioteca Digital Dioscórides de la Universidad Complutense de Madrid, http://dioscorides.ucm.es/proyecto_digitalizacion/index.php?5315923966. Select the publication tagged "Patrimonio Digital Complutense" for the highest-resolution copy. For an introduction to the Complutensian Polyglot Bible with links to high-resolution images of each of its six volumes, see José Luís Gonzalo Sánchez-Molero, "La Biblia Políglota Complutense: Un monumento cultural y tipográfico," Biblioteca Histórica Marqués de Valdecilla, https://biblioteca.ucm.es/historica/vetus-testamentum. The Universidad Complutense de Madrid (UCM) collection also includes a letter written by García de Bobadilla to Cisneros in 1516 recommending the inclusion of Erasmus in whatever work remained for the Polyglot project: https://biblioteca.ucm.es/historica/carta-de-bobadilla. For those interested in knowing more about its historical context and sources, the Biblioteca Histórica Marqués de Valdecilla held an exposition to mark the quincentennial of the printing of the NT volume of the Complutensian Polyglot called Exposición V Centenario de la Biblia Políglota Complutense: Indice de secciones (find it at https://biblioteca.ucm.es/historica/indice-de-secciones). Of particular interest might be "Las fuentes de la Biblia Políglota en lengua griega," but do not expect to find the Greek sources for the NT there. They remain undiscovered, and it is unlikely they were ever sent to Alcalá de Henares from the Vatican Library. Presentations made at the Marqués de Valdecilla Library in November 2014 were published with side-by-side Spanish and English text. The volume titled *V Centenario de la Biblia Políglota Complutense. La Universidad del Renacimiento. El Renacimiento de la Universidad* is available at https://www.ucm.es/data/cont/docs/web-EstudiosBibliav9.pdf. Another conference was held in Alcalá de Henares in October 2014. Presentations were published in Antonio Alvar Ezquerra, ed., *La Biblia Políglota Complutense en su contexto* (Alcalá de Henares: Universidad de Alcalá, 2015). Unfortunately, it is unavailable in electronic format. Of particular importance are chapters by Luis Gil Fernández ("La columna griega de la Biblia Políglota Complutense") and Antonio Piñero Sáenz ("La columna griega del Nuevo Testamento en la Biblia Políglota Complutense").

When it comes to language acquisition, though, doing a refresher through online tutorials of a beginning Greek grammar is not a bad place to start. Beginning Greek students are probably already aware of the online tools associated with the textbook they used, but a quick refresher might be helpful here. And even though a student used one introductory grammar, the electronic tools available for another Greek grammar might end up being more profitable. The following are for introductory Greek grammars by William D. Mounce and David Alan Black:

1. Companion lectures for each of William Mounce's chapters (thirty-seven total) in *Basics of Biblical Greek*. Both a physical copy of the book and a yearlong online subscription are available for purchase.[10]
2. David Alan Black's Greek course recorded in Addis Ababa, Ethiopia, following his *Learn to Read New Testament Greek*. The DVD set (twenty-four total, covering all twenty-six chapters) is available for purchase.[11]
3. Rob Plummer's "Learn Biblical Greek" tutorials at Daily Dose of Greek.[12]

For building your knowledge of Greek vocabulary, a number of resources exist. First-year students are probably familiar with at least one vocabulary app like Quizlet (www.quizlet.com). Besides just refreshing or getting a head start with Bruce M. Metzger's lists, students should begin to look at vocabulary in different ways.[13] Instead of learning the glosses for words occurring ten times or more, then nine times or more, and so on, why not choose one New Testament text and focus on its vocabulary? In Logos Bible Software, the "Word List" feature will isolate all the words for any New Testament text. In Logos 8, just select "Docs," then "New," and scroll down to "Word List." From the new window that opens up, select "Add," make sure the resource

10. Bill Mounce, "First Year Greek," https://www.billmounce.com/firstyeargreek. According to the author's website, these materials are free for those who are incarcerated. The fourth edition of the textbook came out in February 2019. The videos correspond to the previous edition. Mounce has also put together a number of screencasts corresponding to his workbook that are incorporated into his online Greek class (also for sale). Three samples (corresponding to the workbook exercises for chaps. 3, 4, and 6) are currently available online. See "Screencast for Chapter 3," https://www.billmounce.com/workbook/3; substitute "3" with "4" or "6" to access the other samples.
11. See David Alan Black, "Greek DVDs Now Available," Dave Black Online, April 13, 2009, https://www.daveblackonline.com/greek_dvds_now_available.htm; for a sample, see "Clip from the Greek Teaching DVDs," DaveBlackGreek, March 4, 2010, https://www.youtube.com/watch?v=SGFADaCSxj8.
12. Robert L. Plummer, "Learn Biblical Greek," Daily Dose of Greek, https://dailydoseofgreek.com/learn-biblical-greek/.
13. Bruce M. Metzger, *Lexical Aids for Students of New Testament Greek*, 3rd ed. (Grand Rapids: Baker, 1997).

is set to an edition of the Greek New Testament, and then specify the New Testament text (e.g., Philippians). Video tutorials for different Logos features, including "Word List," and step-by-step instructions known as wikis (www .wiki.logos.com) are helpful for navigating the platform.

Utilizing some sort of morphological search can reinforce and increase your knowledge of grammatical forms. In Logos Bible Software, you can use something called a "visual filter" if you want a refresher on differentiating between two grammatical forms (e.g., aorist and imperfect). If you set the filter up in such a way that both the aorist and imperfect indicative, for example, are highlighted in blue, then you can open your Greek New Testament (or even other biblical and nonbiblical Greek texts)[14] and start practicing. You could also utilize an analytical lexicon like the *Lexham Analytical Lexicon of the New Testament* and practice forming the different forms of Greek words (e.g., βάλλω), checking the lexicon to see if you are forming them correctly. Choose a Greek word, write out the inflections for yourself, then check the analytical lexicon for those that appear in the New Testament and/or Septuagint. The lexicon becomes your answer key.

■ Textual Criticism

Not surprisingly, the focus of Greek grammars is Greek grammar. That explains how many students learn very little about a subject called textual criticism in their beginning Greek grammars and introductory Greek courses.[15] Nevertheless, numerous electronic resources are available online, from introductions

14. Visit the Logos Bible Software website, log in, and be sure the "Perseus Classics Collection (1,114 vols.)" is in your package: Logos Bible Software, https://www.logos.com/product /9940/perseus-classics-collection. And even though it was published in 2011, see the "How to Study with the Free Perseus Classics Collection," Logos Bible Software, September 16, 2011, https://www.youtube.com/watch?v=Yo8MgoI2p6k.

15. For example, N. Clayton Croy, when discussing the LXX exercises found in *A Primer of Biblical Greek* (Grand Rapids: Eerdmans, 1999), only mentions that the LXX "does not always have a fixed text" and has "varying manuscript traditions" (6). This could give a student the impression that the NT text is fixed, which it is not. David Alan Black provides a paragraph in the epilogue of his beginning grammar (*Learn to Read New Testament Greek*, 3rd ed. [Nashville: B&H Academic, 2009], 213) that points readers to Bruce M. Metzger's *A Textual Commentary on the Greek New Testament*, 2nd ed. (New York: United Bible Societies, 1994) and to Black's *New Testament Textual Criticism* (Grand Rapids: Baker, 1994). Jeremy Duff (*The Elements of New Testament Greek*, 3rd ed. [Cambridge: Cambridge University Press, 2005], ccxvii) suggests reading an introduction by Kurt and Barbara Aland or the one written by Metzger. Stanley E. Porter, Jeffrey T. Reed, and Matthew Brook O'Donnell mention only that at the time *Fundamentals of New Testament Greek* (Grand Rapids: Eerdmans, 2010) was published, *Fundamentals of New Testament Textual Criticism* (Grand Rapids: Eerdmans, 2015) was in development (Porter, Reed, and O'Donnell, *Fundamentals of New Testament Greek*, x). Again, the purpose of Greek grammars is the grammar, but perhaps there could be a new kind

to what textual criticism is to web platforms where you can view images of the thousands of extant New Testament manuscripts. To get started, check out David Alan Black's short chapter titled "Textual Criticism of the New Testament."[16] He discusses the types of textual issues found in New Testament manuscripts and also provides the framework by which textual issues should be analyzed (e.g., which reading has wider geographical support).[17] Then move to the Center for the Study of New Testament Manuscripts (CSNTM) resources, which are available free through iTunes.[18] There are six topics:

1. The Basics of New Testament Textual Criticism (fifteen videos)
2. Scribal Methods and Materials (five videos)
3. Disputed New Testament Passages: Textual Criticism Put into Practice (seven videos)
4. Famous Manuscripts and the Stories behind Them (four videos)
5. Pioneers of the Trade: Famous Text-Critical Scholars (eleven videos)
6. Insider's Look into the Work of CSNTM (eleven videos)

The introductory videos include topics like why textual criticism exists, the difference between internal and external evidence, and how many variants there are in the New Testament.[19]

---

of grammar that takes into consideration the tasks a student of Greek will need to perform as a result of the course and teaches grammar in tandem with those tasks.

16. David Alan Black, "Textual Criticism of the New Testament," in *Foundations for Biblical Interpretation*, ed. David S. Dockery et al. (Nashville: Broadman & Holman, 1994), 396–413, http://newtestamentgreekportal.blogspot.com/p/textual-criticism.html. Members of the University of Hamburg's Comparative Oriental Manuscript Studies research group produced a book titled *Comparative Oriental Manuscript Studies: An Introduction*, ed. Alessandro Bausi et al., Comparative Oriental Manuscript Studies (Hamburg: Tredition, 2015). The chapters on paleography (69–266) and textual criticism (321–466) might be of interest to those looking for a more technical and broad-in-scope presentation of what is involved in textual studies. Find the full text at https://www.aai.uni-hamburg.de/en/comst/publications/handbook.html.

17. Two studies by David Alan Black are available under "My Greek Tools," *New Testament Greek Portal* (blog), http://newtestamentgreekportal.blogspot.com/p/dave-blacks-greek-tools.html: "The Text of John 3:13," *Grace Theological Journal* 6 (1985): 49–66; and "Jesus on Anger: The Text of Matthew 5:22a Revisited," *Novum Testamentum* 30 (1988): 1–8. Black and I also studied the issue of εἰκῇ in 2013: "Jesus on Anger (Matt 5,22a): A History of Recent Scholarship," in *Greeks, Jews, and Christians: Historical, Religious, and Philological Studies in Honor of Jesús Peláez del Rosal*, ed. L. Roig Lanzillotta and I. Muñoz Gallarte (Córdoba: El Almendro, 2013), 91–104.

18. Center for the Study of New Testament Manuscripts, http://www.csntm.org. Click the iTunes link at the top of the page.

19. Concerning the number of textual variants in the NT, see also Peter J. Gurry, "The Number of Variants in the Greek New Testament: A Proposed Estimate," *New Testament Studies* 62 (2016): 97–121, https://www.repository.cam.ac.uk/handle/1810/250445.

Robert Waltz's online encyclopedia of New Testament textual criticism was last updated over a decade ago, but it is a good introduction to text-critical topics and issues.[20] You can find all of the guiding principles (better not to say "rules") behind external and internal evidence under the entry "Canons of Criticism."[21]

Ralph Bruce Terry developed an open-access orientation to textual issues in the New Testament titled "A Student's Guide to New Testament Textual Variants." His purpose was to provide those who have never studied Greek with an explanation of "textual footnotes that are found in several modern translations of the Bible."[22] What he provides is similar to Metzger's *Textual Commentary on the Greek New Testament*[23] as well as the adaptation of it by Roger L. Omanson[24] and *The Lexham Textual Notes on the Bible* by Rick Brannan and Israel Loken.[25] Terry provides the translation of the adopted reading in the New Analytical Version with a selection of supportive evidence. Below this is an alternative reading (marked "Notes") with a selection of supportive evidence. With each textual issue, Terry provides an explanation of how he interprets the evidence. The issue surrounding εἰκῇ ("without cause") in Matthew 5:22, for example, is presented in the following manner:

Text: "everyone who is angry with his brother shall be liable to judgment"
Evidence: $\mathfrak{P}^{67vid}$ S* B 2174^{vid} vg
Translations: ASV RSV NASB NIV NEB TEV
Rank: C
Notes: "everyone who is angry with his brother without cause shall be liable to judgment"
Evidence: S^c D K L W Delta Theta Pi f1 f13 28 33 565 700 892 1010 1241 Byz Lect lat syr cop
Translations: KJV ASVn RSVn NASBn NIVn NEBn TEVn

20. Robert Waltz, "A Site Inspired by The Encyclopedia of New Testament Textual Criticism," http://www.skypoint.com/members/waltzmn/.

21. See also Daniel B. Wallace, "Challenges in New Testament Textual Criticism for the Twenty-First Century," *JETS* 52 (2009): 79–100, https://www.etsjets.org/files/JETS-PDFs/52/52-1/JETS%2052-1%2079-100%20Wallace.pdf.

22. Ralph Bruce Terry, "A Student's Guide to New Testament Textual Variants," Ohio Valley University, http://bible.ovc.edu/tc.

23. Metzger, *Textual Commentary on the Greek New Testament*.

24. Roger L. Omanson, *A Textual Guide to the Greek New Testament: An Adaptation of Bruce M. Metzger's Textual Commentary for the Needs of Translators* (Stuttgart: Deutsche Bibelgesellschaft, 2006). The front matter and a sample of the notes from Matt. 1:7–8 to 7:24 are available at https://www.die-bibel.de/media/articles/pdf/6044_Leseprobe.pdf.

25. Rick Brannan and Israel Loken, *The Lexham Textual Notes on the Bible* (Bellingham, WA: Lexham, 2014).

Comments: It seems more likely that copyists would soften the teaching by adding "without cause" than leave it out and thus make it more difficult. However, it is also possible that it was accidently omitted when a copyist's eye jumped from *eike* "without cause" to the next word *enokhos* "liable."[26]

Another free resource, more helpful than Terry's simply because of the amount of information provided, is Wieland Willker's "An Online Textual Commentary on the Greek Gospels."[27] For Matthew 5:22, Willker presents the readings found in the NA[28] and Robinson-Pierpont, provides a translation of εἰκῇ, and presents the manuscript evidence as follows:

Byz   01[C2-mg], D, K, Π, L, W, Δ, Θ, Σ, 0233, 0287, f1, f13, 33, 700, 892, Maj, it, Sy, Co, arm, geo, goth, Ir, Eus, [Trg]

txt   𝔓[67vid] = 𝔓[64](200 CE), 01*, B, Ω, 372, 1424[mg], 2737, al[25], aur, vg, aeth, Justin, Cl, Or, Hier[mss], Basil(4th CE), Trg[mg]

Below this information, Willker provides some annotation on select manuscripts (e.g., regarding 𝔓[67] and Δ, including a link to an image of the manuscript demonstrating his point). The manuscript 𝔓[67] is mentioned, for example, because the issue of εἰκῇ is found on the last line of the fragment. He demonstrates how the very tips of the upper halves of the letters corresponding to -υτου ενοχος are visible and support the reading without εἰκῇ. Greek-English quotations of patristic sources follow, and he concludes with an analysis of the evidence, including a reference to Black's 1988 article.[28]

The resources mentioned so far will help you identify where textual issues are present in the texts of the New Testament, and they will help you to start thinking through the evidence also. What about viewing actual New Testament manuscripts? There was a time when philologists had to spend exuberant amounts of money or travel great distances by ship, four-legged creatures, and foot just to view them. That is not the case today. The New Testament Virtual Manuscript Room (NTVMR) is the most user-friendly database of

26. From http://bible.ovc.edu/tc/lay01mat.htm. Scroll down to the issue in Matt. 5:22.

27. Wieland Willker, "TCG: An Online Textual Commentary on the Greek Gospels," http://www.willker.de/wie/TCG/index.html. There is a lot of information on Willker's site, not just the textual commentaries for the Gospels (e.g., see "Top Textual Variants of the Gospels" and "The Pericope Adulterae").

28. See Black, "Jesus on Anger." Willker includes the following note: "[Black] argues for the inclusion of εἰκῇ, but the arguments are not convincing." Unfortunately, he does not explain why Black's arguments are not convincing, nor does he reference the up-to-date analysis of the originality of εἰκῇ that I coauthored with Black; see Black and Hudgins, "Jesus on Anger (Matt 5,22a)."

digitized images of New Testament manuscripts.[29] Actually, it is a workspace where text critics index, transcribe, and evaluate textual evidence. If you have never consulted a New Testament manuscript before, start by viewing a thirteen-minute introductory tutorial video on YouTube titled "NTVMR Introduction."[30] Greg Paulson, on the *INTF* blog, has a script tutorial on how to view manuscripts using the database.[31] Set your modern critical edition aside for a week or two (or more), and take a look at Miniscule 2,[32] which Erasmus used for his edition of the Greek New Testament. For those ready for more, choose a manuscript that has not been indexed, and start by identifying its contents (e.g., Matt. 5:1–18).[33] With some practice and exposure, you could become one of the manuscript transcribers. To do this, though, it is necessary to consult "IGNTP Guidelines for the Transcription of Manuscripts Using the Online Transcription Editor" (2016) by Amy C. Myshrall and others.[34]

Besides the sheer nostalgia of using one of the manuscripts Erasmus used between 1514 and 1516, when you start taking a look at the actual manuscripts, you can begin to imagine the birth of some textual issues, such as how a short word could have been accidentally left off had it been abbreviated and occurred at the end of a justified line in the copy's source. Expect a bit of a learning curve. Remember that the so-called majuscules are written in all capital letters and the shorthand found in minuscules can appear unrecognizable at first. Fordham University has a table showing typographical ligatures (i.e., combinations of Greek letters written into single glyphs) that helps overcome this small obstacle.[35] Students of the New Testament should be more comfort-

29. See http://ntvmr.uni-muenster.de.

30. "NTVMR Introduction," Scribe7777, June 10, 2013, https://youtu.be/j0-B4NgKveY.

31. For a tutorial with screenshots, see Greg Paulson, "How to View Greek New Testament Manuscripts in the VMR," *INTF* (blog), December 14, 2018, http://ntvmr.uni-muenster.de/intf blog/-/blogs/how-to-view-greek-new-testament-manuscripts-in-the-vmr.

32. Once you select "Liste" on the main page, type the number 2 in the "Name" field below the words "Quick Lookup." A list of manuscripts containing the number 2 will populate, the first of which is DocID "30002" Name "2" Date "XI/XII," consisting of 248 pages. To the right is a box that includes additional information pertaining to the selected manuscript, such as the number of written lines per page and page height and width. The latter is interesting because some of these manuscripts are physically small. When I consulted manuscripts in the Vatican Library's Rare Manuscript Room, sometimes I found it easier to read an online image than to use the actual manuscript in front of me.

33. This needs to be done a particular way, so please see Greg Paulson, "How to Index Manuscripts on the VMR," *INTF* (blog), January 21, 2019, http://ntvmr.uni-muenster.de/intf blog/-/blogs/how-to-index-a-manuscript-on-the-vmr.

34. Amy C. Myshrall, Rachel Kevern, and H. A. G. Houghton, "IGNTP Guidelines for the Transcription of Manuscripts Using the Online Transcription Editor" (Birmingham, UK: International Greek New Testament Project, 2016), http://epapers.bham.ac.uk/2161.

35. Paul Halsall, "Greek Letter Combinations (Ligatures, Etc.)," Internet History Sourcebooks Project, https://sourcebooks.fordham.edu/ikon/greekligs.asp. Read a miniscule for just a

able in consulting actual manuscripts. The need that existed for consulting a standardized Greek text—for example, in the sixteenth century, when the Spaniards and Erasmus printed and published their editions of the Greek New Testament—is not the same today. The real value of modern critical editions, especially the NA[28] and UBS[5] editions, is found in their critical apparatuses. Today, New Testament students should be exposed more and more to the manuscripts, consulting NA[28] and UBS[5] to identify textual issues and as one step in the evaluation of external evidence. Keep in mind, if you are working on Acts, the INTF has made the apparatus of the ECM available online.[36]

You can access higher-resolution images of New Testament manuscripts than those found in the INTF New Testament Virtual Manuscript Room. For example, the Center for the Study of New Testament Manuscripts (http:// www.csntm.org) in cooperation with proprietors of New Testament manuscripts has photographed some of the most renowned collections, one example being the Chester Beatty papyri.[37] Their work at preserving texts is unparalleled, and they have a number of manuscripts (e.g., Miniscule 2907) not available via the INTF.[38] Entire websites are devoted to certain renowned manuscripts, such as Codex Sinaiticus, Codex Vaticanus, and Codex Bezae.[39]

To stay up to date on current issues and publications, visit the *Evangelical Textual Criticism* blog, which is updated almost on a daily basis,[40] and *TC: A Journal of Biblical Textual Criticism*.[41]

---

few minutes. The brain can make sense of what is written with minimal effort, especially with a first-year knowledge of Greek vocabulary. The Fordham chart is most helpful with superposition ligatures. Note how the ε sometimes looks like a σ.

36. See http://ntvmr.uni-muenster.de/nt-transcripts. Simply type the specific verse (e.g., Acts 28:1), and the ECM box below the Greek text will populate with the apparatus; manuscripts in the apparatus are hyperlinked to transcriptions of the Greek text in that particular manuscript. Note also that if you click on a Greek word in the text, it will populate the Liddell-Scott lexicon entry in an adjacent box (see *A Greek-English Lexicon*, 9th ed. with revised supplement, ed. H. G. Liddell and R. Scott [London: Clarendon, 1996]). For further explanation on how to use this resource, see Greg Paulson, "An Interactive Textual Commentary on Acts," *INTF* (blog), September 14, 2018, http://ntvmr.uni-muenster.de/intfblog/-/blogs/an-interactive-textual -commentary-on-acts.

37. The Chester Beatty papyri can also be found via the Chester Beatty Digital Collections, Chester Beatty Library, https://viewer.cbl.ie/viewer/. Select "Biblical Papyri collection."

38. Be sure to consult the files titled "Informational Document" on the manuscript's main page.

39. Codex Sinaiticus, http://www.codexsinaiticus.org/en/; Codex Vaticanus, "Manuscript— Vat.gr.1209," Digital Vatican Library, https://digi.vatlib.it/view/MSS_Vat.gr.1209; and Codex Bezae, "Codex Bezae (MS Nn.2.41)," University of Cambridge Digital Library, https://cudl.lib .cam.ac.uk/view/MS-NN-00002-00041/12.

40. *Evangelical Textual Criticism* (blog), http://evangelicaltextualcriticism.blogspot.com.

41. *TC: A Journal of Biblical Textual Criticism*, http://jbtc.org/index.html#page=home.

▪ Lexical Analysis

In a perfect world, I would be able to point you to a free version of *A Greek-English Lexicon of the New Testament and Other Early Christian Literature* (3rd ed.), also known as BDAG. There are a number of resources in the public domain, but not everything out there is worth incorporating into your studies. Bible software is probably more important with lexical and syntactical analysis than with other areas of exegesis. I simply cannot imagine doing a word study today without the "Bible Word Study" feature in Logos Bible Software.[42] Becoming a regular at Logos and Accordance blogs will keep you engaged with original language studies and knowledgeable on different functions of the software and how to leverage their features.[43]

Logos 8 Basic Academic (free) is a good place to start if you do not have Bible software yet.[44] You can open the SBLGNT directly or use something called the "English-Greek reverse interlinear,"[45] albeit with the free version it will be the Lexham (i.e., Logos) translation or the King James Version. Get in the habit, though, of consulting multiple translations in as many languages as you know. The free version comes with more resources, including Brannan and Loken's *Lexham Textual Notes on the Bible* and Souter's *Pocket Lexicon to the Greek New Testament*.[46] The former is similar to Metzger's *Textual Commentary on the Greek New Testament*, just free. Souter's lexicon might be dated, but since it links to the SBLGNT and English translations, you will be able to see how the Bible Word Study feature works. Just imagine how it would work if you had more lexicons (e.g., BDAG, Louw-Nida).

42. For a short introduction to this feature, see the Logos 8 tutorial at https://youtu.be/MI-ucYSJGNk.

43. For Logos, see *Logos Talk: The Logos Bible Software Blog*, https://blog.logos.com, and *The Logos Academic Blog*, https://academic.logos.com. For Accordance, see *Accordance Blog*, https://www.accordancebible.com/blog/index.html. For word studies, see Mark Ward, "How to Do Bible Word Studies: A Fool-Proof Guide," *Logos Talk* (blog), February 3, 2016, https://blog.logos.com/2016/02/how-to-do-bible-word-studies-a-fool-proof-guide.

44. The download is available at https://www.logos.com/academic-basic. I would recommend a download here of Accordance Lite, but the free version hardly compares to the Logos free version. Accordance, for example, provides only a sample (Matt. 1–3) of the Nestle-Aland Greek text (not including the textual apparatus). The Logos free version does not have the Nestle-Aland text, but it does provide the SBLGNT in its entirety. And the only difference between the NA[28] and the SBLGNT in Matt. 1–3 is a few instances of final ν (2:14, 16, 21).

45. This is available with a number of major translations, all of which are included with Logos 8 Basic. This type of interlinear keeps the English as the primary text and includes the corresponding Greek text in separate space below.

46. Alexander Souter, *A Pocket Lexicon to the Greek New Testament* (Oxford: Clarendon, 1917).

Lexicographers are changing the way they present lexical data. Laparola. net has a feature that allows you to see the domains and subdomains found in Louw and Nida's *Greek-English Lexicon of the New Testament: Based on Semantic Domains*.[47] You can also search the glosses, but it lacks the definitions and discussion found in the actual text. The members of the Semantic Analysis Research Group of Cordoba continue their work on the *Diccionario griego-español del Nuevo Testamento (DGENT)*.[48] Recently, they began to publish their findings online.[49] This is a huge development. Hopefully, work on the online edition will continue and remain free. The *DGENT* entry for ἀγαπάω[50] includes a general definition, sample glosses, three different sememes with specific definitions pertaining to each, and corresponding verses in Greek and Spanish. The bibliographic page features a number of publications worth exploring, such as Marta Merino Hernández's study on ἀπό and Jesús Peláez's study on βασιλεία.[51] The influence of the Iberian Peninsula on Greek philology even in modern times should be impossible to overlook, but for some reason it sometimes escapes the notice of researchers in the twenty-first century. You will probably be interested in the *Diccionario griego-español (DGE)*, a modern lexicon of ancient Greek produced under the direction of Francisco R. Adrados and Juan Rodríguez Somolinos. The *DGE* is also available via the Thesaurus Linguae Graecae (TLG). Familiarize yourself with this resource.

47. J. P. Louw and Eugene Nida, *Greek-English Lexicon of the New Testament: Based on Semantic Domains* (New York: United Bible Societies, 1996). To see the domains, visit https://www.laparola.net/greco/louwnida.php?LNGloss=. Logos has a three-minute introduction for the lexicon ("Louw-Nida," Logos Bible Software, https://www.logos.com/logos-pro/louw-nida). Another video introduces BDAG ("BDAG," Logos Bible Software, https://www.logos.com/logos -pro/bdag). In addition to these, see Rodney J. Decker, "An Introduction to the Bauer/Danker *Greek-English Lexicon of the New Testament*," *NT Resources* (blog), 2003, http://ntresour ces.com/blog/documents/UsingBDAG.pdf; and Vern S. Poythress, "Greek Lexicography and Translation: Comparing Bauer's and Louw-Nida's Lexicons," *JETS* 44 (June 2001): 285–96, https://www.etsjets.org/files/JETS-PDFs/44/44-2/44-2-PP285-296_JETS.pdf.

48. Andrew Bowden's translation and expansion of Juan Mateos's *Método de análisis semántico aplicado al griego del Nuevo Testamento* (Córdoba: El Almendro, 1989) and Jesús Peláez's *Metodología del Diccionario griego-español del Nuevo Testamento* (Córdoba: El Almendro, 1996) was published with the title *New Testament Lexicography: Introduction, Theory, Method* (Berlin: de Gruyter, 2018).

49. See the Diccionario griego-español del Nuevo Testamento at https://www.dgent.es. It is an excellent representation of a new shift in lexicography since even the publication of Louw-Nida. If you are studying a Greek word that begins with anything from α to δ, it would be wise to see what the Cordoba team has published online. If you cannot read Spanish, drop the web address into Google Translate. The translation will not be perfect but is still very helpful.

50. "ἀγαπάω," https://www.dgent.es/α/ἀγαπάω.

51. The bibliographic page is accessible through the sidebar. Look for those entries with "PDF" at the end.

For our purposes here, let me just encourage you to register for the free account and then find "Lexica" on the topic bar under the red header. When you click that word, a text box appears underneath the words "Lexicographical Resources." Begin typing "agapa . . ." The Greek word ἀγαπάω is one of the words the system auto-suggests. From here you can access not only the *DGE* but also the online Liddell-Scott *Greek-English Lexicon*, short definitions from Bauer's lexicon, and some other non-English lexicons.[52]

Words have ranges of meaning. And their meanings are always found in context. Exchanging a receptor-language gloss for a Greek lexeme is not the equivalent of studying the meaning of a word. More is required in historical research, and the study of the New Testament should be no different. I recommend reading Benjamin J. Baxter's articles in the *McMaster Journal of Theology and Ministry*: (1) "The Meanings of Biblical Words"[53] and (2) "Hebrew and Greek Word-Study Fallacies,"[54] and Daniel Wallace's "Lexical Fallacies by Linguists."[55] Mark Strauss has a twenty-five-minute discussion on what constitutes a word study and how to avoid three lexical fallacies:[56]

1. Meaning is determined by context, not by word roots.
2. Study sentences, not Greek words.
3. Read for the big idea, not for the hidden meaning.
4. Compare various English versions.
5. Check the better commentaries.

I recommend comparing as many translations as you possibly can. That includes paraphrases, and it means getting away from a preferred translation: ESV, KJV, NASB, or whichever it is.[57] Translations, in my experience, tend to

52. Thesaurus Linguae Graecae, http://stephanus.tlg.uci.edu/Iris/demo/lexica.jsp.

53. Benjamin J. Baxter, "The Meaning of Biblical Words," *MJTM* (2009–10): 89–120, https://www.mcmaster.ca/mjtm/pdfs/vol11/articles/MJTM_11.5_BaxterBiblicalWords.pdf.

54. Benjamin J. Baxter, "Hebrew and Greek Word-Study Fallacies," *MJTM* (2010–11): 3–32, https://www.mcmaster.ca/mjtm/documents/MJTM_12.1_BaxterFallacies_001.pdf.

55. Daniel B. Wallace, "Lexical Fallacies by Linguists," DanielBWallace.com, December 8, 2014, https://danielbwallace.com/2014/12/08/lexical-fallacies-by-linguists/. Every student still needs to read the chapter on lexical fallacies in D. A. Carson, *Exegetical Fallacies*, 2nd ed. (Grand Rapids: Baker, 1996).

56. Mark Strauss, "Lecture 6: Word Studies," Biblical Training, https://www.biblicaltraining.org/word-studies/how-study-your-bible.

57. Crossway released a promotional video for the ESV in 2010 ("ESV Trusted by Leaders," https://vimeo.com/16535086). It features some well-known Christians. In the video, Matt Chandler says he loves the ESV "because of the scholarship behind it and the accuracy of the translation." Thabiti Anyabwile calls it "an accurate and faithful attempt to mine the Word of God as it really is." Janet Parshall says, "It's crystal clear and with clarity I can understand

be more or less intentionally ambiguous, not more or less literal. We need to work harder at identifying the ambiguity and clearing out the fog, not using our Greek knowledge as a megaphone for preferred translations.

■ Syntactical Analysis

Syntax is everything. And analyzing the syntax of the Greek New Testament requires more tools than what you can find on the Blue Letter Bible website. It requires a knowledge of Greek grammar or at the least an ability (and willingness) to go back to the Greek grammars, to reach into exegetical commentaries, to identify interpretive options, and to evaluate their strengths and weaknesses until you are comfortable enough to settle on the one you think the author intended. There are ranges of meaning in syntax, as there are for individual words. Authorial intent assigns a finite meaning, and context is what assists hearers and readers—both near and distant—in identifying that meaning. The goal in syntactical analysis is to move from ambiguity to clarity, from the position of reader or hearer to the position of the author and understanding the author's choice in a discourse.

Think about Romans 5:8: "God demonstrates his own love toward us in that while we were yet sinners, Christ died for us." First, what aspect (imperfective or aoristic)[58] does Paul intend with συνίστησιν ("demonstrates" *or* "is demonstrating")? And what about the phrase ὑπὲρ ἡμῶν ("for us")? The translation "for us" is ambiguous. Sometimes it helps to think about the syntax we find in our English translations and just carry it over to a completely different setting. For example, what if I said, "I am going to the store to get a present *for John*." What do I mean? Is it that I am going to the store to get a present that I intend to give to John, or that I am going

---

exactly what our heavenly Father is trying to teach us." And John Piper says, "There isn't any version better in striking that balance in accuracy and usability and understandability." A balance between accuracy and usability? Viewing translations as "literal" or "word-for-word" might have a place, but associating the word "accuracy" with one of them is problematic. A better way to view translations, including paraphrases, is on a scale of ambiguity. Translations like the NASB and ESV are what I call "intentionally ambiguous," not literal and certainly not more "accurate" than, say, the NKJV or the NIV. Think about 2 Cor. 5:21: "For our sake he made him to be sin who knew no sin, so that in him we might become the righteousness of God" (ESV). The translations are not inaccurate so much as they are ambiguous. This ambiguity is intended by the editors so that teachers do not have to correct translations where ambiguity has been removed. But again, this should not be presented as accuracy.

58. For a simplified discussion on aspect, see the chart provided by Black in *Learn to Read New Testament Greek*, 15. Black indicates that the present is "basically imperfective" but that it can sometimes be aoristic.

to the store to get a present because John, for whatever reason, is unable to do it himself? Our goal is to remove the ambiguity.

Most of us need a grid for thinking about syntax before we even know what we are looking for, though. Start asking yourself why an author chose that syntax, and work toward being able to explain how the meaning might have been different or nuanced had another selection been made (e.g., the use of the imperfect ἐγίνωσκεν in Matt. 1:25 instead of the aorist ἔγνω). What are some electronic resources or places online that can help you as you begin to engage the syntax of the New Testament? Here are just a few:

1. A. T. Robertson's *Word Pictures of the New Testament* (1933)[59] and *A Grammar of the Greek New Testament in the Light of Historical Research*:[60] These remain valuable to modern researchers despite being published before the Second World War. The latter is long and heavy, the author regularly and effortlessly switching between languages (without translation) and using an unfamiliar vocabulary for most novice students of Greek. Nevertheless, it is worth its weight in gold. The only way to get full access to the best Greek grammars is to buy them individually or buy a Bible software package that contains them.

2. Google Books (www.books.google.com): This has search features that, while not exhaustive, will help identify syntactical discussions. In Robertson's grammar, for example, you can search for the word "imperfect," and it will take you directly to where he discusses its different functions. If you type "Greek grammar AND imperfect" into the search bar on Google Books, a number of other public domain works come up. Keep scrolling down until you find Daniel Wallace's *Greek Grammar beyond the Basics*.[61] Click on that resource, and then look to the left sidebar, where you will find another small search box under the book image and title. In that search box, type "imperfect." The results and how much is shown will vary, but my experience has been that Google Books will surprise you with how much of a book's content publishers have made available. When I did this search right now, I was taken to page 541, where Wallace discusses the relationship of the imperfect tense to time, and to page 544, where he contrasts the imperfect and aorist tenses. If you do the same thing for David Alan Black's *It's*

59. A. T. Robertson, *Word Pictures in the New Testament* (Nashville: Broadman, 1933), https://www.biblestudytools.com/commentaries/robertsons-word-pictures/.

60. The third edition is available through Google Books: A. T. Robertson, *A Grammar of the Greek New Testament in the Light of Historical Research*, 3rd ed. (New York: Hodder & Stoughton, 1919), https://books.google.com/books?id=n5ikBxAloW8C&dq=robertson%20greek%20grammar&pg=PR4#v=onepage&q&f=false, or just search for the title.

61. Daniel B. Wallace, *Greek Grammar beyond the Basics: An Exegetical Syntax of the New Testament* (Grand Rapids: Zondervan, 1996).

Still Greek to Me,[62] hopefully you will be able to see pages 105–6, where he identifies four clear uses of the imperfect—progressive, iterative, tendential, and inceptive. In Matthew 1:25, the translation "he kept her" obscures the fact that Matthew used the imperfect and not the aorist, and the translation "he was keeping her" would simply be ambiguous. Our goal is to remove that ambiguity. And knowing how to leverage Google Books helps us, even at the very beginning stages of our learning, in making practical and informed use of our study of the Greek language. Here are just a few more suggestions:

- Search for commentaries in Google Books on the specific New Testament text you are studying (e.g., "commentary on Matthew"). From there, use different searches to find relevant material, such as "1:25" for the verse where the imperfect in question is found.
- Sometimes the search will let you down. When you are searching in a commentary, for example, try to navigate via scrolling to the section where your discourse unit is discussed.
- Take notes while you can. Just because a set of pages is available one day does not mean they will be there the next time you visit the preview.
- Search for Greek words (e.g., ἐγίνωσκεν) and transliterated forms (e.g., *eginōsken*). Try those searches in conjunction with other queries like "Gospel of Matthew" or "Matthew." You might also try the lexical form since sometimes authors use those by default.

Be creative and come up with other ways to help you get to the relevant data.

3. The journal *Biblical and Ancient Greek Linguistics* (www.bagl.org): This open-access scholarly journal contains articles like Stanley E. Porter's "θαυμάζω in Mark 6:6 and Luke 11:38: A Note on Monosemy" (2013) and Paul L. Danove's "The Conceptualization of Communication in the New Testament: A Feature Description" (2017).

4. OpenText.org: This electronic resource actually outdoes Bible software with how it categorizes and displays syntactical and discourse relationships—and it's free. You need to read Matthew Brook O'Donnell's "Introducing the OpenText.org Syntactically Analyzed Greek New Testament" to understand all the features of this analyzed Greek New Testament.[63]

---

62. David Alan Black, *It's Still Greek to Me: An Easy-to-Understand Guide to Intermediate Greek* (Grand Rapids: Baker, 1998).
63. Matthew Brook O'Donnell, "Introducing the OpenText.org Syntactically Analyzed Greek New Testament," OpenText.org, September 22, 2005, http://www.opentext.org/resources/articles/a8.html.

5. Michael W. Palmer's "Comprehensive Bibliography of Hellenistic Greek Linguistics."[64]

6. J. Harold Greenlee's page:[65] You can access some very interesting articles, such as "The Importance of Syntax for the Proper Understanding of the Sacred Text of the New Testament."[66]

7. The journal *Filología Neotestamentaria* (www.bsw.org/filologia-neo testamentaria/): Articles like David I. Yoon's "Prominence in New Testament Discourse: Galatians 1,11–2,10 as a Test Case" are available to read online for free.

■ Conclusion

You have to decide where you invest your time and energies. My own experience, and the path I recommend for others, is to learn Greek as you study the New Testament. Leverage the resources available to you. Carry your Greek New Testament with you everywhere you go. Or better yet, take a trip back in time and just start using volume five of the Complutensian Polyglot or Erasmus's edition. Read broadly. Push yourself beyond the free resources on BibleGateway.com. Think past the glosses. Keep going back to your Greek grammars. More than identifying the tense, voice, or mood of a verb, ask why a New Testament author used that one, and be willing to figure out how the meaning would have been different had he chosen something else. Learn about textual criticism. Look at the manuscripts for yourselves. Trust me, you will enjoy looking at a Greek manuscript (especially one with some historical significance) more than you will a modern critical edition. As tempting as it is to have shelves and shelves of books, go digital. New Testament students who live in the world of nostalgia do themselves no favors. Living in the past—that is, doing New Testament studies with paper books alone—is dangerous to your pursuit of knowledge. Today our tools are changing. The best students of the New Testament will be those who change with it.

64. Michael W. Palmer, "A Comprehensive Bibliography of Hellenistic Greek Linguistics," Greek Language and Linguistics, https://greek-language.com/Palmer-bibliography.html. Sometimes the links are broken. If this happens, try searching for the title, and you might get lucky, as I did with Carl Conrad's "New Observations on Voice in the Ancient Greek Verb."

65. "J. Harold Greenlee (1918–)," Theologicalstudies.org.uk, https://www.theologicalstudies .org.uk/theo_greenlee.php.

66. J. Harold Greenlee, "The Importance of Syntax for the Proper Understanding of the Sacred Text of the New Testament," *Evangelical Quarterly* 44, no. 3 (1972): 131–46.

10

An Ideal Beginning Greek Grammar?

ROBERT L. PLUMMER

I s there an ideal beginning Greek grammar? I will answer this question by discussing two caveats and six essential characteristics of an ideal beginning Greek grammar.

■ Caveat 1: Wisdom from a Child's Stationery: Embrace Your Reality

I have an eleven-year-old daughter, Anabelle, who recently showed me a postcard with a beautiful picture of a unicorn on it and these words: "Always be yourself, unless you can be a unicorn. Then always be a unicorn."

From the perspective of a young girl, it would be an amazing experience to be a unicorn, wouldn't it? But it's an impossibility. So rather than seeking an unattainable ideal, one should embrace the reality that God has providentially given you. In the case of the unicorn question, the providential reality God has given you is a human body rather than a unicorn body.

This conference paper has been edited extensively for publication, but the author has attempted to maintain an elevated conversational tone in keeping with the topic of the paper and the context of its original delivery.

We might compare this existential question to our search for the "ideal" Greek grammar. There is *no* ideal Greek grammar. Yes, there are some better than others. But, to my target audience of students or alumni who have completed at least one year of Greek, the grammar you should embrace is the one on your shelf. Or, better yet, hold closely the Greek grammar that your teacher selected. In giving these blunt instructions, I am countering the tendency of students or pastors to think that if they just purchase the next or better resource, then they will finally learn Greek (or Hebrew) as they should have. Nevertheless, the essential element that the student or pastor is usually lacking is willpower, time, and hard work.

I'd like to create my own inspirational stationery cards that say: "Use the ideal Greek grammar, unless you can't find it—and then use whatever you've got . . . or whatever you were assigned." Embracing the Greek textbook that God has already put in your hands actually touches on the doctrine of vocation, perhaps best articulated postbiblically, nearly five hundred years ago, by the great Reformer Martin Luther.

The doctrine of vocation speaks to the intersection of God's providence with our daily roles and tasks. God is not sovereign just over the nations. (And indeed he is: "Surely the nations are like a drop in a bucket; / they are regarded as dust on the scales; / he weighs the islands as though they were fine dust," Isa. 40:15 NIV). God is also sovereign over the seminary you attend, the Greek professor you study under, and the Greek textbook that your professor chose.

Not a sparrow falls to the ground apart from the knowledge and will of your heavenly Father (Matt. 10:29). He feeds the birds, which neither sow nor reap, and he clothes the flowers of the field with a splendor that surpasses that of Solomon (6:25–29). How much more so then, little children, does he oversee the Greek resources at your disposal!

If I may continue to address my reader directly: one of *your* divinely given roles is to be a student and reader of the Greek New Testament. God's providence extends to the small details of that role, and in it he is calling *you* to love and trust him—and to love your neighbor—your teacher, your fellow students, your future neighbors (i.e., church members who will be relying on you to teach them the Scriptures accurately).

At a recent missionary conference, I wanted to give the attendees a visual image to help them understand the doctrine of vocation. I showed them a picture of the resurrected Christ with his palms up, arms stretched out toward them. In Jesus's hands (in this image) he holds a list, and on that list there are their various roles: language student, mother, business owner, missionary. I reminded the missionaries that biblically, each day, Jesus is specifically commissioning each one of them to fulfill these roles in faith and love. How would laundry, cooking, or memorizing Greek paradigms look different if one embraced these tasks as part of the roles given by our great Savior? How would the struggle of learning language look different if one really believed, "God has appointed me in this particular time and place to learn Koine Greek"? And, as you work diligently as a student, you are loving your teacher, you are loving your fellow students, you are loving the people who sacrificed to send you here, and you are loving future church members (decades from now) who will hear the gospel message more faithfully and passionately because of your diligent study.

At the same time, if you determine that you are not being instructed well—or that your learning style is incompatible with your teacher's pedagogy—it has never been easier to supplement your instruction. Here are three websites to supplement your formal Greek education:

- www.dailydoseofgreek.com
- biblearc.com
- biblicaltraining.org

■ Caveat 2: The Economic Problem of "Lock In" and Its Relation to Greek Pedagogy

As we consider the "ideal Greek grammar," we must consider another caveat. The teaching of Greek—whether in person or through a textbook—faces a problem that economists call the problem of "lock in." We can illustrate this with the QWERTY keyboard.[1]

Before iPads and laptops, there were electronic typewriters. And before electronic typewriters, there were manual typewriters. The QWERTY order of the keys that we all find as the default setting on our electronic devices dates from the late 1800s. The order was designed not for speed but for the transcription of telegraph messages. Yet that order soon dominated the market. It became "locked in."

A gentleman named August Dvorak patented a different keyboard layout in 1936 that multiple studies have shown allows superior typing speed— especially with modern computer keyboards, in which there is no concern

---

1. I am drawing heavily here on a recent podcast by Tim Hartford about the QWERTY keyboard: Tim Hartford, "QWERTY," April 20, 2019, in *50 Things That Made the Modern Economy*, produced by Ben Crighton, podcast, MP3 audio, 9:00, https://www.bbc.co.uk/sounds /play/w3csz2w5.

about physical key levers becoming stuck together. Yet, even though objective studies have shown that it is economically worthwhile to retrain typists to type on Dvorak keyboards, and (with computers now) it's easy to change any keyboard to work on the Dvorak pattern, and there are countless free videos online teaching how to retool yourself to the Dvorak keyboard, why do 99.9 percent of us still use the QWERTY keyboard? We're "locked in." When we took a typing class online or in high school, that's the keyboard we learned. Every keyboard we buy—virtual or real—comes set up default with the QWERTY layout. So we don't care that it will make us slightly faster to learn to type on the Dvorak model. Such a transition would be annoying and slow us down for a few weeks. We judge that any potential increase in efficiency is not worth the short-term pain.

The comparison of QWERTY and Dvorak keyboards is similar to a number of issues in Greek pedagogy. Let's look at them from the viewpoint of professors:

- **Textbooks:** Yes, there are newer and better Greek textbooks out there, but most established professors must admit that all of their quizzes and notes and PowerPoint presentations are keyed to a slightly inferior grammar that they have been using for twenty years. They are "locked in," and they'd rather have extra time to write a scholarly article or go biking than retool their classes for a better textbook. The result? Over decades, hundreds of students suffer from pedagogical inertia. Also, the sales numbers of new and wonderfully designed beginning Greek textbooks are shockingly low.

- **Pronunciation:** The majority of current Greek professors learned and employ Erasmian pronunciation. It works fine. But, from an objective perspective, modern pronunciation or reconstructed Koine pronunciation is better. If a professor were to shift to reconstructed Koine pronunciation, perhaps in an incremental way it would help hundreds of new and future students, but the professor would also face the danger of alienating colleagues and alumni. The result? Most New Testament Greek professors are locked into a pronunciation system that works well enough, and the intense incremental pain of changing—and the resultant disconnect from other Erasmian speakers—makes them continue to stay "locked in."

- **The Living Language Method:** As an undergraduate at Duke University, I learned Greek under a traditional pedagogy that focused on memorizing paradigms, parsing, and translation. In high school and college, I also learned French—but as a spoken language. I can still speak and think in French, and it's wired differently in my brain than Greek. It's more immediate and intuitive. No doubt, it is the superior way to know language. For the last year, I've been studying Latin in a spoken-language method, and I find that the Latin language is becoming wired in my brain similar to French. However, regarding Greek, I find that I am "locked in" to the traditional pedagogy, and if I were to switch, the students would not be able to take a different professor at our seminary for the second semester of the course. It would create scheduling nightmares and collegial tension. Is it possible that being inescapably "locked in" to a good, robust traditional pedagogy could, in fact, be the enemy of a superior living language method?

So, we've begun our discussion of the "ideal Greek grammar" with two caveats. To recap, these are the following:

- Use the ideal Greek grammar, unless you can't find it—and then use whatever you've got . . . or whatever you were assigned.
- Writing or adopting the ideal Greek grammar faces the challenge that professors, alumni, and students are already irrevocably "locked in" to good, but perhaps inferior, textbooks, pronunciation systems, and pedagogical methods.

Given those caveats, let us now consider six essential characteristics of the "ideal beginning Greek grammar."

■ Characteristic 1: The Ideal Grammar Will Inspire Students to Seek Spiritual Nourishment in the Greek New Testament

Seminary students regularly ask me why they should learn Greek. Sometimes I respond in a parable: Imagine, I say, that you meet someone who teaches French literature at the local university. You chat with him, and you say, "Oh, that's interesting. When did you learn French?" He responds, "Oh, I don't know French. You know, the translations are so good. There's no need to learn it."

You might not show it in your facial expression (because you're a pastor, and you've learned to hide your shock and disgust), but in your heart you'd think, "This guy is a fake! He claims to teach French literature, and he doesn't even read French?!"

Imagine now that you have a pastor who says, "I believe that the Bible is the very Word of God!" We may reply, "That's fantastic, but when did you take the time to learn to read the actual Greek and Hebrew words that God breathed out?" Doesn't the doctrine of verbal plenary inspiration demand an attention to the biblical languages?

Sadly, it's not uncommon to find seminaries so streamlining their degrees and curricula that they are making the biblical languages optional. Under President Obama, we had a competitive national educational program titled "Race to the Top." In our current seminary environment, we find something more akin to "Race to the Bottom," with schools falling over themselves for a greater market share of a shrinking demographic, seeking to provide the least and easiest education in the shortest amount of time. Amazingly, it is not uncommon for people to earn an MDiv degree at reputable evangelical or nonevangelical institutions having never learned any Greek. Μὴ γένοιτο ("May it never be!").

With schools themselves providing the marketing against biblical languages, it is incumbent upon the professor and textbook to make a constant advertisement for the benefit of learning the biblical languages. One reason Benjamin Merkle and I wrote *Greek for Life* (Baker Academic, 2017) was to put an inspirational tool in the hands of other professors or discouraged students themselves—and to supplement the majority of textbooks that leave the inspiring to the instructing professor.

Philipp Melanchthon (1497–1560), the great contemporary of Luther, said it well:

> Since the Bible is written in part in Hebrew and in part in Greek, . . . we drink from the stream of both—we must learn these languages, unless we want to be "silent persons" as theologians. Once we understand the significance and the weight of the words, the true meaning of Scripture will light up for us as the midday sun. Only if we have clearly understood the language will we clearly understand the content. . . . If we put our minds to the [Greek and Hebrew] sources, we will begin to understand Christ rightly.[2]

Many students do not come into a beginning Greek class having thought through the value of learning the biblical languages and, in fact, often come with a plurality of voices that have told them that Greek and Hebrew are not worth the effort. We, the Greek professors, must inspire them—in the

---

2. Melanchthon's inaugural address on "The Reform of the Education of Youth" (1518), cited in Hans J. Hillerbrand, ed., *The Reformation: A Narrative History Related by Contemporary Observers and Participants* (Grand Rapids: Baker, 1987), 59–60.

classroom *and* in the textbook—with many, many examples of where knowing Greek makes a difference in our understanding or guards us against a superficial or flawed reading. Greek matters!

This is one reason I'm very excited about Merkle's book *Exegetical Gems from Biblical Greek* (Baker Academic, 2019). Throughout this entire book, Merkle maintains a tight connection between grammatical concept and payoff in exegetical significance. This book is a model of characteristic 1 for an ideal Greek grammar.

◼ Characteristic 2: The Ideal Grammar Will Incorporate Mnemonic Devices[3]

Just as students often come uninspired to their study of the Greek language—not really having a vision or passion for why they are learning—so also they come without having previously acquired the specific skills needed for learning a foreign language. Professors need not only to teach Greek accurately but also to teach students *how* to learn Greek—that is, how to remember foreign language vocabulary, conjugations, and paradigms.

Students have different abilities to learn foreign languages. I see this variation even among my three daughters. One daughter can just recite Latin or Greek vocabulary a few times, and then she seems to be able to recall the words with almost photographic accuracy. Another daughter can repeat words over and over again, but they slide off her neural synapses like a fried egg off a Teflon-coated skillet.

A while back, one of my daughters was struggling to remember that the Latin word *agnus* means "lamb." I personally have found that English cognates or theological phrases that seem familiar to me, like *agnus Dei* (lamb of God), are completely unhelpful to my children. "What does it sound like to you?" I asked my daughter. "*Agnus . . . agnus . . . ,*" she repeated thoughtfully. Then she said, "*A goose*! It sounds like *a goose*!" So, I told her, imagine a little lamb walking around and bleating: "Baaaa . . . baaaa." Then suddenly—poof—it turns into a goose!" We not only visualized the scene; we got down on the ground and acted it out—at first walking about bleating like sheep and then, suddenly, flapping our arms like wings and making honking noises. The meaning of *agnus* was imprinted upon her memory through multiple sensory experiences.

Many students need to learn basic memory techniques of association, visual memory palaces, and employing songs to memorize word endings.

---

3. A mnemonic device is, of course, a device used to help memorize something more quickly or effectively.

Unless textbook authors and professors incorporate these mnemonic materials into their instruction, students are usually at a loss to supplement their education on their own.

Whether you are a professor or student looking to incorporate more memory helps, let me recommend the following:

- Benjamin L. Merkle and Robert L. Plummer, *Greek for Life: Strategies for Learning, Retaining, and Reviving New Testament Greek* (Grand Rapids: Baker Academic, 2017)
- Danny Zacharias's YouTube channel, "The Singing Grammarian," https://www.youtube.com/playlist?list=PLO-USksx-puxxltOhjEK-tS EjbEX1XepZ
- Mullenmemory.com

■ Characteristic 3: The Ideal Grammar Will Be Written Clearly and Simply

Sadly, many grammarians write for each other. It is perhaps the minority of scholars who can write in such a way that the nonspecialist is informed, inspired, and even delighted. Let's look at a sample of writing from an unnamed introductory Greek grammar (not written by any of the speakers at the conference where this paper was read, I assure you):

> Οὗτος and ἐκεῖνος are frequently used with nouns. When they are so used, the noun with which they are used has the article, and they themselves stand in the predicate, not in the attributive, position.

Let's consider this same paragraph after some editing done with the beginning student in mind:

> The demonstrative pronouns οὗτος ("this") and ἐκεῖνος ("that") frequently occur as modifiers of explicit nouns. (For example: οὗτος ὁ λόγος, "this word," or ἐκεῖνοι οἱ λόγοι, "those words.") Note in these examples that the words οὗτος and ἐκεῖνοι (the demonstrative pronouns) do not have articles in front of them. The nouns they modify (λόγος and λόγοι), however, do have articles in front of them. This is the normal way for demonstrative pronouns to occur when modifying explicit nouns.

For beginning students, who have trouble remembering the meaning of "predicate position" and "attributive position," taking the time to spell these matters out in a bit more simplistic detail is advisable.

When I was seeking endorsements for my *40 Questions about Interpreting the Bible* (Kregel, 2010), I took a chance and asked the famous theologian and hermeneutics scholar Kevin Vanhoozer. He very kindly wrote an endorsement, but he made the offhand comment that he and I were writing for different audiences, which I think was a polite way of saying that I had written a children's book while he wrote for grownups. I do think that Dr. Vanhoozer and I are writing for the same audience, but perhaps I have a bit more realistic appraisal of my audience's ability to digest new and difficult concepts. Authors of Greek textbooks need a realistic appraisal of students' lack of grammatical knowledge.

Not long ago, I taught a Greek review course to about eighty-five students from all over the United States and Canada. One of them had recently graduated from a well-known evangelical seminary. He came to me during a class break to tell me how astounded and overjoyed he was to finally know what a "declension" was—that it was just a fancy word for a grammatical pattern. He was a smart and curious student. Isn't that almost unimaginable—that a good student could get through several Greek classes and still be unable to define the word "declension"?

Because too many introductory Greek grammars assume too much grammatical ability on the part of their users, there has arisen an entire cottage industry of producing supplementary books on rudimentary English grammar. These include the following:

- *A Dictionary of English Grammar for Students of Biblical Languages* by Kyle R. Greenwood (Grand Rapids: Zondervan, 2020)
- *English Grammar to Ace New Testament Greek* by Samuel Lamerson (Grand Rapids: Zondervan, 2004)
- *Grammatical Concepts 101 for Biblical Greek* by Gary A. Long (Grand Rapids: Baker Academic, 2006)

And the classic booklet for English speakers learning any foreign language (ancient or modern):

English Grammar for Language Students: Basic Grammatical Terminology Defined and Alphabetically Arranged by Frank X. Braun (Ann Arbor, MI: Ulrich's Books; repr., Eugene, OR: Wipf & Stock, 2013)

If you did not learn Greek with the "ideal" grammar (as none of us did!), perhaps these books will help shore up your grammatical foundation.

■ Characteristic 4: The Ideal Grammar Will Be Accurate

Every elementary Greek grammar will include oversimplification, yet there is a need to *not* introduce too many oversimplifications. Every oversimplification is a distortion that the beginning student will have to overcome at the intermediate or advanced level.

Merkle and I are fighting this battle as we finish up our beginning Greek grammar manuscript. For example, it is quite common when teaching the aorist tense to speak about the aorist active, aorist middle, and aorist passive forms as distinct—as if there is no overlap among them. But, if you actually consider Koine writers' usage, the aorist passive form is frequently found in the New Testament period conveying a middle idea. Let's look at an illustrative text from Revelation 12:18:

Καὶ **ἐστάθη** ἐπὶ τὴν ἄμμον τῆς θαλάσσης.
And **he stood** on the sand of the sea.

Ἐστάθη is from the lexical form ἵστημι and is translated "he stood." Clearly, a middle sense is intended. As you may remember, the middle voice is used to convey an action that the subject both executes and is affected by—a voice that fits well with the activity of standing.

Based on the discussion of the aorist in many introductory grammars, beginning students can be excused if they translate this as "he was stood" or "he was placed" on the sand of the sea. Certainly, that would be an "accurate" literalistic rendering of the aorist passive form. Beginning students might then speculate on the providential activity conveyed by this divine passive—in fact, they could write an entire paragraph of theologically rich thoughts . . . and they would be entirely mistaken—from a *grammatical* standpoint. This aorist passive form in Revelation 12:18, as in many other places in the New Testament, conveys a middle idea. Would it not be more accurate, then, to teach this common nuance to beginning students and perhaps call the aorist passive forms "medio-passive" (a suggestion of a colleague) to remind students of this reality? Or, to follow my preferred nomenclature, we can say that ἐστάθη is an aorist passive *form* used to convey a middle *idea*.

Let's consider another example of misleading oversimplification. In beginning grammars, it's not uncommon to teach that present imperatives are used for a general practice and aorist imperatives are used for a discrete occasion. This is somewhat true, but equally important in determining why an author has selected the present or aorist imperative is to note the inherent procedural nature of the verbal activity described. Telic, or bounded, activity (like hitting someone) has a strong preference for the aorist imperative; atelic, or unbounded, activity (like walking) has a strong predilection for the present imperative. This observation is not difficult to understand, is easy to illustrate with multiple examples, and will guard Greek students from many misunderstandings and overstatements.

At a Greek conference like the one where this paper was originally read, the variety of speakers provide a living, visual reminder that there are disagreements among Greek grammarians about secondary and tertiary issues. Yet there are also many points of agreement, and it is on those agreements and undeniable linguistic patterns that the ideal beginning Greek grammar should focus. I especially appreciate the way that fellow conference participant Steve Runge has sought to find common ground with previous generations of grammarians. It is true that, in certain cases, the academic discipline of linguistics can provide a more precise description of various phenomena in the Greek language, but a previous generation of scholars and commentators did often have an accurate sense of the same patterns, which they described in the terms and categories available to them.

■ Characteristic 5: The Ideal Grammar Will Have an Online Portal of Supporting Resources

To the author of the "ideal beginning Greek textbook," we can say this: it is foolish for you to think that you can write a print Greek textbook— even an ideal one—and *on this basis alone* it will be widely adopted and influence the proper reading of the Greek New Testament. What's the use of writing an "ideal" textbook if it is not in the hands of many students and professors and if it does not result in a deeper knowledge of God's Word, a greater love for the Lord, and more faithful teaching in the church? Imagine writing an ideal book and then sealing it in a crypt. What's the purpose in that?

We write to teach and influence, and so we *must* think about how to make that textbook accessible, desirable, and adopted. In the twenty-first century, authors of textbooks must have a vision and a passion to impart knowledge and inspire. The printed textbook is one leg of a three-legged stool. An online portal of resources is another of those legs.[4] (I realize that technology may

---

4. Perhaps the third leg is the author—through the author's character, life, passion, teaching, and influence.

change so quickly in the coming decades that the terminology I am using will sound outdated, but the basic idea will endure.)

Every book has its flaws, and *Going Deeper with New Testament Greek*, a book coauthored by me, certainly has its shortcomings. But one thing I think we did well was have a webpage in place when the book launched. I recommend that you look at www.deepergreek.com. For the elementary text, *Beginning with New Testament Greek*, see www.beginninggreek.com.

Ideally, a textbook-linked website address should be prominently displayed on the book's cover and opening pages; and the website should be up and running before the publishing of the book. An online portal of this sort is needed to ease the adoption of the book by professors—to fight against the inertia of "lock in" to a current grammar. If a professor is provided with PowerPoint presentations, quizzes, tests, answer keys, and so on, it will greatly increase the chance of the textbook's adoption. Also, students can be provided with digital flashcards, chapter summaries, study aids, PDFs of PowerPoint lessons, and many other helpful ancillary resources.

The author of the ideal textbook must not simply aim to write an excellent textbook. That goal is too small. The goal is to change the world. To change the world, you must have a vision for capturing people's desires—and teaching and mentoring them in the most effective methods possible. That includes a printed textbook but goes far beyond it.

■ Characteristic 6: The Ideal Grammar Will Be Written by Authors Who Are Growing as Disciples of Christ

When I was finishing my PhD program at Southern Baptist Seminary, my wife and I had a wonderful job. We lived in the basement of the guesthouse on campus. This was the housing facility where chapel speakers, prospective faculty, and other VIP guests stayed. One of our weekly guests was a famous professor who traveled in on a regular basis. (He has now passed away.) He has written quite a few famous books.

This professor had the reputation of being angry and rude. I heard a story secondhand that this professor had been extremely rude to one of the secretaries in the dean's office at our school. When the dean met with this rude professor about this incident, he made it very clear that if that ever happened again, the rude professor's employment would be terminated.

Over the years, I've seen this man's books many times. I've never read one, nor do I think I ever will. No matter how accurate, pedagogically engaging, and helpful a beginning Greek textbook is, if we, the authors, are not people who genuinely love God and love people, who walk with humility and integrity, who seek to share the gospel with our lost neighbors and are remembered by our students as people who loved them, then we are nothing but noisy gongs, clanging cymbals. We are nothing. We gain nothing.

Yet, by God's grace, by the empowering of his Holy Spirit, may we be people who love the Lord Jesus with an undying love and teach Greek with infective passion, pedagogical skill, and scholarly accuracy. Μαράνα θά (1 Cor. 16:22).

11

Biblical Exegesis and Linguistics

A Prodigal History

NICHOLAS J. ELLIS

A t the crossroad of biblical exegesis, we find an intersection of language, history, and theology. I have walked these roads as a historian, a theologian, and a grammarian, working most of my life within cross-cultural, multilanguage contexts. I have been increasingly drawn to the explanatory power of linguistics. In my case, the draw to linguistics arose from the need for better resources for engagement with biblical languages and exegesis in English, Portuguese, Spanish, and lately East African languages. The need was cemented by overseeing a failed four-year project of translating Daniel Wallace's *Greek Grammar beyond the Basics* into Portuguese, by the end of which I had realized that it simply was not sufficient to translate English-interfaced grammatical/semantic tools for the study of Greek and Hebrew into global languages of wider communication. And yet this remains the predominant method of resourcing the global church: the focus is on the production and commercialization of products, which are then exported into the global context, with an emphasis on increased distribution and less-than-satisfactory thought to target-language linguistic accuracy.

And yet, we are called into a global mission, for the resourcing of the Christian church. In response, I find myself reevaluating my own, primarily English-language programs and curricula in order to contribute to better global engagement with Greek and Hebrew. This has led to a turn (and in some ways a turn back, as we will see), to crosslinguistic, deeply contextual, typological engagement with biblical texts and the languages of wider communication in which the global church is now engaging.

At the same time, however, this crosslinguistic emphasis has proven difficult to defend in my own professional guild of biblical and theological studies. We have inherited a legacy of hesitance at such work, stemming in no small part from the ongoing influence of James Barr and the linguistic work pioneered in the early twentieth century.

It is against this background that, when asked to contribute a chapter on linguistics and exegesis, I chose this specific question: How should the biblical and theological studies guild, and its cousin the Bible translation community, engage with the constantly evolving and highly productive field of linguistics, for the broad purpose of accurate engagement with the biblical text? I will examine this question diachronically, placing us within a history of research.

■ The Linguistic Terrain

When Dirk Geeraerts describes, in his seminal work on lexical semantics, a mental journey through the historical landscape of linguistic theory, there is within this landscape an unmentioned territory of biblical and theological studies that is perhaps most notable for the deep canyons and fissures that run through its terrain.[1] These canyons separate this territory into camps: the general population of biblical scholars, a smaller camp of "biblical linguists," and the Bible translation community, with the whole territory almost entirely separated from the wider field of linguistics.

I was trained within the first camp, oriented historically and by long influence to the reflections of the biblical philologists—that is, the "Dead Grammarians," such as A. T. Robertson and James Hope Moulton. Indeed, my guild continues to use the tools and resources developed within the area of the Dead Grammarians: from these minds came our core lexicons, grammars, and syntaxes.

On the other hand, it has become entirely unfashionable to engage in the linguistic conclusions of these older grammarians, especially since the 1960s and Barr's structuralist reprimand to the biblical studies guild on their use (or misuse) of biblical languages.[2] However, with the exception of the oc-

---

1. Dirk Geeraerts, *Theories of Lexical Semantics* (Oxford: Oxford University Press, 2010), xiii.

2. James Barr, *The Semantics of Biblical Language* (Oxford: Oxford University Press, 1961).

casional cautionary glance back to Barr about the dangers of crosslinguistic or typological analysis, the biblical studies guild has in large part failed to engage with formal linguistics as a basic expectation of its practitioners. There are indeed isolated groups of scholars who have embraced certain schools of linguistics. Perhaps most famous in North America is Stanley Porter, who built a circle of students within a particular Systemic Functional Linguistic camp that has attained a certain degree of internal cohesion. However, this group has remained quite small, especially in comparison to the wider field.

This is all the more acutely felt by the exception that proves the rule: notably, the deep engagement with linguistic theory in the work of Bible translation, a community fundamentally inclined toward crosslinguistic analysis, diachronic study, and other such things that Barr's specter has made unfashionable in the biblical studies guild. And yet, the Bible translation guild has, for the most part and until recently, been seemingly unwilling and uninterested in engaging with the biblical studies academic guild, and vice versa, possibly due to an increasing gap in mutually unintelligible vocabulary and theoretical frameworks that would enable the two communities to collaborate in their biblical analyses.

And so, as exegetes we find ourselves in a strangely compromised situation—both dependent upon and yet alienated from our philological past, anxious as to the criticisms of the early modern linguists but for the most part unwilling or unable to engage with ongoing current research in linguistics, and separated culturally and terminologically from our fellow workers in the field of Bible translation.

■ Linguistics, Exegesis, and Historical Influence

One of the problems in the biblical studies guild has been the isolation of linguistic interests to a small section of its membership. This has resulted both in an imbalance of power and an inability to evaluate linguistic claims. A parallel can be found in the field of New Testament scholarship: for two centuries, the study of the New Testament was dominated by a cutting-edge historical reconstruction, birthed in Tübingen by F. C. Baur and his colleagues. This historical reconstruction, in which Paul and Peter represented conflicting camps, became the foundation for much of New Testament exegesis. In fact, it became almost impossible to do critical academic work in the New Testament field outside of those historical and philosophical expectations. Only when biblical scholars moved past purely "exegetical work" and took the time and energy to invest in working within the historical and philosophical presuppositions that had informed much of the modern German and indeed the liberal Protestant project, only then could New Testament studies productively engage in scholarly readings of the New Testament outside of the historical framework of Baur and his followers. Just as exegetes and theologians had to become historians and philosophers, willing to critique and engage outside of narrow exegetical work, so also we must engage with linguistics.

There are, then, embedded within the study and use of linguistics, questions of power, the ability to evaluate truth claims on proper use of language, and exegetical responsibility. Just as we could no longer afford *to neglect history and philosophy* within our exegetical process, we must now acknowledge that biblical scholars can no longer afford *not to do linguistics* and be able to evaluate linguistic truth claims, which increasingly seek to wield exegetical influence.

This is not simply a question of access to new linguistic data. Exegetical engagement with linguistics also addresses questions of power (i.e., who controls our theories and analysis), accountability (i.e., who holds us accountable for our linguistic and exegetical decisions), and responsibility (i.e., how well are we caring for those under our pedagogical or exegetical influence?). All these demand that we gain better access to the linguistic thought that influences our engagement with the biblical text and our own communication of that text. Indeed, linguistic systems are making their way into exegetical method, commentaries, and discussions on exegetical disputes. However, the advocates of these systems frequently beg the linguistic questions, with little accountability from the guild to evaluate or critique the linguistic assumptions. Much of this comes from the relatively isolated engagement of our field with linguistics, the idiosyncrasies that have arisen within our small camp of linguists, and the inability to self-police and synthesize linguistic checks and balances.

Take, for instance, a few unhappy examples. In Jan Nylund's recent review of Dave Mathewson's commentary on Revelation, we find Nylund begging the very linguistic questions under investigation.[3] Here is Nylund's critique of Mathewson's claims on markedness:

> In the aspectual network the Perfective (Aorist) is the least marked, whereas the Imperfective (Present, Imperfect) are more marked. The stative aspect (Perfect, Pluperfect) is the most heavily marked aspect. . . . The aspects are markers of degrees of prominence in discourse, where the perfective is used for backgrounding, the imperfective is used for foregrounding and the stative is used for frontground, which means that the Aorist is used for narrative, the Imperfect

---

3. David L. Mathewson, *Verbal Aspect in the Book of Revelation: The Function of Greek Verb Tenses in John's Apocalypse*, Linguistic Biblical Studies 4 (Leiden: Brill, 2010).

for marked past contexts, the Present for climactic points and the Perfect and Pluperfect for what is highly prominent.[4]

Here Nylund follows a particular symmetrical approach to markedness. There is no mention in the review that this is a contested theory of markedness, indeed one in the minority position outside biblical linguistics. As a result, the review reads either as a promotional piece for the author's linguistic school or as simply unaware of other voices within the broader Greek linguistics field.

Porter's linguistic influence within biblical studies is in particular danger in this regard, which is understandable given his own voluminous publishing record. In a recent SBL presentation, Porter attempted to appeal to a "Kuhnian shift" that had taken place in support of his own linguistic framework. Yet, referencing the "wrong-headed linguistic approach" of alternating approaches such as typological studies, cognitive studies, and prototype theory, he ends up assuming the validity of his Systemic Functional Linguistic (SFL) school as the governing model within biblical studies. A further example of this can be seen, for instance, in a 2008 article, coauthored by Porter, which reads much as though we should treat Porter's preferred linguistic school as the fixed leg of the drafting compass, against which other linguistic work should be evaluated and judged.[5] The danger here, both for the field and for our foremost biblical linguists such as Porter, is to believe that such a linguistic hegemony is actually in force. Such flattening of the linguistic landscape does justice neither to the broader field nor to Porter's own broad-ranging and creative work. The fact that the biblical studies field has failed to engage with these linguistic schools or to hold them accountable has led to mutual detriment and increased isolation, rather than engagement and synthesis.

Accordingly, as I will argue below, it is the duty of the exegete to respond to such truth claims with sober engagement, to avoid either being led around by the proverbial linguistic nose or conversely ignoring serious linguistic theories. When we understand the theoretical and historical camps from which these linguistic arguments are emerging, the biblical studies guild will be far more prepared to build a framework for engagement and analysis. The benefits— indeed, the absolute necessity—of exegetes reengaging with the linguistic schools, rather than simply referring to their favorite linguistically informed biblical scholar, is to bring these theories into the light of discussion and

4. Jan Nylund, "Review of Dave Matthewson, *Verbal Aspect in the Book of Revelation: The Function of Greek Verbal Tenses in John's Apocalypse*," *Svensk exegetisk årsbok* 78 (2013): 243–45.

5. Stanley E. Porter and Andrew W. Pitts, "New Testament Greek Language and Linguistics in Recent Research," *Currents in Research* 6, no. 2 (June 2008): 214–55.

analysis, for evaluation, sharpening, synthesis, and then dissemination and reevaluation of knowledge.

And so, much as the turn to serious historical study provided a well-needed corrective to the Tübingen school's "cutting edge" historical reconstruction, so also a turn to serious linguistic study has the power to provide an antidote to the chaos of our own general linguistic ignorance, while also guarding us from the sectarian tendencies of those wielding, whether intentionally or unintentionally, the trappings of exegetical power.

I believe, or at least dare to hope, that the true Kuhnian shift taking place is a reengagement with modern linguistics and that isolated tribes, in their valleys and coves, can no longer claim a monopoly on our exegetical frameworks.

■ Situating Ourselves within the Historical Conversation

With such questions of history, power, and exegetical responsibility in mind, how did we arrive at this place, where most of our Greek and Hebrew scholars have generally disengaged from the linguistic conversation? There is a history here, and by revisiting this history of scholarship we may find opportunity to engage questions of why we, as exegetes, have in general abandoned the linguistic field and how we might reverse this trend.

Earlier in this volume, Porter provided an excellent high-level review of linguistic schools. For this exercise, let us take the field of lexical semantics as a point of comparison. This section is not intended to be comprehensive, but rather heuristic. I find here the work of Geeraerts to be particularly helpful in tracing these historical influences.[6]

The Philologists

Historical-philological semantics dominated the scene for much of the nineteenth century. Although the study of lexical semantics was taking place before 1830, at this time research into word meanings came into its own. Here we find representative scholars such as Michel Bréal, Hermann Paul, and Gustaf Stern. In biblical linguistics, the early giants of the field can be positioned here as well, including the work of scholars such as A. T. Robertson and James Hope Moulton for Greek, and Wilhelm Gesenius and Samuel Driver for Hebrew, scholars who produced some of the cutting-edge language research of their day. The theological dictionaries such as Gerhard Kittel's

6. Geeraerts, *Theories of Lexical Semantics.*

likewise emerged from this period.[7] Their method of semantic research was keenly interested in the diachronic development of words, including a deeply psychological and socially contextualized interest. Geeraerts characterizes their work along three lines.

First, their orientation was diachronic: they were interested in changes of meaning manifested across different cultures, contexts, and time periods. In other words, semantic meaning was considered to be deeply *contextualized*. Second, change of meaning was mostly narrowed down to changes in individual words. Third, the dominant conception of meaning was psychological, resulting from psychological processes.[8]

In terms of legacy within the biblical studies guild, the historical-philological scholars were very much in sync with, and indeed were leaders within, broader philological and linguistic development. The quality of their work continues to provide us with a legacy of resources. However, as the wider linguistic field migrated away from comparative philology and toward structuralism, the biblical studies community, inherently conservative in its exegetical decisions, found it difficult to commit to the migration.

Structuralism

The origins of formal structuralist semantics may be attributed to Jost Trier (1931) and Leo Weisgerber (1927), taking theoretical inspiration from the work of Ferdinand de Saussure. Weisgerber criticized historical-philological semantics, specifically arguing that the study of meaning should be synchronic instead of diachronic and focused on the structural nature of words rather than on a psychological representation of the term.[9]

We can see here three important distinctions from the earlier philologists: a shift from diachronic study to the study of a language's synchronic structure; a focus on the abstract language structure as opposed to linguistic behavior or performance; and a focus on the signifier versus signified. Likewise, the focus began to shift away from language comparisons. As Geeraerts proposes, structuralism was at its core a shift toward *decontextualization*, attempting to strip away the psychological, diachronic, and performative properties of the language.

---

7. Gerhard Kittel, Otto Bauernfeind, and Gerhard Friedrich, *Theologisches Wörterbuch zum Neuen Testament* (Stuttgart: Kohlhammer, 1932–79).

8. Geeraerts, *Theories of Lexical Semantics*, 1–42, 273.

9. Cf. Geeraerts, *Theories of Lexical Semantics*, 48; and especially Leo Weisgerber, "Die Bedeutungslehre: Ein Irrweg der Sprachwissenschaft?," *Germanisch-Romanische Monatsschrift* 15 (1927): 170.

In the biblical studies world, this "decontextualizing impulse" was heightened by the perceived misuses of the philologists: overly theological and arbitrary readings of terms and etymological fallacies abounded, and a structuralist response provided a corrective.

Participating in this linguistic migration, Barr's seminal structuralist work *Comparative Philology and the Text of the Old Testament* had an irreversible impact: to this day it is considered in biblical studies to be a seminal and even governing work for linguistic analysis.[10] Barr's view is consonant with the contemporary migration within the field of linguistics to a structuralist camp. Comparative philology as a discipline fell almost entirely out of vogue in research on the biblical languages, at least in contemporary scholarly literature. Scholars such as Moisés Silva took up Barr's mantle, helping to integrate his concerns into the collective consciousness of the field. Nevertheless, the vast majority of the core tools such as lexicons and commentaries remained essentially philological in their orientation; the field lacked the necessary critical mass to uproot an entire exegetical tradition.

Though in recent years the structuralist approach has waned in influence, it continues to have an ongoing legacy within generative grammar, functional linguistics, and even cognitive linguistics. In biblical studies, Barr's legacy made it unfashionable to utilize overwrought etymologies and theologized word studies. But his legacy has also embedded a compulsive reaction against crosslinguistic, typological, or comparative studies (i.e., the ability to analyze and learn from comparisons with other languages). In the process, we may have jettisoned much learned from diachronic changes in meaning and organic and contextual usage over the centuries.

Functional Linguistics

When we turn from structuralist linguistics to functional linguistics, we find a central concern for what language does and how it works in a given context.[11] This approach contrasts with more formalist approaches that are

10. James Barr, *Comparative Philology and the Text of the Old Testament* (Oxford: Clarendon, 1968).

11. For the sake of time, I will only briefly comment on generative semantics and biblical linguistics. Generative semantics was developed by Noam Chomsky's early students as a branch of generative grammar. Generative grammar seeks to describe a language in terms of a set of logical rules formulated so as to be capable of generating the infinite number of possible sentences of that language and providing them with the correct structural description. Noam Chomsky is certainly the most famous of the generative grammarians, but there is a wide range of development and branches of generative grammar. Katzian semantics combined a structuralist method of analysis, a formalist system of description, and a mentalist conception of meaning. Accordingly, it reflects both the history and the legacy of structuralism, but it has an

primarily concerned with linguistic structures. Functional linguistics is focused on deriving grammatical, syntactic, and textual structures from the ways in which language is used. Many functional linguists trace their work to the British linguist J. R. Firth and/or the early twentieth-century Prague School of linguists.

On the one hand, the legacy of a structuralist emphasis on language as a system is clearly apparent in approaches like Systemic Functional Linguistics. On the other hand, in functionalism we see an interesting return to the contextualizing impulse of the philologists, which, as we shall see, will be maximized in cognitive linguistics. For example, as Brigitte Nerlich and David Clarke state, "Natural allies of Cognitive Linguistics are functionalists and contextualists of all persuasions from the Prague School onward: Functional Grammarians such as Simon Dik, Systemic-Functional Grammarians such as Halliday, and functional-typological theorists such as Givón."[12]

Thus, a number of functional approaches should be noted here, including Functional Grammar, Systemic Functional Linguistics, and Role and Reference Grammar. Functional Grammar is interested in both identifying rules to construct linguistic utterances, such as semantic, syntactic, morphological, and phonological rules, and also in determining the pragmatic rules that govern the patterns of verbal interaction, thereby connecting form with function.[13] Systemic Functional Linguistics likewise has a dual goal of developing both a theory about language as social process and an analytical methodology that permits the detailed and systematic description of language patterns, though this creates a highly complex system of analysis. Role and Reference Grammar (RRG) grew out of an attempt to answer two basic questions: (1) What would linguistic theory look like if it were based on the analysis of diverse languages rather than a single language such as English? and (2) How can the interaction of syntax, semantics, and pragmatics in different grammatical systems best be explained?[14]

---

explicit interest in the psychological reality of meaning (specifically, the language user's ability to interpret sentences). This ties in with the Chomskyan interest in the linguistic competence of the language user as the proper object of linguistics. Little has been produced to impact biblical studies from a generativist perspective.

12. Brigitte Nerlich and David D. Clarke, "Cognitive Linguistics and the History of Linguistics," in *The Oxford Handbook of Cognitive Linguistics*, ed. Dirk Geeraerts and Hubert Cuyckens (Oxford: Oxford University Press, 2007), 590.

13. So Simon C. Dik, *The Theory of Functional Grammar, Part 1: The Structure of the Clause* (Berlin: de Gruyter, 1997), 2–3.

14. On these frameworks for linguistic schools of thought, cf. Douglas Mangum and Josh Westbury, eds., *Linguistics and Biblical Exegesis* (Bellingham, WA: Lexham, 2017), esp. chap. 5 (Thompson and Widder, "Major Approaches to Linguistics," 87–133): "We can anticipate that cross-linguistic, typological concerns will play a much more important role in RRG than in other functional approaches" (106).

Three key concepts emerging from functionalism include markedness, topic, and comment, as well as linguistic typology and language universals. As we might expect, given its crosslinguistic interest, functional linguistics has had a strong impact within the field of Bible translation at places such as SIL's Graduate School of Linguistics. In Greek, we can see the massive influence in semantics by such giants as the South African Johannes Louw. Porter's work operates from within this school, while Steve Runge's *Discourse Grammar* and more seminally Stephen Levinsohn's *Discourse Features of the New Testament* have significantly increased broad exposure to functionalism in recent years.

Within the functional schools, we find an increased interest in language choice and therefore the contextual factors that lead to choice. Accordingly, we can perceive a movement away from the decontextualizing impulse of the structuralists and a move back toward contextualization. This is paralleled by a strong current emphasis on cognitive linguistics within the linguistic community outside of biblical studies, a sort of maximizing of the contextualizing impulse.

Cognitive Linguistics

Cognitive linguistics emerged in the 1980s as an explicitly "maximalist" attempt to "integrate rather than separate meaning and cognition."[15] This approach seeks to integrate rather than to separate semantics (what other schools of thought might describe as the meaning of words and their meaning within a sentence) and pragmatics (what other schools might describe as the meaning of words within context, in actual situations); indeed, cognitive linguistics would doubt whether such a distinction is even possible. As we can perhaps anticipate, cognitive linguistics sits on the opposite end of the spectrum from structuralism in that it denies whether meaning is even accessible in a purely structural form, outside of an inherent context. Through the introduction of new models of description and analysis such as prototype theory, frame semantics, and conceptual metaphor theory, it has proved to be a highly productive approach, with a wide appeal among lexical semanticists.

The "shared perspective" of cognitive linguists revolves around a basic principle and four tenets. The basic principle is that language is entirely about meaning in use, rather than in form. Understandably, then, semantics has been the focus of much of the research of cognitive linguists (though there is recent work evaluating cognitive grammar as well). The four basic tenets of cognitive linguistics are that (1) meaning is perspectival and language "embodies"

15. Here, and in what follows, see Geeraerts, *Theories of Lexical Semantics*, 275.

these different perspectives; (2) meaning is dynamic and flexible; (3) meaning is encyclopedic and nonautonomous—that is, neither a separate structure (so Saussure) nor an independent component in the mind (so Chomsky); rather, meaning entails our knowledge of the world and reflects what we experience; and finally (4) meaning is based on usage and experience, not abstract structures. Thus, grammatical patterns and structures, while perhaps useful in theory, are always part of actual usage, utterances, and conversations.

Cognitive Linguistics and Historical-Philological Semantics

Tracing the history of semantics, Geeraerts posits that cognitive semantics reacts against the "restrictive and autonomist" aspects of generativist semantics but at the same time links up with prestructuralist historical-philological semantics due to a shared interest in psychology, context, and mental process. Although this link is obscured by the unfamiliarity and inaccessibility of the historical-philological tradition to modern nonbiblical linguists, Geeraerts sees a remarkable correspondence between the basic positions of historical-philological and cognitive semantics. Cognitive semantics and traditional historical semantics share a psychological conception of meaning. Both approaches hold that lexical meaning is inextricably bound up with the individual, cultural, social, and historical experience of the language user. Both approaches are specifically interested in the flexibility and polysemy of meaning and the mechanisms underlying those phenomena.[16] Striking similarities exist between the older philological literature and newer cognitive studies. For example, Geeraerts notes how modern descriptions of the vagueness of word boundaries read like early statements on cognitive prototype effects, while the regular patterns of metaphor and metonymy investigated in cognitive semantics may sometimes be found almost literally forecasted in the older philological literature.

Geeraerts sees here a more or less cyclical process, in which cognitive semantics seems to return to some of the basic concerns and the fundamental conceptions of historical-philological semantics, recognizing a number of tensions and oppositions throughout the history of linguistics, starting with the structuralists: tensions between usage and structure, between so-called pragmatics and semantics, between context and system, and between flexibility and permanence. If Geeraert's historical interpretation is correct, the overall history of lexical semantics can be written as a cyclical process of decontextualization and recontextualization, a pattern that to some extent also characterizes the migratory history of linguistics.

16. Geeraerts, *Theories of Lexical Semantics*, 277.

Contextualization and Decontextualization: A Linguistic Legacy in Biblical Studies

As Mike Aubrey notes, the linguists and lexicographers among the histori-cal philologists, both secular and biblical, "recognized an important fact about the nature of language that was lost (or ignored) during much of the twen-tieth century, namely, that the linguistic phenomena under study were seen as revealing characteristics of the human mind and its shared experiences." The significance of this relationship between a word and the larger cultural, social, and psychological associations with that word was highlighted, and the contextualized, associative meaning was viewed as highly valuable to understanding language and semantic change. These early linguists recog-nized that words are not "self-contained phonetic vessels, but complex mental representations of human knowledge."[17]

Thus, when a linguist such as Barr, coming from a newer structuralist framework, heavily criticized the theological lexicography of the philolo-gists in general or works such as Kittel's *Theological Dictionary of the New Testament* in particular, we may accept Barr's criticism of theologians doing poor, undisciplined linguistics (such as Kittel's moving beyond sociocultural assumptions implicit in Biblical Greek lexemes into making illegitimate theo-logical claims about those particular lexemes and thus encouraging the lexical fallacy of illegitimate totality transfer, in which all associative meanings that might be evoked by a particular lexeme are always all evoked by a particular lexeme, etc.). At the same time, however, we should also recognize that Barr's criticisms reflect the structuralist migration of the 1930s, 1940s, and 1950s, which were fundamentally at odds with the contextualizing perspective on language that existed in the nineteenth and early twentieth centuries. This structural reaction against the excesses of certain historical philologists, in decontextualizing meaning into formal structure, opened the door to other excesses and extremes.

Personally, I have increasingly been drawn into the explanatory power and contextualizing flexibility of cognitive linguistics. Perhaps this is due to the improvements that cognitive linguistics makes to the encyclopedic, contextual-izing interests of my old philological friends, but I believe it goes beyond this. Cognitive linguistics provides a framework for engaging within and across cultures and languages, even as I engage with the Greek and Hebrew texts. Indeed, this approach to linguistics needs to be given greater exposure. Re-cent surveys of linguistics and biblical studies—for example, Constantine

---

17. Michael Aubrey, "Linguistic Issues in Biblical Greek," in Mangum and Westbury, *Lin-guistics and Biblical Exegesis*, 161–89.

Campbell's book on advances in Greek linguistics or the 2008 article by Porter and Andrew Pitts—have failed to mention this approach, and this undervalues the widespread impact of cognitive studies within nonbiblical linguistics.[18]

◼ Spanning the Canyon of Linguistics, Biblical Studies, and Bible Translation

In light of the preceding historical and theoretical discussion, we are in a better place to understand the historical migrations and resulting tribalism that emerged among linguists, biblical scholars, and the Bible translation community. What seems to have happened in these past fifty or so years is threefold:

1. The biblical and theological studies guilds took seriously the concerns of Barr and generally adopted his structuralist recommendations. For most biblical scholars, however, the linguistic engagement then calcified: shallow readings of Saussurean structuralism became more a cautionary note for linguistic analysis than a productive one.

2. Productive use of linguistic theory within biblical studies has been limited and often highly cliquish, and (in North America at least) has been frequently isolated to Porter's quasi-monopoly within his particular SFL-type "Schule," a tribe that has tended toward self-authentication and self-replication, with frequently idiosyncratic results. Nevertheless, much of the linguistic scholarship that we have in biblical studies today is due to Porter's influence, and if we are to criticize the results, then we must be willing to do similarly productive work.

3. The Bible translation community—by its very nature typological, functional, and crosslinguistic—continued to engage deeply with linguistic research, though oftentimes abandoning the biblical and theological studies guild to its own devices. This has been accompanied with certain detrimental effects, frequently disconnected with historical and theological developments in the study of the biblical text, and frequently undervaluing even the study of Greek and Hebrew, given the focus on modern-language typology and crosslinguistic analysis. In fact, the drifting of the biblical studies and Bible translation cousins is close to resulting in mutually unintelligible dialects. In this matter, we stand as

18. See Constantine R. Campbell, *Advances in the Study of Greek: New Insights for Reading the New Testament* (Grand Rapids: Zondervan, 2015); Porter and Pitts, "New Testament Greek Language."

children of a divorce, watching our parents live separate lives, and this is to be mourned as one of the most tragic results of this linguistic history. In the meanwhile, the broader nonbiblical linguistic conversations have for the most part moved on, no longer connected with the philological conversations of the past; as most in the New Testament field either are uninterested/unaware of the conversations or are firmly entrenched in their own positions, they have little contact with our work.

Pursuing Linguistic Reconciliation

Despite this history, there are signs of a reconciliation, with a willingness for certain scholars within the Bible translation community to take steps to reengage the biblical studies guild. Examples include the bridging work of Stephen Levinsohn, the pedagogical influence of Randall Buth, and new leadership at SIL/Wycliffe that seeks to engage with biblical studies and biblical languages scholarship. There has also been a growing awareness and interest in the diversity of thought and need for engagement with linguistics to provide answers to impasses on such topics as verbal aspect, semantics, information structure, word order, and deponency.

We have also seen a growing reassessment of our linguistic starting points, especially with the influx of scholars from the majority world asking questions of how we engage with languages in general, including the interface between one's own mother language, an ancient language, and other languages of broader communication. If we are called to communicate "to all the world"—that is, "to all human communities"—are we prepared to communicate the gospel message in a meaningful, linguistically accurate, historically, and theologically informed manner? Language, and specifically the linguistic analysis of the biblical text for all languages and for all peoples, is critically important to the very heart of the Christian mission: our understanding of these ancient texts and how we communicate to the global community. Unfortunately, I fear that we are far behind in the need to retool in such a way that reflects an updated understanding of both source and receptor languages and how we engage with biblical texts. Biblical studies and linguistics must reunite to serve this unified mission.

Practical Contributions of Linguistics to Biblical Studies

Now that we have briefly charted the historical landscape of semantic studies, hopefully we have gained some greater clarity on the migratory influences that continue to govern our work and have created many of these perceived tribal identities. I would like to close by highlighting key, practical contributions that this history of linguistics can provide, noting especially recent work on prototype theory from cognitive linguistics, as well as discourse grammar; constituent order, information structure, and word order; and crosslinguistic and typological analysis.

Prototype Theory

In prototype theory, a prototype serves as a point of reference for a particular category and enables people to navigate the category's not-so-clear instances with relative ease. As described by Jeremy Thompson and Wendy Widder, prototype theory has four basic concepts regarding mental categories.[19] First, every mental category has an exemplar that depicts the category's relevant features (e.g., "robin" for the category "bird"). Second, there are good and bad (or marginal) members in every category (e.g., "robin" and "penguin"). Third, every category has features that are important but not necessarily essential (e.g., "birds fly"). Finally, the boundaries of a category are blurry, so something may actually be a member of more than one category at a time (e.g., an eighteen-year-old can be considered both an "adult" and a "youth" or "teen").

As Chris Fresch explained in a recent interview, "Cognitive categories of prototypes encourage usage-based categories that allow for non-prototypical uses as well as fuzzy boundaries between various categories. This holds true for both semantics, and also in Stoic Greek grammar: the Stoics formally regarded and categorized the aorist indicative form as past perfective, while fully aware that this form could be pragmatically used in non-past contexts."[20] So, we may find a verbal form grammaticalized for past tense, prototypically marking past perfective aspect, but with non-prototypical uses for pragmatic effect. Rather than trying to create a single *structural* category that accounts for every possible meaning of a term (e.g., proposals that the Greek verbal form should in fact not be seen to mark past tense, given the exceptions), prototype theory provides a framework for integrating functional pragmatics into form and use.[21]

19. Thompson and Widder, "Major Approaches to Linguistics," in Mangum and Westbury, *Linguistics and Biblical Exegesis*, 87–133.

20. Christopher J. Fresch, interview with ExegeticalTools.com, http://exegeticaltools.com /2017/06/13/greek-verb-greek-linguist-chris-fresch.

21. For an in-depth analysis of the above feature of Greek grammar, see Christopher J. Fresch, "Typology, Polysemy, and Prototypes: Situating Nonpast Aorist Indicatives," in *The Greek Verb*

Discourse Grammar

Second, we have witnessed the recent impact of discourse grammar within our field. Runge's book on discourse grammar brought this approach to the fore of the New Testament guild's popular imagination, building from his predecessors such as Levinsohn and others. Discourse grammar provides the critical tools to discuss features such as markedness, constituent order, information structure and word order, and other fields that were for the most part out of sight and mind during my school years.

Most textbooks continue to approach Greek exegesis by having students evaluate the function and meaning of words and grammatical elements one at a time in a linear order. This is essentially how grammar is laid out in Wallace's *Greek Grammar beyond the Basics*, itself building from Friedrich Blass, Albert Debrunner, and Robert Funk's earlier seminal work (BDF). In this framework, each word is evaluated on its own, and every semantic function of the dative case, for example, is evaluated as a potential option; students learn to sort and categorize meaning via an encyclopedic accounting of all possible usages. This list of options could be quite challenging, and indeed such an approach seems to me an exercise in futility: there is no ontological manner of categorizing all ranges of meaning, as meaning is based on use and is dynamic and constantly evolving. What Wallace calls an "exegetical syntax" is really a dive into semantic, exegetically derived usage. I am increasingly convinced that trying to attach (what appear to students as) ontological categories to describe polysemous, contextually derived meaning is not a helpful way forward.

In contrast, a discourse grammar approach focuses on the clause as a whole, recognizing that the manner in which verbs engage with noun phrases, prepositional phrases, and subordinate clauses will constrain the interpretation from the start. An awareness of contextualized meaning then naturally leads to the study of larger chunks of texts (namely, discourse), which have improved our understanding of the nature of grammar and language above the sentence level.[22]

Constituent Order, Information Structure, and Word Order

Flowing as a function of discourse, the ordering of words or constituents is directly related to how information flows from one sentence to another.

Revisited: A Fresh Approach for Biblical Exegesis, ed. Steven E. Runge and Christopher J. Fresch (Bellingham, WA: Lexham, 2016), 379–415.

22. See Michael Aubrey, "The Value of Linguistically Informed Exegesis," in Mangum and Westbury, _Linguistics and Biblical Exegesis_, 191–202.

These are other areas that, during my training years, were left unaddressed. Greek was explained simply via "word order is fluid and doesn't matter."

However, this has increasingly been shown to be far from correct, especially from crosslinguistic analysis. As Runge explains: "Although there is tremendous diversity among languages, every language has to accomplish certain basic tasks. . . . Since there is a common set of tasks that need to be accomplished across all languages, the task list can inform our description of what the different grammatical choices accomplish."[23] Biblical studies students can now understand, with confidence and clarity, not only that word order has meaning in Greek but that we can access this meaning.

Since discourse grammar is fundamentally interested in the basic structure for human communication across languages, this then leads to my final recommendation for linguistics and exegesis: reengaging in crosslinguistic and typological analysis.

Crosslinguistic and Typological Analysis

When we begin to ask questions of information structure, and how a language communicates meaning, we are *forced* to reckon with variations between ancient languages and our own language of analysis. Bluntly, unless we understand language typology and crosslinguistic frameworks, we are making our work unusable for an increasingly global church, whose members are maturing and which is developing into serious centers of study. From my perspective, there may be no more urgent area for linguistic analysis and integration than within the biblical studies guild. Due to Barr's structuralist legacy, there remains an odor of general skepticism toward the idea that crosslinguistic analysis can shed light on how a language communicates meaning. This is the perspective of a guild that is still operating under the linguistic assumptions that were in place at the turn of the twentieth century.

Although no two languages are exactly the same, whether in their lexicon, their morphology, or their syntax, this does not mean that there are no limits to language variation.[24] Linguists have been examining and comparing the languages of the world with an ever-growing understanding of language variation and similarity. This information about typology and crosslinguistic similarities and differences can shed significant light on what we can expect within Hebrew and Greek. Not only does this help us understand Greek and Hebrew, but it provides accurate frameworks for communicating these

23. Steven E. Runge, *Discourse Grammar of the Greek New Testament* (Peabody, MA: Hendrickson, 2010), 6–7.
24. So Aubrey, "Value of Linguistically Informed Exegesis," §8.3.

languages into other global languages, which from a Bible translation perspective is a critical task. To resume beating a particularly dead horse, as Mike Aubrey assesses: when a scholar claims that Koine Greek does not have the grammatical category of tense, we can ask, Are there other languages of the world that lack the category of tense? When we analyze other languages, we find the answer to this: yes, there are languages that lack the category of tense in their verbal morphology. This then leads to a follow-up question: Do any of those languages that lack tense look anything like Greek in terms of the structure of its verbal system? This certainly appears to not be the case: tenseless languages do not look like Koine Greek.[25] When I, then, teach Greek using a language such as Portuguese, typology provides me with the typological tools to avoid explaining Greek from a Portuguese framework, or, even worse, creating a Portuguese description of an English-based analysis of Greek! Knowing how language works in a crosslinguistic framework prepares us to create meaningful tools and frameworks for a global audience and to avoid exporting nonsense.

■ Conclusion

Given Porter's summary of linguistic schools earlier in this volume, and what we have seen here specifically in lexical semantics, we may conclude in agreement that biblical scholars must not operate blind to the presence of linguistic schools and those schools' influence on our thinking. An awareness of scholarly diversity on the questions at hand frees us from the perceived hegemony of a particular linguistic school within our guild. In keeping with the best of those scholars who have come before us, we must continue to adapt and engage with the linguistic conversation. If we are truly to follow in the legacy of Barr, for instance, it must be in his willingness to engage in new thinking in linguistics, rather than adhering to the conclusions of Barr's structuralist school. We now have additional tools within our reach, and I urge the reader to consider tools capable of helping us engage in a manner that is sensitive to a topic dear to our exegetical hearts—linguistic analysis that is contextual, organic, and attuned to the usage of its communities. Biblical scholars should reengage with the idea that language is not merely system or structure; language is organic and biological. Language is use, and as such it is embodied, in that it describes experiential access to knowledge; it is therefore cognitive (not merely grounded in arbitrary sign, but rather in cognition and experience) and

25. Aubrey, "Value of Linguistically Informed Exegesis," §8.3 (my paraphrase).

perspectival (in that language expresses the contexts, history, and culture of real people and specifically their shared human experience); it is encyclopedic (as it encompasses semantics, the lexicon, and syntax as unified, functional features of meaning). And finally, because language is use, language changes constantly, unpredictably, and outside of the control of those who would seek to contain or constrain it through formal structure.

To close, I find this quote from Rachel Aubrey deeply resonating:

> One of the difficulties of coming to linguistics as a biblical scholar is that it may often seem that certain linguistic theories, texts, or articles are not relevant at all to the aims of the biblical scholar who is primarily interested in exegesis, preaching, teaching, or personal Bible study. However, if the field [of linguistics] as a whole is serious about understanding how Greek and/or Hebrew grammar works then nothing could be farther from the truth. If we study a language, wanting to know about its structure, its word order, and the function of its categories, then linguistics as a field is always relevant. . . .
>
> Linguistic principles, research goals, methodology, philosophy, and descriptive frameworks are ignored, glossed over, or pushed aside to the detriment of biblical language studies. Short-changing linguistic texts, frameworks, or articles because they do not appear, at first, to have any immediate relevance to exegetical conclusions . . . puts the cart before the horse. It steps over the necessary work of learning about how language works in order to rush on to the goal that seeks to conclude something about the meaning of a text based on how the language works.[26]

As for me, a scholar working in primarily cross-cultural, crosslinguistic communities, I receive this exhortation as a demand for a reconnection with a contextualizing, typologically aware, and crosslinguistic understanding of the ancient languages, my own language, and the wider languages of communication. Indeed, this is the very essence of biblical exegesis, in fulfilling our Great Commission mandate.

---

26. Kris Lyle, "Scholars in Press: An Interview with Rachel Aubrey," Koine-Greek: Studies in Greek Language & Linguistics, January 23, 2019, https://koine-greek.com/2019/01/23/schol ars-in-press-an-interview-with-rachel-aubrey.

Postscript

Where Do We Go from Here?

BENJAMIN L. MERKLE

Like the modern political scene, New Testament scholars, grammarians, and linguists can often appear divided, with the various sides firmly entrenched to defend the ground they've gained. With such a diversity of opinions, which often leads to linguistic shrapnel, one wonders if the application of linguistics to New Testament studies is worth all the trouble. Such diversity of thought and resulting polemics in writing, however, can often be overstated. The science of linguistics as applied to New Testament studies has paid amazing dividends over the past thirty years. Furthermore, the influence of linguistics finally appears to be gaining ground so that it is not merely New Testament scholars who are dabbling in linguistics but also linguists who are applying their expertise to the arena of New Testament studies. Consequently, those who teach New Testament Greek can no longer ignore the influence of linguistics—nor would it be wise or responsible to do so. Furthermore, students of New Testament Greek can benefit greatly by familiarizing themselves with the fruit that linguistics has produced. This book has been an attempt to do just that.

The goal of this postscript is not merely to recount or summarize the chapters of this book. Rather, my goal is to synthesize some of the chapters and perspectives, assess the current landscape of linguistics and New Testament studies, and then offer what I believe is a fruitful way forward. Particularly,

I want to address three of the main issues on which this book has focused: linguistic schools, verbal aspect, and pedagogy.

■ Linguistic Schools

When I tell people that I ride a motorcycle, my statement often elicits a question from my dialogue partner: "What type of motorcycle do you ride?" Saying that I ride a motorcycle triggers a follow-up question since not all bikes are created equal. The kind of bike a person rides often reveals other truths about that person. So it is with linguistics. A person cannot simply claim to be a linguist without fielding the necessary follow-up question regarding the linguistic school that they were trained in or are currently employing. Not all linguistic models are created equal. In relation to New Testament studies, which methods are the most productive or useful? From my perspective (and it is limited), the two most popular methods are Systemic Functional Linguistics (SFL) and some eclectic model that includes cognitive linguistics or a cognitive-functional approach.

Stanley Porter claims to be the first person, along with Nigel J. C. Gotteri, to introduce SFL to New Testament studies (1985).[1] Along with his landmark volume on verbal aspect, he wrote three subsequent volumes where SFL was utilized.[2] While admitting that this linguistic model is both "very complex" and not readily adaptable to aspectual languages like Greek, Porter is surprised that more do not embrace SFL. For him, the strength of this approach is its "robust concept of context," which includes "being a discourse analytic model" (35). Porter is skeptical of the practice of linguistic eclecticism, especially when such practices cross the boundaries of the major schools (formalist, cognitive, and functional). Consequently, he is predisposed to reject a cognitive-functional model, since it is by definition a hybrid.

Others, such as Stephen Levinsohn, Steve Runge, and Nicholas Ellis, find more value in the approach of cognitive linguistics or a cognitive-functional (or even a crosslinguistic) approach. Levinsohn, a Bible translator and trained linguist, was schooled in a variety of approaches, including Syntagmatics or

---

1. Nigel J. C. Gotteri and Stanley E. Porter, "Ambiguity, Vagueness and the Working Systemic Linguist," *Sheffield Working Papers in Language and Linguistics* 2 (1985): 105–18.

2. Stanley E. Porter, *Verbal Aspect in the Greek of the New Testament, with Reference to Tense and Mood* (New York: Peter Lang, 1989); Stanley E. Porter, *Idioms of the Greek New Testament*, 2nd ed. (Sheffield: Sheffield Academic, 1994); Stanley E. Porter, *Linguistic Analysis of the Greek New Testament: Studies in Tools, Methods, and Practice* (Grand Rapids: Baker Academic, 2016); Stanley E. Porter, *Letter to the Romans: A Literary and Linguistic Commentary* (Sheffield: Sheffield Phoenix, 2016).

Structure-Function (John Bendor-Samuel), transformational generative grammar (Noam Chomsky), Tagmemics (Kenneth Pike and Robert Longacre), comparative historicism (Prague School: E. Beneš, Jan Firbas), language types (Matthew Dryer), constituent order (Simon Dik), and relevance theory (V. Zegarač, Anne Reboul, and Jacques Moeschler), among others. Thus, Levinsohn embraces an eclectic approach with a focus on discourse features of the Greek New Testament from a *functional* perspective. More specifically, his aim is "to discover and describe what linguistic structures are used for; the functions they serve, the factors that condition their use."[3] Additionally, Levinsohn emphasizes the basic principle that *choice implies meaning*. In other words, by choosing one expression, the author is *not* choosing a different expression—a choice that indicates a difference in meaning (even if it is a slight difference).

Steve Runge, a disciple of Levinsohn, has also been influenced by a number of linguistic approaches as a means of better understanding the Greek of the New Testament. His approach is an eclectic and crosslinguistic approach that focuses on how languages, not just Koine Greek, generally operate (a trend seen in the recent discussion of typology). Consequently, he is leery of letting one's presuppositions, based on a favored linguistic approach, interpret data in a way that runs roughshod over other important details and nuances of a text. For instance, regarding constituent order, Runge claims that Porter "has posited an inverse correlation between statistical frequency and prominence but achieves mixed results" (129). For Runge, the function of language, including the pragmatics of constituent order, must take into consideration context and cannot be reduced to a simple table. His approach is based on "linguistically sound and typologically attested principles" that are more fruitful and reliable (130).

So which option is better: embracing a single linguistic model (such as SFL) or employing an eclectic or hybrid model (such as a cognitive-functional approach)? From one perspective, it makes sense to employ the methodology of a single approach since each school has a different set of presuppositions and aims for internal consistency and coherence. For example, Porter notes, "Linguistic models . . . are attempts to find conceptual structures by which to examine language without accepting what we have been told or what we assumed without further reflection and without imposing our own language upon another" (12). Rather, such models "provide a linguistic framework that acknowledges its presuppositions and helps us to think about language

---

3. Stephen H. Levinsohn, *Discourse Features of New Testament Greek: A Coursebook on the Information Structure of New Testament Greek*, 2nd ed. (Dallas: SIL International, 2000), vii.

in new ways, using the resources of the linguistic model" (12). In contrast, eclecticism "has helped to dilute the effectiveness of the field" (35).

But when one commits to a single model, there is the danger that it can become the master instead of the servant. Once a scholar commits to, employs, and defends a particular model, there can be a reluctance to see the value and use of other approaches. There is no perfect model, and embracing one model to the exclusion of others might keep one from helpful insights that lead to a more faithful interpretation of a text. New theories are offered to address perceived inadequacies in other systems. But theories that were once new and "cutting edge" are later shown to have inherent weaknesses. Thus, as Runge states, we must be open to "incorporating new insights from other approaches" (143). If we do not, then we are in danger of isolating ourselves from the broader community of linguists. Furthermore, such an eclectic approach has widespread practice within the broader field of linguistics. As such, Runge's warning is worth repeating: "Language is messy, and our understanding about it is constantly developing. Demands for theoretical purity within biblical studies will relegate linguistics to the ivory tower of theoretical contemplation instead of the messy trenches of practical application. The complexities of language, coupled with our constantly evolving understanding of how it works, means that methodologies and theories need to keep pace" (144). Those who pick one model and stick with it will eventually fall behind into the irrelevancy of the older theories that they often criticize.

Finally, although Porter maintains that SFL is "the most productive school of linguistics in New Testament Greek studies" (35), such a claim can be misleading. According to Ellis, Porter and his camp have "remained quite small, especially in comparison to the wider field" (229). Porter's linguistic influence has led to an imbalance in regard to New Testament studies and linguistics, giving the appearance that there is a linguistic hegemony based on the number of works that Porter and his disciples have produced. Ellis concludes, "Such flattening of the linguistic landscape does justice neither to the broader linguistic field nor to Porter's own broad-ranging and creative work" (231). In the end, the apostle Paul's advice seems appropriate here: "Test all things. Hold on to what is good" (1 Thess. 5:21 CSB).

■ Verbal Aspect

Areas of Consensus

Although there are still many places of disagreement and debate, scholars have reached near consensus with many issues relating to verbal aspect:

(1) its definition, (2) its prominence over tense, and (3) the meaning of the perfective and imperfective aspects. First, almost all modern New Testament Greek scholars or linguists agree that aspect is best defined as the *viewpoint* or *perspective* that the author chooses to portray an action (or state).

- **Stanley E. Porter:** "[Verbal aspect is] a semantic (meaning) category by which a speaker or writer grammaticalizes (i.e., represents a meaning by choice of a word-form) *a perspective on an action by the selection of a particular tense-form in the verbal system.*"[4]
- **Buist M. Fanning:** "Verbal aspect in NT Greek is that category in the grammar of the verb which reflects the focus or viewpoint of the speaker in regard to the action or condition which the verb describes. . . . It shows the perspective from which the occurrence is regarded or the portrayal of the occurrence apart from the actual or perceived nature of the situation itself."[5]
- **K. L. McKay:** "Aspect in ancient Greek is that category of the verb system by means of which *an author (or speaker) shows how he views each event or activity* he mentions in relation to its context."[6]
- **Constantine R. Campbell:** "Verbal aspect refers to the manner in which verbs are used *to view* an action or state."[7]

Based on these (and other) definitions, the central idea of aspect is the subjective perspective (viewpoint) by which the author communicates the action of the verb.

A second area of consensus is that aspect has prominence over tense—that is, the aspect or viewpoint of the author is what is grammaticalized in all moods, whereas the tense (or time) of the verb is limited to the indicative mood (if at all). Because time is indicated in the indicative mood by the presence or absence of the augment, the fact that the augment is found only

---

4. Porter, *Idioms of the Greek New Testament*, 21 (emphasis added). Elsewhere Porter defines verbal aspect as "a synthetic category (realized in the forms of verbs) used of meaningful oppositions in a network of tense systems to grammaticalize the author's reasoned subjective choice of conception of a process." Porter, *Verbal Aspect*, 88.

5. Buist M. Fanning, *Verbal Aspect in New Testament Greek*, Oxford Theological Monographs (Oxford: Clarendon, 1990), 84–85 (emphasis added).

6. K. L. McKay, *A New Syntax of the Verb in New Testament Greek: An Aspectual Approach*, Studies in Biblical Greek 5 (New York: Peter Lang, 1994), 27 (emphasis added).

7. Constantine R. Campbell, *Verbal Aspect and Non-Indicative Verbs: Further Soundings in the Greek of the New Testament*, Studies in Biblical Greek 15 (New York: Peter Lang, 2008), 6 (emphasis added).

in the indicative suggests that time is not communicated by the verbal form in non-indicative moods. But this understanding is not a modern development. Over a hundred years ago, A. T. Robertson recognized that tense was not prominent: "Since the pres[ent] ind[icative] occurs for past, present and future time it is clear that 'time' is secondary even in the ind[icative]. In the other moods it has, of course, no time at all."[8] Earlier Robertson wrote that the term "tense" is "a misnomer and a hindrance to the understanding of this aspect of verb-form. Time does come finally to enter relatively into the indicative. . . . But it is not the original nor the general idea of what we call tense."[9] More recently, Ellis rightly notes, "Aspect is more grammaticalized, more paradigmatic, more obligatory, and more pervasive than tense or mood."[10]

A third area of consensus relates to the meaning of the perfective and imperfective aspects. The perfective aspect, signified by the aorist tense-form, views the action externally, as a whole, or in summary form.[11] The imperfective aspect, signified by the present and imperfect tense-forms, views the action internally, as in progress or unfolding.[12] Although perhaps somewhat overstating it, Campbell is on track when he writes, "All Greek scholars agree that the aorist is perfective in aspect, while the present and imperfect are imperfective in aspect" (42).

8. A. T. Robertson, *A Grammar of the Greek New Testament in the Light of Historical Research*, 4th ed. (Nashville: Broadman, 1923), 881–82.

9. Robertson, *Grammar of the Greek New Testament*, 343. See also Friedrich Blass, Albert Debrunner, and Robert W. Funk, *A Greek Grammar of the New Testament and Other Early Christian Literature* (Chicago: University of Chicago Press, 1961), 166–67 (§318); James A. Brooks and Carlton L. Winbery, *Syntax of New Testament Greek* (Washington, DC: University Press of America, 1979), 76; Ernest De Witt Burton, *Syntax of the Moods and Tenses in New Testament Greek*, 3rd ed. (Edinburgh: T&T Clark, 1898), 6; H. E. Dana and Julius R. Mantey, *A Manual Grammar of the Greek New Testament* (Toronto: Macmillan, 1927), 177–79; C. F. D. Moule, *An Idiom Book of New Testament Greek* (Cambridge: Cambridge University Press, 1953), 5; James Hope Moulton, *Prolegomena*, vol. 1 of *A Grammar of New Testament Greek*, 3rd ed. (Edinburgh: T&T Clark, 1908), 108–10. For more recent works, see D. N. S. Bhat, *The Prominence of Tense, Aspect and Mood*, Studies in Language Companion Series 49 (Philadelphia: Benjamins, 1999); Constantine R. Campbell, *Basics of Verbal Aspect in Biblical Greek* (Grand Rapids: Zondervan, 2008), 32; Fanning, *Verbal Aspect in New Testament Greek*, 325; Albert Rijksbaron, *The Syntax and Semantics of the Verb in Classical Greek: An Introduction*, 3rd ed. (Chicago: University of Chicago Press, 2007).

10. See Nicholas J. Ellis, "Aspect-Prominence, Morpho-Syntax, and a Cognitive-Linguistic Framework for the Greek Verb," in *The Greek Verb Revisited: A Fresh Approach for Biblical Exegesis*, ed. Steven E. Runge and Christopher J. Fresch (Bellingham, WA: Lexham, 2016), 136.

11. See Porter, *Verbal Aspect*, 106; Porter, *Idioms of the Greek New Testament*, 35; Fanning, *Verbal Aspect in New Testament Greek*, 97.

12. See Porter, *Idioms of the Greek New Testament*, 29; Fanning, *Verbal Aspect in New Testament Greek*, 103.

Areas of Ongoing Debate

Unfortunately, areas of significant disagreement and debate still exist in relation to verbal aspect and the Greek verbal system. These include (1) the number of aspects, (2) temporality in the indicative mood, (3) the influence of lexical meaning on aspectual choice, and (4) prominence. First, the number of aspects is still unsettled among scholars. Although nearly all affirm at least two aspects (perfective and imperfective), the number and function of any additional aspects remains open to debate. Thus, the issue at hand relates to the function of the perfect, pluperfect, and future tense-forms. The following chart catalogs the various views of Greek tense-forms and the aspectual terminology that is employed by key scholars.

Comparison of Verbal Aspect Terminology[13]

	Present	Imperfect	Aorist	Future	Perfect	Pluperfect
McKay	Imperfective		Aoristic	Future	Perfect (Stative)	
Porter	Imperfective		Perfective	—	Stative	
Fanning	Internal		External	—	—	—
Campbell	Imperfective		Perfective		Imperfective	

The perfect tense-form has garnered the largest amount of attention, from journal articles to study groups and debates at conferences. Does the perfect (or pluperfect) convey a stative aspect (McKay and Porter), an imperfective aspect (Campbell), or a combination of perfective aspect, stative *Aktionsart*, and present tense (Fanning)? Personally, I think the best way to think about the perfect is to view it as a combination of the perfective and imperfective aspects ("combinative" aspect) that correlates a previous event (or state) with its resulting imperfective state. This position is closest to Fanning and has been embraced by many others.[14]

The aspectual nature of the future is also debated. Interestingly, both Porter and Fanning agree that the future is non-aspectual.[15] And since most of the contested issues have them on opposite sides, one wonders if their agreement

13. See McKay, *New Syntax of the Verb*, 27–34; Porter, *Verbal Aspect*, 89, 105; Porter, *Idioms of the Greek New Testament*, 21–22, 29–42; Fanning, *Verbal Aspect in New Testament Greek*, 84–125; Campbell, *Basics of Verbal Aspect*; Campbell, *Verbal Aspect and Non-Indicative Verbs*, 11.

14. Runge and Fresch, *Greek Verb Revisited*, esp. 122–60; Andreas J. Köstenberger, Benjamin L. Merkle, and Robert L. Plummer, *Going Deeper with New Testament Greek: An Intermediate Study of the Grammar and Syntax of the New Testament* (Nashville: B&H Academic, 2016), 230–31.

15. For example, Porter argues that the future is distinct in that it is does not constitute "*a verbal aspect in its full sense.*" Instead, the future grammaticalizes the author's expectation

at this point should be given extra weight. On the other hand, Campbell maintains that the future form portrays perfective aspect. Ellis holds a similar view in that he suggests the "perfective aspect suffix" (i.e., -κ) should be understood as conveying "a nonpast version of the perfective aspect."[16] Although many scholars agree that the future originates historically from modal forms that express desire, obligation, and ability, there is no consensus as to its aspectual function in Koine Greek.

A second area of debate is whether or not Greek verbs grammaticalize temporality in the indicative mood. Once again, Porter and Fanning are at odds. Porter insists that the indicative mood conveys only aspect and not time. Temporal reference is conveyed by the aspect working in conjunction with context (especially deictic markers such as temporal adverbs).[17] Thus, for Porter, the Greek augment that is prefixed to imperfect, aorist, and some pluperfect indicative verbs does not communicate that the time of the action necessarily occurred in the past.

Campbell and others agree with Porter's conclusions based on the fact that many verbs do not conform to their expected temporal reference (e.g., an aorist verb does not always indicate an action in the past from the perspective of the author). Campbell calls the statistics "quite overwhelming" (46) since aorist verbs correspond to the past tense only 85 percent of the time, present verbs correspond to the present tense only 70 percent of the time, and perfect verbs correspond to a past action with present consequences less than 50 percent of the time. Campbell adds that "there are other languages that do not encode tense in their verbal system" (46). Thus, many scholars argue that time is not conveyed by the verb's grammatical form.

The majority of Greek grammarians, however, affirm that time is normally communicated by the grammatical form of indicative verbs.[18] Regarding the exceptions that are found in the tense-forms, Christopher Fresch comments, "Porter wants a verbal system that can account for every possible use, but this is simply not how humans conceive of grammatical categories."[19] Finally, Ellis's words are worth repeating: "When a scholar claims that Koine Greek

---

regarding a possible event (similar to the uses of the various moods in Greek). Porter, *Idioms of the Greek New Testament*, 24.

16. See Ellis, "Aspect-Prominence," 148.

17. Porter, *Verbal Aspect*, 76–83, 98–102.

18. Constantine R. Campbell comments, "The 'tenseless' position is still the minority, being rejected by most grammarians." Constantine R. Campbell, *Advances in the Study of Greek: New Insights for Reading the New Testament* (Grand Rapids: Zondervan, 2015), 111.

19. Christopher J. Fresch, "Typology, Polysemy, and Prototypes: Situating Nonpast Aorist Indicatives," in Runge and Fresch, *Greek Verb Revisited*, 409. See also Peter J. Gentry, "The Function of the Augment in Hellenistic Greek," in Runge and Fresch, *Greek Verb Revisited*, 353–78.

does not have the grammatical category of tense, we can ask, Are there other languages of the world that lack the category of tense? When we analyze other languages, we find the answer to this: yes, there are languages that lack the category of tense in their verbal morphology. This then leads to a follow-up question: Do any of those languages that lack tense look anything like Greek in terms of the structure of its verbal system? This certainly appears to not be the case: tenseless languages do not look like Koine Greek" (244).[20]

A third area of debate relates to the influence of lexical meaning on aspectual choice. In other words, does the lexical meaning of a verb (i.e., the type of action conveyed by the lexeme) affect the tense-form chosen by the author? Porter insists that, except for certain verbs such as εἰμί, φημί, and κεῖμαι that are "aspectually vague,"[21] tense-form "is not dependent upon lexis."[22] In Porter's view, the author has a purely subjective (usually) binary aspectual choice, and other factors do not influence that choice.

On the other hand, Fanning maintains that grammatical, lexical, and contextual factors do influence the author's aspectual choice. He writes, "Porter has insisted too much on the subjective conception of the occurrence, without realizing the limits on the optional choice available to the speaker under many circumstances."[23] Earlier he notes, "In many instances the degree of optional choice is reduced and the speaker is limited to one aspect rather than another because of the combination of aspect with other features. . . . Aspect operates so closely with other linguistic features and is so significantly affected by them that no treatment of aspect can be complete without attention to these interactions."[24] Consequently, Fanning believes that one must not only have a basic understanding of verbal aspect but also consider various linguistic

20. Here Ellis is summarizing Michael Aubrey, "The Value of Linguistically Informed Exegesis," in Douglas Mangum and Josh Westbury, eds., *Linguistics and Biblical Exegesis* (Bellingham, WA: Lexham, 2017), §8.3.

21. Porter, *Verbal Aspect*, 447.

22. Porter, *Verbal Aspect*, 87. Porter later states, "Lexical semantics does not appear to be determinative in the selection of tense-forms of New Testament Greek" (Stanley E. Porter, "Aspect Theory and Lexicography," in *Biblical Greek Language and Lexicography: Essays in Honor of Frederick W. Danker*, ed. Bernard A. Taylor et al. [Grand Rapids: Eerdmans, 2004], 215). See also Stanley E. Porter and Matthew Brook O'Donnell, who argue that the "selection of Greek verbal aspect is not statistically significantly affected by selection of these other verbal semantic features." Stanley E. Porter and Matthew Brook O'Donnell, "The Greek Verbal Network Viewed from a Probabilistic Standpoint: An Exercise in Hallidayan Linguistics," *Filología Neotestamentaria* 14, no. 27–28 (2001): 39.

23. Buist M. Fanning, "Approaches to Verbal Aspect in New Testament Greek: Issues in Definition and Method," in *Biblical Greek Language and Linguistics: Open Questions in Current Research*, ed. Stanley E. Porter and D. A. Carson (Sheffield: Sheffield Academic, 1993), 60.

24. Fanning, "Approaches to Verbal Aspect," 51–52; see also Fanning, *Verbal Aspect in New Testament Greek*, 126.

features that may influence why one aspect was chosen over another (especially in non-indicative moods, where temporality is not a factor).[25] Therefore, he is convinced that "verbal aspect is too dependent on other features of the context for it alone to be determinative in interpretation."[26]

Campbell, among others such as McKay, Daniel Wallace, D. A. Carson, Moisés Silva, Daryl Schmidt, and Robert Picirilli,[27] likewise acknowledges the influence of other factors, especially lexeme, on tense-form choice. In his chapter in this book, Campbell states, "Aspect does not operate alone within a text but interacts with lexeme and context to create *Aktionsart* expressions or implicatures" (51).[28] In his book *Advances in the Study of Greek*, he likewise explains that it is useful to observe "predictable patterns that emerge from the combinations of aspects with lexical types. The combination of aspect, lexeme, and context work together to create pragmatic *Aktionsart* expressions, or implicatures."[29]

With a near consensus that lexical meaning (and other factors such as context) influence tense-form choice, it is surprising that some (such as Porter) continue to deny this connection. Porter's position regarding verbal aspect is that "each semantic selection must be considered in relation to opposition and choice."[30] But, as mentioned earlier, his system protects this choice as being completely free, not open to other influences. At this point it appears that Porter's linguistic model, rather than the data, is driving his conclusions. Verbal aspect involves the perspective of the author, but oftentimes the nature of the verb's semantic meaning limits or influences the perspective.[31]

25. Fanning, "Approaches to Verbal Aspect," 56.
26. Fanning, *Verbal Aspect in New Testament Greek*, vi; cf. also 46–49.
27. K. L. McKay, "Time and Aspect in New Testament Greek," *Novum Testamentum* 34, no. 3 (1992): 225; K. L. McKay, "Aspect in Imperatival Constructions in New Testament Greek," *Novum Testamentum* 27, no. 3 (1985): 202; Daniel B. Wallace, *Greek Grammar beyond the Basics: An Exegetical Syntax of the New Testament* (Grand Rapids: Zondervan, 1996), 503–4; D. A. Carson, "An Introduction to the Porter/Fanning Debate," in Porter and Carson, *Biblical Greek Language and Linguistics*, 25–26; Moisés Silva, "A Response to Fanning and Porter on Verbal Aspect," in Porter and Carson, *Biblical Greek Language and Linguistics*, 79; Daryl D. Schmidt, "Verbal Aspect in Greek: Two Approaches," in Porter and Carson, *Biblical Greek Language and Linguistics*, 72; Robert E. Picirilli, "The Meaning of the Tenses in New Testament Greek: Where Are We?," *JETS* 48, no. 3 (2005): 547.
28. See also, Campbell, *Basics of Verbal Aspect*, 55–117.
29. Campbell, *Advances in the Study of Greek*, 120.
30. Porter, *Verbal Aspect*, 97.
31. See Benjamin L. Merkle, "The Abused Aspect: Neglecting the Influence of a Verb's Lexical Meaning on Tense-Form Choice," *Bulletin of Biblical Research* 26, no. 1 (2016): 57–74, 83; Benjamin L. Merkle, "Verbal Aspect and Imperatives: Ephesians as a Test Case," in *New Testament Philology: Essays in Honor of David Alan Black*, ed. Melton Bennett Winstead (Eugene, OR: Pickwick, 2018), 34–51.

As I have written in *New Testament Philology*,

This influence is due to the overlap in function of the verb's aspect and the inherent meaning of the verb. In other words, because the perfective aspect (aorist tense-form) is used by the author to portray the action as a whole, it is more natural to use the perfective aspect with verbs whose actions are normally completed in a relatively short period of time. For example, in the NT the imperative of βάλλω occurs fourteen times as an aorist but never as a present. This usage is expected when one considers that the action to "throw" or "put" takes place almost instantaneously. Indeed, it is difficult to conceive of the imperfective aspect being used when there would be virtually no time to portray the action as in progress or incomplete.

Conversely, because the imperfective aspect (present tense-form) is used by the author to portray the action as in progress, it is more natural to use the imperfective aspect with verbs whose actions normally are viewed as having no natural end point or are stative verbs. For example, in the NT the imperative of γρηγορέω occurs eleven times as a present but only once as an aorist. Again, this usage is expected when one considers that the action of "keeping watch" is not normally completed in a short period of time but is an action that has no natural terminus. Indeed, it is difficult to conceive of the perfective aspect being used when the action is not easily portrayed as a whole.[32]

The final area of debate that I will discuss is prominence—that is, how do we know when a word (in this current discussion, a verb) is heavily weighted in a particular context? One theory, affirmed by Porter, suggests that prominence is grammaticalized—that is, based on its tense-form (aspect), a verb should be viewed as more or less weighted than others. In Porter's schema, the perfective aspect (aorist tense-form) is the "least heavily marked" or "default" form, the imperfective aspect (the present or imperfect tense-form) is more marked, and the stative aspect (the perfect or pluperfect tense-form) is the most heavily marked.[33] Porter does not limit the application of this literary analysis to narratives but claims that it applies to exposition (i.e., epistles) and to non-indicative verbs.[34]

But does the Greek language grammaticalize not only aspect but also prominence? Such a simplistic or wooden view of language seems to run contrary to the textual evidence. Is it true that the more heavily marked perfect or pluperfect is *always* more prominent in a text? In *Advances in the Study of Greek*, Campbell cites several scholars who have tested Porter's thesis and

32. Merkle, "Verbal Aspect and Imperatives," 36–37.
33. Porter, *Idioms of the Greek New Testament*, 22; see also Porter, *Verbal Aspect*, 90–91.
34. Porter, *Verbal Aspect*, 92, 351, 357; Porter, *Idioms of the Greek New Testament*, 23.

found it insufficient to account for the data.[35] Instead of viewing prominence as a morphological function of grammar (semantics), it is better to view it as a function of context (pragmatics). Based on an analysis of the pluperfect, Campbell concludes, "Porter's conception of morphological bulk, and its role in indicating prominence, seems somewhat contrived. . . . This markedness . . . does not necessarily result in the prominence of the pluperfect."[36] Instead, many other factors need to be considered in the context to determine the function (and prominence) of various aspects.

Properly understanding the Greek verbal system is key for having a firm grasp of the language. Thankfully, New Testament Greek studies has produced several areas of consensus such as the definition of verbal aspect and its prominence over tense, as well as the meaning of the perfective and imperfective aspects. Additionally, we could add the function of the middle voice as demonstrated in Jonathan Pennington's chapter. And yet, much more work needs to be done to develop consensus and confidence regarding areas still under debate.

■ Pedagogy and the Living Language Approach

I taught my first Greek class while completing my MDiv in seminary (1995). Since then, I have consistently taught Greek in several institutions and even outside of the US. I have coauthored an intermediate Greek grammar[37] and, more recently, a beginning Greek grammar.[38] I include these details to demonstrate that I am concerned about Koine Greek and its relation to linguistics not merely as an academic or theoretician. Those of us who spend a large part of our time in the classroom are deeply concerned about the transferability of

---

35. Thomas R. Hatina, "The Perfect Tense-Form in Recent Debate: Galatians as a Case Study," *Filología Neotestamentaria* 15, no. 8 (1995): 3–22; Thomas R. Hatina, "The Perfect Tense-Form in Colossians: Verbal Aspect, Temporality and the Challenge of Translation," in *Translating the Bible: Problems and Prospects*, ed. Stanley E. Porter and Richard S. Hess, JSNTSup 173 (Sheffield: Sheffield Academic, 1999), 249–50; Jeffery T. Reed and Ruth A. Reese, "Verbal Aspect, Discourse Prominence, and the Letter of Jude," *Filología Neotestamentaria* 18, no. 9 (1996): 181–99; Moisés Silva, *God, Language, and Scripture: Reading the Bible in the Light of General Linguistics*, Foundations of Contemporary Interpretation 4 (Grand Rapids: Zondervan, 1990), 115, 118; Moisés Silva, "Discourse Analysis and Philippians," in *Discourse Analysis and Other Topics in Biblical Studies*, ed. Stanley E. Porter and D. A. Carson (Sheffield: Sheffield Academic, 1995), 102–6.
36. Campbell, *Advances in the Study of Greek*, 129.
37. Köstenberger, Merkle, and Plummer, *Going Deeper with New Testament Greek*.
38. Benjamin L. Merkle and Robert L. Plummer, *Beginning with New Testament Greek: An Introductory Study of the Grammar and Syntax of the New Testament* (Nashville: B&H Academic, 2020).

the concepts mentioned in this book to our students. In this last section, I will discuss linguistics and New Testament Greek from a pedagogical perspective.

Having learned another spoken (living) language as an adult, I know and appreciate the advantage of the living-language approach to learning Koine Greek. In a relatively short time (less than a year), I was able, with some difficulty, to teach and preach in this other language. I even remember telling a fellow New Testament professor that my abilities in my newly learned language surpassed my abilities in New Testament Greek. His response was, "Well, I guess you don't know Greek very well." At that point, I had a PhD in New Testament Studies, had studied Greek somewhat rigorously for more than a decade, and had taught Greek about ten times. I did know Greek well; I just didn't think or speak it like I did my newly learned language. What made the difference? It's not complicated. I was immersed in this new language for a year as a full-time language student, spending three to four hours a day in class five days a week. Additionally, I was forced to practice my language skills outside the classroom, since I lived in a context where English was not widely spoken. Can this experience be reproduced in a classroom with a dead language?

In a sense the answer is, "Of course it can—since it has been and is being done." There are, however, tremendous obstacles that make it quite difficult to achieve, including (1) time, (2) teachers, and (3) total immersion. First, students normally don't take enough Greek because most schools require only a minimal level of Greek to graduate. If someone takes only two semesters of Greek, then the living-language approach cannot expect to achieve a satisfactory level of fluency. Second, most teachers, even if they are convinced that the living-language approach is best, could not use such methodology. Such teachers would need to attain a high level of fluency first, something that almost no Greek professor has. Third, unless students are in a total-immersion context, they will inevitably struggle with the living-language approach. Three hours a week in a classroom setting for two (or even four) semesters is not a sufficient setting to gain the needed skills.

Sometimes the ideal and the reality live in two separate worlds. It would be great if students could be immersed in Hebrew or Greek, studying that language full time for a semester or year. But, as Michael Halcomb has argued, we should not view this dilemma as requiring an all-or-nothing approach. As instructors, teachers, or professors, we must be willing to assess our pedagogy, knowing that there is always room for improvement and growth. Halcomb calls us to a "more holistic and embodied approach"—that is, an approach that includes "imitation, listening, reading, writing, speaking, grammar study [inductively → deductively], or translation" (166). This type of class "should be conducted by a master teacher" (166). Again, all these thoughts are great, but just how many "master teachers" are out there? Halcomb rightly notes that such a method will require hard work and risk taking. This includes future Greek teachers having degrees in linguistics (and biblical studies, since most schools require professors to also teach New Testament courses) and adding linguistics courses to curricula.

As teachers we can improve our pedagogy. We can learn from others and grow in our understanding of ancient Greek. We can apply the science of linguistics to our discipline and reap tremendous results that can help sharpen and even correct our understanding of Greek. Our comprehension of verbal aspect, middle voice (and deponency), discourse analysis, constituent order, pronunciation, and pedagogy have benefited greatly from the application of linguistics to Greek studies. And although there is still much work left to do, we can celebrate what has been accomplished. The ideal teacher and the ideal grammar don't exist. But improving teachers and improving grammars do. May this book help to speed along that process.

Glossary

ablaut: The process by which the inflected form of a word is changed by modifying its stem vowel (e.g., sing, sang, sung; Greek: λείπω, ἔλιπον, λέλοιπα).

agent: The entity that is the cause of the action in the predicate (e.g., "The course was taught by the guest lecturer").

Aktionsart: The kind of action described by a particular verb (e.g., punctiliar, iterative, constative, etc.).

aspect: The perspective or viewpoint encoded in language, especially in verbs (e.g., imperfective, perfective, stative).

Attic Greek: The Greek dialect of the ancient city-state of Athens.

bilabial: A sound that is produced by the use of both lips (e.g., English *p* and *b*; Greek π and β).

case grammar: A system of linguistic analysis that focuses on the function that noun phrases play with respect to the event, process, or state expressed by the verb.

cataphoric: The relation between a unit of language and another unit that follows it.

coding: The process of converting one signaling system into another.

cognitive linguistics: A cluster of overlapping approaches to the study of language as a cognitive phenomenon.

comparative philology: A branch of historical linguistics that is concerned with comparing languages to establish their historical relatedness.

constituent order: The relative order of subject, verb, object, and adjuncts.

diphthong: A phonetic sequence consisting of a vowel and an upward glide (e.g., oil; Greek: οἶκος).

discourse: Any structured stretch of language that is longer than a single sentence.

discourse analysis: A research method for studying language in relation to its social context, sometimes defined as analysis of language beyond the sentence.

Erasmian pronunciation: A method of pronouncing ancient Greek derived from one of Erasmus's dialogues.

exegesis: The critical explanation or interpretation of a text.

fricative: A type of consonant made by the friction of breath in a narrow opening (e.g., English *f*; Greek φ).

implicature: Anything inferred from an utterance that is not also a condition for the truth of that utterance.

Koine Greek: The common form of Greek spoken and written during the Hellenistic, Roman, and early Byzantine periods.

lexeme: The minimal unit of language that has a semantic interpretation; lexemes are frequently listed in dictionaries as separate entries.

markedness: A state in which one linguistic element is more distinctively identified than another.

middle voice: A voice that indicates the subject is acting upon him- or herself reflexively or for his or her own benefit.

mnemonic device: A technique used to help one remember something.

morpheme: The smallest component of a word that contributes some sort of meaning (e.g., "disagreement" has three: dis, agree, and ment; Greek: ἔχομεν = εχ + ο + μεν).

morphology: The branch of linguistics that studies the structure or form of words.

palatal: A sound produced by raising the tongue toward the hard palate (e.g., German *ich*; Greek γ and κ).

phoneme: The smallest unit of language by which one word can be distinguished from another (e.g., "ten" versus "pen"; Greek: χαίρω versus καιρῷ).

phonology: The branch of linguistics that studies the sounds and sound systems of languages.

receptor language: The language that a text is being translated into.

Restored Attic pronunciation: A system for pronouncing Attic Greek.

rheme: The part of a clause that gives information about the theme.

salient information: Information that the speaker assumes will most likely capture the receptor's attention in a given situation and have the greatest influence on the receptor's understanding about that information.

semantics: The study of the meaning of linguistic expressions.

Septuagint: A Greek version of the Hebrew Bible produced for Greek-speaking Jews in Egypt in the third and second centuries BCE.

source language: The language one is translating from.

stative verb: A verb that expresses a state of affairs or a state of being rather than an action.

Systemic Functional Linguistics: An approach to linguistics that considers language as a social semiotic system organized by hierarchy and that differentiates the functions of language in use.

target language: The language one is translating into.

tense: A grammatical category that refers to the time of the event or state denoted by a verb.

tense-form: A variation in the morphological form of a verb (e.g., present, aorist, imperfect, future, etc.).

theme: Topic; the entity about which something is said.

transitivity: A property of verbs that relates to whether a particular verb can take a direct object and how many such objects that verb can take.

umlaut: A sound change in which a vowel is pronounced more like a following vowel or semivowel.

velar: A sound pronounced near the back of the tongue near the velum or soft palate.

Contributors

Michael G. Aubrey earned an MA in linguistics and exegesis from Trinity Western University in British Columbia, Canada. His thesis was titled "The Greek Perfect and the Categorization of Tense and Aspect: Toward a Descriptive Apparatus for Operators in Role and Reference Grammar." He also studied at the Canada Institute of Linguistics. He specializes in cognitive-functional approaches to language, with particular interest in Koine Greek. Currently, he works as a language editor for Logos Bible Software and is in the process of transitioning to Wycliffe Bible Translators/SIL International. He is also the senior editor for Koine-Greek.com, which focuses on making technical linguistic research more accessible and available for students and scholars.

David Alan Black received his doctor of theology (DTheol) degree at the University of Basel in Switzerland in 1983. He currently serves as senior professor of New Testament and Greek and is the Dr. M. O. Owens Jr. Chair of New Testament Studies at Southeastern Baptist Theological Seminary in Wake Forest, North Carolina. His publications include *Learn to Read New Testament Greek*, *Linguistics for Students of New Testament Greek: A Survey of Basic Concepts and Applications*, and *It's Still Greek to Me: An Easy-to-Understand Guide to Intermediate Greek*. He has also edited or co-edited numerous books, including *Linguistics and New Testament Interpretation: Essays on Discourse Analysis* and *Interpreting the New Testament: Essays on Methods and Issues*.

Randall Buth earned a PhD in Near Eastern languages and cultures from UCLA and has become a recognized voice in the academic field of biblical studies, linguistics, and discourse analysis. He worked in Bible translation with the Summer Institute of Linguistics and the United Bible Societies. He is the founder and director the Biblical Language Center and the academic provost of the Institute for Biblical Languages and Translation in Jerusalem. He is the author of *Living Biblical Hebrew*, parts 1, 2, and 3 and *Living Koine Greek*, parts 1, 2a, and 2b. He more recently co-edited *The Language Environment of First Century Judaea*, vol. 2 of *Jerusalem Studies in the Synoptic Gospels*, and he is a pioneer in the use of second-language acquisition methods to study biblical languages.

Constantine R. Campbell is senior vice president of Global Content and Bible Teaching at Our Daily Bread Ministries. He previously served as professor of New Testament at Trinity Evangelical Divinity School. He holds a PhD from Macquarie University. His publications include *Basics of Verbal Aspect in Biblical Greek*, *Advances in the Study of Greek: New Insights for Reading the New Testament*, and *Paul and Union with Christ: An Exegetical and Theological Study*, which was the 2014 *Christianity Today* Book of the Year in biblical studies.

Nicholas J. Ellis has degrees from Union University, Trinity Western University, and the University of Oxford, where he earned a DPhil in theology (New Testament). He is the author of *The Hermeneutics of Divine Testing: Cosmic Trials and Biblical Interpretation in the Epistle of James and Other Jewish Literature*. He has also contributed chapters to several scholarly books, including *The Greek Verb Revisited*. He currently serves as the CEO of EDi-Global, an organization promoting biblical and theological education across the global Christian community.

T. Michael W. Halcomb is professor of biblical languages at Pacific Rim Christian University (Honolulu, Hawaii). He is also lead pastor at The Bridge Church (Nazarene) in Honolulu. He holds a bachelor of science (Kentucky Christian University), an MDiv (Lexington Theological Seminary), an MA in biblical studies (Asbury Theological Seminary), an MA in linguistic theory (University of Kentucky), and a PhD in biblical studies (Asbury Theological Seminary), focused on the New Testament. Halcomb founded the Conversational Koine Institute and cofounded GlossaHouse, which publishes works in the areas of language, hermeneutics, and pedagogy. He is the author of several books, including *Speak Koine Greek* and *Entering the Fray: A Primer on New Testament Issues for the Church and Academy*. He is the editor of *Kingdom Rhetoric: New Testament Explorations in Honor of Ben Witherington III*.

Thomas W. Hudgins completed a PhD in ancient world studies at the Complutense University of Madrid and an EdD from Southeastern Baptist

Theological Seminary. He is a professor in the Modern Languages Institute at Nebrija University and a member of the theology faculty of Saint Louis University in Madrid, Spain. His New Testament publications include *Those Footnotes in Your New Testament: A Textual Criticism Primer for Everyone* and the Spanish translation of David Alan Black's *Learn to Read New Testament Greek* (*Aprenda a Leer el Griego del Nuevo Testamento*).

Stephen H. Levinsohn holds a PhD in linguistic science from the University of Reading, UK. He is a member of Wycliffe Bible Translators and, with his wife, Nessie, worked as a linguist and translator from 1968 to 1995 with the Inga people of Colombia. As a senior linguistic consultant with SIL International, he has directed "Discourse for Translation" workshops in over twenty countries for linguist-translators working with over 450 languages. Levinsohn is the author of *Textual Connections in Acts* and *Discourse Features of New Testament Greek*.

Benjamin L. Merkle is professor of New Testament and Greek at Southeastern Baptist Theological Seminary. He earned a PhD at Southern Baptist Theological Seminary. He is the author of the Ephesians volume of the Exegetical Guide to the Greek New Testament series and *Exegetical Gems from Biblical Greek*. He is also the coauthor of *Going Deeper with New Testament Greek: An Intermediate Study of the Grammar and Syntax of the New Testament*, *Greek for Life: Strategies for Learning, Retaining, and Reviving New Testament Greek*, and, most recently, *Beginning with New Testament Greek: An Introductory Study of the Grammar and Syntax of the New Testament*.

Jonathan T. Pennington is associate professor of New Testament interpretation and the director of research doctoral studies at Southern Baptist Theological Seminary. He earned a PhD in New Testament studies from the University of St. Andrews (Scotland). He has published a variety of articles, reviews, and Greek and Hebrew language tools, in addition to the books *Heaven and Earth in the Gospel of Matthew*, *Reading the Gospels Wisely: A Narrative and Theological Introduction*, and *The Sermon on the Mount and Human Flourishing*.

Robert L. Plummer is the Collin and Evelyn Aikman Professor of Biblical Studies at Southern Baptist Theological Seminary. He received his undergraduate degree from Duke University and both his MDiv and PhD from Southern Baptist Theological Seminary. Plummer has authored or coauthored several books, including *Greek for Life: Strategies for Learning, Retaining, and*

Reviving New Testament Greek, Going Deeper with New Testament Greek: An Intermediate Study of the Grammar and Syntax of the New Testament, Beginning with New Testament Greek: An Introductory Study of the Grammar and Syntax of the New Testament, and *40 Questions about Interpreting the Bible*. He also hosts the screencast *Daily Dose of Greek*.

Stanley E. Porter completed his BA (Point Loma College) and MA (Claremont Graduate School) degrees in English before being "converted" to biblical studies, where he earned an MA in New Testament (Trinity Evangelical Divinity School) and a PhD in biblical studies and linguistics (University of Sheffield). Since 2001 he has been president, dean, and professor of New Testament at McMaster Divinity College in Hamilton, Ontario, Canada (the largest Baptist seminary in Canada) and also holds the Roy A. Hope Chair in Christian Worldview. He is a prolific author in the area of linguistics and New Testament Greek, having written *Verbal Aspect in the Greek of the New Testament, Idioms of the Greek New Testament, Studies in the Greek New Testament, Fundamentals of New Testament Greek*, and *Linguistic Analysis of the Greek New Testament*, as well as numerous other books and articles.

Steven E. Runge received his BA in speech communication (Western Washington University), an MTS in biblical languages (Trinity Western Seminary in Langley, BC), and a DLitt in biblical languages (University of Stellenbosch in South Africa). He serves as scholar-in-residence for Logos Bible Software and as a research associate affiliated with the Department of Ancient Studies, University of Stellenbosch. He is the author of *Discourse Grammar of the Greek New Testament: A Practical Introduction for Teaching and Exegesis, High Definition Commentary: Philippians*, and *High Definition Commentary: Romans*. He also edited *Discourse Studies and Biblical Interpretation: A Festschrift in Honor of Stephen H. Levinsohn* and co-edited *The Greek Verb Revisited*.

Scripture and Ancient Writings Index

Author Index

Subject Index